ALSO BY JOHN SANFORD

NOVELS AND OTHER FICTION

The Water Wheel (1933)
The Old Man's Place (1935)
Seventy Times Seven (1939)
The People from Heaven (1943)
A Man Without Shoes (1951, 1982)
The Land That Touches Mine (1953)
Every Island Fled Away (1964)
The $300 Man (1967)
Adirondack Stories (1976)

INTERPRETATIONS OF AMERICAN HISTORY

A More Goodly Country (1975)
View From This Wilderness (1977)
To Feed Their Hopes (1980)
The Winters of That Country (1984)

SCENES FROM AN AMERICAN LIFE

The Color of the Air, Part 1 (Spring 1985)

JOHN
THE SANFORD
WINTERS
OF THAT
COUNTRY
TALES OF THE MAN MADE SEASONS

BLACK SPARROW PRESS
SANTA BARBARA-1984

LIBRARY OF CONGRESS CATALOGING IN PUBLICATION DATA

Sanford, John B., 1904-
    The winters of that country.

    1. United States—History—Literary collections.
    I. Title.
PS3537.A694W5   1984   813'.52   84-4276
ISBN 0-87685-615-6
ISBN 0-87685-616-4 (signed)
ISBN 0-87685-614-8 (pbk.)

To a more perfect Union

For the season it was winter, and they
that know the winters of that country know
them to be sharp and violent, and subject
to cruell and feirce stormes.

  —Bradford: *History of Plymouth Plantation*

TABLE OF CONTENTS

The Winters of That Country

ON THE WATERS OF DARKNESS

There were in that ancient age certain nobles that quitted Norway to dwell in Iceland, in the seas beyond the Western Isles. Such went there as these, Thorolf, and Skalla-Grim, and Ketil Haeng, great ones all, but none more so than Ingolf that came to Reykjanes, where the snowfields were. His life was long and goodly-lived in that place, and his blood descended to many, among them him called Herjulf, high-held in the mouths and minds of men for his daring on the wave. A rover he became, faring in his serpent-ship where oar drew and wind drove him, and when Eric cried up the excellences of Greenland, pleasureless save in its pleasureful name, he hied himself thither, leaving behind Bjarni, the son he had got upon Thorgerd.

They might have been ships themselves, those people — dragons, cranes, things with sixty sweeps and square white wings — and no storm could stun them, no deeps dismay. One such shipman Bjarni was, Herjulf's son. The waters were his element: ashore, he seemed not quite natural, a cast-up mass, tide-abandoned, stranded on its side; at sea, he was of the sea, marine. And being so, one day he braved the season to winter with his sire in Greenland, but it befell that the will of the wind prevailed, and it bore him where it listed, a strange and misted course, and ere its force was spent, the way was lost, and none could say whither the vessel went. There was much conjecture among the men, nor did fear prove rare, for the verge of the world might well be near, but it pleased the gods to rend the veil, and therethrough was land descried, a littoral of small hillocks thickly wooded. Bjarni took the bottom close in, and it was supposed that he meant to try the country for meat and spoil, but in the end he bade the steersman to sheer them off — that loom was not Greenland, Bjarni said, and they turned away to seek that shore.

They were many days making another landfall, and when that came to pass, Bjarni declared it to be likest Greenland, having capes and fjords that he could see from afar, and those were smokes that rose on the sky, as like as not from Herjulf's fire. So it was soon found to be, and son and sire came together there on the scar, where crags grew up from the sea. The company wintered in that country, as Bjarni had said they would, and when the time came for taking leave, it was the occasion for no little solemnity, for all knew the parting would be forever, and then the ship—dragon, serpent, crane—sailed toward the rising sun.

Long later, Bjarni being in Norway, he made mention of the land he had glimpsed through the mist, and some surprise was shown at his not having gone ashore for

> *the grapes grown there*
> *the sweet water and the self-sown wheat,*
> *the lynx whose eyes could see through stone,*

and in time the tale came to Eric's son, the one called Leif. . . .

OF THE PEOPLE OF APALACHE

and those who have gone there
to conquer it
— Garcilaso de la Vega

In that place, the cypress could be found, and the satinwood, and the gumbo limbo tree, from the last of which *cachibu*, meaning resin, and the savin grew there, and the pine and yew, and in its shallows the *manati* dwelt, a sea-thing that was said to have arms and to carry its young, and lizards lazed in the maremmatic bays, and to take salt, lynxes came to the water's edge, and with them bear to fish for pompanos, and there were stilted birds and those that swam and dove, and morphoes made bluer the bluest sky, and fritillaries flew in clouds, clapping their wings, their hands, for that handsome land.

Its naturals were of a race that reverenced the sun and the moon, but with small ceremony or none at all, as though it were vain to point at what was plain to view. But they so adored their dead that they would not bury them, proffering them instead to the day and night until, piece by piece, birds bore them away. Among that people, a man espoused but one woman — two, and he suffered death — and that woman, so that she refrained from adulterous intercourse, remained his licit wife, and though he might take a concubine, that one did not share the right, being fit only to bear the burden of servitude. Of their manner in dress, the accounts of all did call it modest. The women wore the skins of the chamois, well wrought with oils for pliancy, and these concealed the body from knees to gorge. The men wore skins of like sort, but they covered only the parts they thought unseemly for the eye. A decorous and forthright breed, blessed in their residence and, if the truth had been told, blessed as well in plate and gold, in jade and sard and jasper, in all kinds of precious stones. . . .

On the isle of Hispaniola, there was a certain hidalgo captain, by name Pámphilo de Narváez, that did learn of the opulency of the Indians of Apalache. They wore El Oro commonly, he heard, as in Spain sequins were worn for their sheen, and tales came to him of children at play with the substance, tossing it like bones in the jackstone game, or merely tossing it away. To such as they, it was a thing of not much value; indeed, they were reputed to confer it freely on whomso admired it, and in requital they were well pleased with a hawk's bell, a red cap, a bit of colored glass. Fired by these reports, the captain set a course for Eldorado with four hundred men and eighty head of horse.

Be it remembered that this was the same Narváez that had been deputed to Mexico by the Adelantado of Cuba to subdue and supersede Hernan Cortés. Had these ends been won, the fame of Narváez would have run to the latest age, but in all verity, he had hardly landed than, at Cempoalla, he was fallen upon in the rain and soon and signally defeated. For him, the expedition closed in little glory and less beauty, for in the course of the fray he lost an eye. Thus grievously wounded, he had been brought before his conqueror in chains, and he spake these words to him, saying *You have much reason, Señor Cortés, to thank Fortune for having won you the day.* In this manner did Cortés reply, *I hold victory over you to be one of the least of my achievements.* And Narváez, humiliated and in much pain, was amerced the sum of an hundred thousand castellanos and held by all in disdain.

Such, then, was he that sought to fatten a lean purse in Apalache, or Florida, as some called it, for it was a flowered place, truly a feast of flowers, and, debarking there, he marched with his men to a town whereof the ruler was the cacique Hirrihigua. But, alas, for all the gold he saw in that country, he might have left both eyes in the mud at Cempoalla: no gold was found, nor plate, nor the bright and dreamt-of gems, opals, pearls, and chrysoprase. Lo!, he may have cried, behold my empty Eden!, and in a killing frost of rage, he and his company of foot and horse drew the sword against the Indians and slew until the very slain barred the way to those still living.

Numbered with the dead was the cacique's mother, hacked into clods of meat and flung among the Spaniards' dogs, and as for Hirrihigua himself, he was suffered to live with his nose cut off. Sated with blood, if naught else, the soldiers sought now to return to the ships, but the way had been lost, and they wandered, sore beset by nature and sorer by the naturals, and when they came at last to the marge, the waters were as barren as the garden. Thereupon they built small craft and sailed them west until westing ended in a river that ran through the sea, brown and swift and two days wide, and in that stream there were many who died, and one of these had but one good eye.

A PRISONER OF HIRRIHIGUA

*I am a Christian and was born in
Seville.*

—Juan Ortiz

He was one of that complement left by Narváez to guard the ships,
but being gulled into going ashore, he had been seized by the savages
along with three others, and lest more be lost than four, the ships
had sailed away. Their captor, the cacique that Narváez had bereft
of a nose, had not forgotten the name of his maimer, yet so malign
did it make his mind that he could not suffer his ear to hear it. But
even so, unspoken, it was heard, and the word inflamed him until
he could take no ease at the fire nor solace from the hunt, nor did
children seem the sweet companions of before. With Narváez out
of reach, the cacique assuaged his rage with this: he deemed that
each of the Spaniardoes should requite him in part—those four white
lives must pay for his nose.

He charged that they be most lovingly cared for, to the end that
they might be grilled and eaten at a feasting rite a few days thence.
And that time being come, he signified that they be taken naked to
a certain open place and there made to run through flights of
arrows—sharp-billed birds—until the bird-beaks killed them, and as
to three of the four, the fate decreed befell them. The cacique drew
great pleasure from their futile frenzies and their droll dying, and
that he might add to his delight, he now called for the fourth man,
final payment on his short-cut nose.

But Juan Ortiz, for he was the fourth, was hardly yet a man, having seen but eighteen years in this tear-stained vale. In some of the
savages, pity was stirred by his tender age, though none dared speak
but one, and she the wife of Hirrihigua, the simian cacique. Standing boldly before him, she pleaded for the boy's life at the risk of
her own. He had not invaded the country, she said, he had stayed
with the ships and done no harm, and his crime, if one could be laid
against him, was in being less artful than the Indian, indeed, his

crime was innocence — and so ardent was her entreaty, so bitter her anguish, that not even the cacique was proof against yielding.

To pleasure the woman, the boy was spared and made a slave, but so grievously was he tormented that he must often have envied his dead companions and rued the day he was saved. His labors were heavy and endless, and in their performance he was much impeded by buffeting, stoning, and strokes of the lash, and there were times when, to feed the passions of Hirrihigua, he was forced to run before him all the day, from the rising to the setting of the sun, with death in wait for the briefest pause, and had he not, as a Christian, been debarred from suicide, he might thus have tried to die. It was as though the cacique had repented of his weakness in letting the boy live, and whensoever he survived an agony, a new agony was devised for him, more barbarous than the last, more past bearing.

At length, a great fire was kindled and allowed to burn until it became a bed of glowing coals, and above this, on a *barbacoa,* a grid of poles, the boy was placed with the purpose of roasting him alive. His shrieks of torment brought thither the cacique's wife, and once more she besought him for his captive's life. In the end, he relented, but not before the boy had baked until blisters like halves of oranges had formed, many of which had burst and bled, so that they were painful to behold, as if their heat could be felt by the eye.

How endless his calendar of tortures! To Juan Ortiz, in the chronicles of his mind, it must have seemed that he had found hell in life, for what was hell but death without dying, hurt everlasting, crescent pangs and waning hope? What he must have feared most was that he would *not* die, that he would survive all suffering to suffer the more, and had the cacique studied to wreak his worst, he would have assured the boy that he would live forever.

Shall more be told of his many miseries, the blows he took, the odium endured, the dangers, the life he spent on the edge of the knife? Or shall an end be put to the seeming endless, shall it be said that he was one day saved after ten years lost? Ten years was Juan Ortiz among the Indians of Florida, and in that time so far had he changed beyond the change of numbers that when brought before de Soto's captain Baltasar de Gallegos, he scarce could speak the horseman's tongue, saying *Xivilla,* by which he meant Seville. Nor yet in dress was he then a white, being bare but for a cloth at the loins, browned by the sun and the seasons, wearing a plume in his hair, as his captors had done, and bearing wounds that had never healed, and he stank of matter wherein worms swam—ah, Dios!, it was twenty days before he could don a blouse without pain nor stain it through.

He had much reason now to live, but the ways of God have no reason, and one must take what He gives and go. The boy Juan Ortiz had become the man that, ten years since, Hirrihigua would have killed, and with the two tongues that dwelt in his mouth, he sought to make the savage and the Spaniard understand—but understand what? what was there to understand? In all truth, neither understood, for men too have unknown reasons, and there ensued three years of blood and death to the Great River, and somewhere beyond its banks Juan Ortiz began to fail. He grew by slow degrees weaker, as much from old heart-sickness as from new, and in a place called Utiangue, one day he died.

Francis Drake, 1545–96

OFF NOMBRE DE DIOS, IN THE GULF OF DARIEN

He lived by the sea, died on it, and
was buried in it.
—Richard Hakluyt, vol.iii, p. 588

On a certain daye in August, in the yeare of our Lord 1595, he
weighed from Plymmouth with 27 sayle for the plundering of the
dagoes that had plundered Panama. To accomplishe that ende, the
shipps were provisioned thus:

with graynes of sundrie sort,
such as malt and rye and pease and barley,
and biscuit, bread, and beare were taken,
and there were manye flags and streamers,
and budge barrels,
which were for the carrying of powder
safe from flying sparkes,
and muskets went along, and iron shotte,
and petronels, which fired stones,
and almonds were laded,
and 140 double trace of garlick,
and salt and balsam were stored
in the holds,
and oars, and spars, and barricoes,
which were small caskes,
and nayles and pike heads
and cressets and rosin,
and neats tongues for lubricant,
and targets of proof were brought aboard,
and there were chests of medicaments
as well,
electuaries for the scorbutum,
hot Rewms,
tertiary agues,

and diseases of the joynts,
some of these the gentle kinde
and some to be warye of,
and there was Diaphenicon
for infyrmities of the Bowel,
and there was Confectio hamech,
soveraigne for melancholly and salt fleam,
also for scabs,
itch,
leprosies,
and cancers,
etc.,
and there were flaskets
and brasscocks
and funnel pipes,
and there were monmouth caps,
bowes and bowe-strings,
and bottels made of woode,
and there were divers instrumentes
of music,
lutes,
hobboyes,
sagbutes,
cornettes,
opharions bandora,
and such lyke,
and there were pipes of wine
for the captains
and beare for the men
that manned the shipps of the line

Alas, the expedityon gayned but little, a few handfulls of plate,
gold arduouslie won grayne by grayne, and the Admiral became sore
in spirrit, havinge lost manye that he warmly loved, amonge them
Clifford and Brute Browne and John Hawkyns, and as the spirrit
flagged, so the bodye, and being taken of the Fluxe, he soon died
and was committed to the sea in a leaden coffyn no great way off
from Nombre de Dios, where his fleete had been defeated. His
culverins and sakers did not save him, nor did his joynted shotte
and hail shotte, his falcons and his fowlers and his cannons periers,

no, nor was he saved by his chests of cures and remedies, such as Diacatholicon, the cooling purge, nor by caracostina, of which all authors say it taketh away inflammations, nor by the electuary Indum that breaketh the bodye's wynde. He was not saved by his ordnances, his medicines, his twenty-five hundred men. He is dead, and in lead he lies off Darien.

THE PRICE OF THE DOG

> *Thou shalt not bring the price of*
> *a dog into the house of the Lord.*
> —Deut. 23. 18

It must've been a wondrous sight, the ships out there in the roads, the Bight of Benin blacks on the strand, the barracoons with their backs to the trees — a very pretty scene, the canoes coming out from land with slaves to swap for brass and brandy. Everywhere the ships with riches lay, in all the bays of Guinea, in the mouths of christened rios, the maze of nameless streams. At Anashan, the sea seemed to hold them on its breath, to lift and let them fall, at Commenda too and Calabar new and old, and they were seen as well at Calsamanca, at Cormantine and Wyemba, and they were ranged along the Pepper Coast, and on the sea's respiration they rose and fell, waiting to sell their freight for slaves.

> *it is usuall to make some present*
> *to the Kings and great Men*
> *which are called dashes*
> *to the value of an Iron Barr,*
> *if to a King a laced Hatt*
> *or*
> *something else that he shall fancy*
> *for it is usuall*
> *for the Kings and Great Men*
> *to present a Neagroe or two*
> *for their kind entertainment,*
> *and others will present you*
> *with small gifts of Teeth*
> *etc.*

At each vendue, there was much clamor among the people for the marchandizes arrayed upon the decks. They were quite ardent for such things as Venice bugles, which were small glass beads that came in strings, and for false crystal they would offer never so, and their eyes were hot intent on cowries, or cawries, that is, shells meant to go from hand to hand, a pretty kind of money to be spent, and what would they not part with for the dew of the sun, *rosa solis*, a sweet and cordial wine! They were drawn to Scotch pans and barber basons, to porringers and bottles rimmed with tin, to Dutch cutlaces, strait or bow'd, and they were needful too of voyage iron, and most abundantly would they tender for the dye *roucou*, an orange-red, or, since it came from Cayenne, *Rocuyenne*. Round padlocks were sought by all, as were looking-glasses and pewter wrought, and demand was ever made for empty trunks, for chairs of cane and clapper bells,

> *one man died with Scurvy,*
> *one Boy died with the flucks,*
> *a woman died with a Consumption*
> *having been Meagre a long time,*
> *died a Girl Slave with Dropsy,*
> *man Slave jumped over bord,*
> *the Slaves had intention*
> *of taking the Ship*
> *one was shot dead*
> *one trampled to death in the fray*
> *and four wounded*
> *two of which pretty dangerously,*
> *the Weather ends pleasant*

and rarely was there little stir where the scissors and the fish-hooks lay, the Coignac, the coarse red cord called Bure, and somme were scarcely to be consoled if they found no smilax on board, which to the Spainiards was *zarzaparrilla*.

But if they were afire in their desire for wares such as those, what shall be said of their craze for these—the brocadels, the China sattins, the taffeties? The stuffs, the stuffs! They burned for Salempores, a blue cotton cloth from Ind, for buckshaws, which were piece-goods, and for flowered armozeens. They honed for nicanees both fine and common, for chints and frise, for Quaque cloth and Cabo Verdo—stuffs, stuffs, they were consumed by their yearn for stuffs!, silken sashes, platillas, breech-clouts, and when naught of such remained, old sheets would be taken in trade, rags were made to do. For shoddy they did sell their enemies, for pistareens their own—for bright colors, for gastropods from the Indian Ocean, for pins and cups and maccatons, whatever those might be, for *Konings' Kleederen*, clothes for Kings, for flash trash, for nothings at all, they sent their boys and girls, their sons and daughters away.

Sent them in the *Anna*, the *Dolphin*, the *Poultney*, in the *Phillis* and the *Industry*, in the *Diamond*, the *Blessing* (Thos Outlaw capt), in the *Cleopatra*, yes, even in the *Othello*,

> *not uncommon was it for a marchant*
> *in the African trade*
> *to suffer painfull Loss,*
> *for ever on a Guineaman*
> *mortality amongst the slaves*
> *ran high,*
> *yett where a capt had purchas'd*
> *some to his owne accompt*
> *these were seldom knowne*
> *to die*

sent them in brig and brigantine, in sloop and schooner, and they could be seen for sale at 3 of the clocke on a Fryday afternoon at the sign of the Blue Ball, or near the Swinging Bridge, or hard by Mr. Harris's school, they were on display in Trea-mont Street, at Welsteed's Warehouse on the Dock, at the upper end of Scarlett's Wharff, they were at Bermuda Hundred, at Osborne's on the James, at Jacksonburgh Ponpon in Charleston, at Strawberry Ferry and Eliott's Wharff,

And they were stout, young, prime, a likely lot, well set up, handsome featur'd, strait limb'd, good natur'd, speak some English, had the small-Pox, a choice parcel from Majumba, Gambia, Quamboo, the Coast of Gold,

> *and being cold season*
> *will be sold*
> *very cheap*

And they wore these names, these lovely names: Tilla, Juba, Abra, and Quammo were among them, and Essee, and Ocrasaw, and they answered (like dogs) to Taynay and Primax, to Armenda and Ocreka and Yono Cish, aye, you could say the words or whistle for Acavan and Theribah, for the lame one called A Lame Joseph, for the black bitch Elecata, and you could take your choice of Baynah, Boyya, Abah, Cumba—if you paid the price,

but bring them not to the house of the Lord!

MASTER OF THE *SALOMON*

In a public way of Plymmouth, which is on the river Plym in the shire of Devon, it befell that a certain John Hawkins, a youth of honorable descent, did openly and *vi et armis* assault a commoner. thereby causing a great effusion of blood, with death ensuing. Being hued against by passersby, he was made to stand his triall, whereat he deposed in manner following: *I struck the man* (meaning one White, a barber) *because I could not avoid him.*

White had no first name, it seemeth, or if White was the first, no last. One White, he was called (though, being half-christened, he might have been half-White), and it was thus that he quitted history, but questions remained in his train, a hum as from a swarm come and gone. How had his life run out — through the gorge? the gizzard? the privities? And had a weapon been used or only the mortal empty hand? And what offense had he given — had he shorn the Hawkins beard too short, or, finding but down to work on, had he ventured a jest and laughed?

I struck the man, said John Hawkins, *because I could not avoid him*, whereupon he was declared to be innocent of felony.

Mariner and merchant became he now, and with such it was the custom to lade ware and woven stuffs and sail it oversea for trade that promised gain. Beyond Cape Verde was a place where rarities were said to be displayed on the sands, as the teeth of olyphants, and malaguette pepper, and Guinea grains, that pungent spice that some well-named the grains of Paradise. All these things could be got of the people there for such bait as hatchets, combs, nightcaps, and, more enticing still, copper and lead in the lump, to be beaten into the earrings and armlets (*manillios*, these last) that so delighted them.

I struck the man . . ., said he.

He prospered in that commerce, but long did he long to traffick in one thing more that Afric offered — the Africanoes. Abundant, they were, and on display like their goods and granules, black and blinding, a living kind of jet, and in time his mind was turned, as once it turned for White.

I struck the man . . ., he said.

He was thirty years old when his fleet of three sail stood out from Plymmouth and cleared The Sound—the flagship *Salomon*, 130 tonne, the *Swallow*, 100 tonne, and the 40-tonne sloop, the *Jonas*. They made for Tenerife in the Grand Canaries, and there they took on board the pilot Juan Martinez, a sailor much lauded for his knowledge of West Indian navigation. The next land raised was the coast of Guinea.

I struck the man, Hawkins said, *because I could not avoid. . . .*

In the river Caces, he could not avoid taking 200 blacks from the Portingales, and in and about the river Mtombi, he could not avoid taking a like number from shore and ship, nor at Sierra Leone could he avoid laying hands on 500 more, to which were unavoidably added 32,000 ducats, a store of wax and ivory, and a certain great galleon for his 900 blacks. The hard spoil was sent to England; the soft went westward with the fleet.

From Guinea, the winds and Juan Martinez took the merchandise to the isle of Hispaniola, where, at such ports as Isabella and Puerto de Plata and Monte Christi, all Spain in the Indies awaited the cargo. When placed on view, bull and cow alike drew cries of admiration, for here were no Indian slaves, tameless Caribs or timid Tainos that died too soon of broken hearts. These were fauna of another color, all of them lofty and well-set, prime seed and likely breeders. They found much favor and fetched handsomely under the hammer.

> *he made vend of the whole number of his Negroes, for which he received in those 3. places by way of exchange such quantitie of merchandise that hee did not onely lade his owne 3. shippes with hides, ginger, sugars, and some quantities of perles, but fraighted also two other hulkes with hides and the like commodities. And so with prosperous successe and much gaine to himselfe, he came home, and arrived in the moneth of September 1563*

The Queen spoke Hawkins fair for his achievement, in recognition whereof she granted the blackbirder a coat of arms after this fashion: Sable, on a point wavy a lion passant or; in chief, three bezants; and for a crest, a demi-Moor proper bound in a cord. No one had told Her Majesty that a slave ship stank from three leagues off.

His feats, his fortune, his crest and coat of arms—Sable, on a point wavy!—none of these things stayed the passage of time, and at three-and-sixty years of age, the Queen's shipman died at sea. He was committed to it from the deck of the *Garland*, and even as one White, no man knows where he lies.

I struck the man, Death said, *because I could not avoid him.*

ALL LEARNED AND VIRTUOUS MEN

concerning a letter from Brother
Luis Brandaon to Father Sandoval

Brother Brandaon was rector of the College of the Society of Jesus at Loando in Angola, whence some twelve thousand blacks had been sent forth to be vended in the New Isles, the *Ilhas Novas,* where the Portingales grew the cane they used in the making of rum. To the said Brandaon, the priest Sandoval had addressed some lines, lost now or sequestered from the eye, in which certain doubts were raised concerning the aforementioned traffick, but, God be praised!, the reply of Brother Luis has survived the willed and random shots of time. Enwound in its words, the dead letter's ghost can still be found and readily read.

Known therefrom is this, that the priestly heart was sorely panged by the commerce between the Gulf of Guinea and the Indies: to him, such trucking in souls, even in those that were not yet saved, was a most unseemly merchantry, a far remove from decent usage and plainly repugnant to the precepts of Christ. Where he wrote from is uncertainly known—from nearby Fernando Po, it may have been, or from faraway Brazil—but write he did to the rector, and as his saddened spirit inclined him, so he must have phrased.

In this wise did Brother Luis seek to suage the father's heart, thus his mitigation for the mind. He had taken counsel of his clerical brethren, wrote the rector, some near at hand in Loando, and some offshore in Sao Thomé, aye, he had even addressed himself to the Board of Conscience at Lisboa, *all learned and virtuous men,* and none had scrupled at jobbery in slaves. For his own part, he had been forty years there in the Kingdom of the Congo, and amongst his peers and superiors in the College, he had never seen the practice frowned on, never read that it lacked canonical sanction, never heard the merest word.

Nor need his Reverence, said he, be discomposed under another head—that the Neagroes in question had been illegally acquired, in fine, stolen by the traders who sold them for shipment over the sea. He could vouch for the sellers, a likely lot in the main, given to buying in good faith and in good faith vending. None of them could know which of his many wares had a cloud on its title, and if one existed, none could prove it away. Moreover, wrote brother Luis, all blacks claimed illegal capture, and if on that account every slave were freed, little service would be done to God, who would have no souls to save. . . .

There ends the letter of brother Brandaon to Father Sandoval, and no trace remains of a further exchange. It is unknown, therefore, whether the qualms of the priest were stilled by the rector, the brethren of Sao Thomé and Cape Verde, and the Bishops of the Board of Conscience at Lisboa, *all learned and virtuous men.* There ensued only silence, except, of course, from the blacks: they continued to cry aloud and die on their way to Brazil.

MUTINY ABOARD THE *DISCOVERY*

Nothing much is known of him before his voyages for London's merchants and the ventures he made with the Dutch. Only this can be shown, a house beside the Thames—he could see the Tower from its windows, they say, and the ships in Katherine's Pool—and this, that he was wedded once and thrice the sire of sons. But none since has said where he was born or when, and none has sworn he died the day his crew rose against him and put him overside with a certain loyal few. Amid the James Bay ice, nine men in a shallop watched the *Discovery* head for home, nine as good as dead four thousand miles from the India docks, four thousand and one from the Pool. And yet, who knows?—maybe they didn't lie down and dream of fire while they froze, maybe they threaded the floes and reached the shore. And there, maybe they found and fed on roots, bark, berries, took birds and hare by hand, maybe tracks led them to holes in the ground where foxes dwelt and bear, maybe they're living yet, who knows? who can say?, beating the tundra's streams and snows and sphagnum bogs for a warm way through the cold— maybe, now four hundred years old, they still seek the way to Cathay.

The mutineers were four months in getting to London, and after seven more years they were tried *for feloniously pinnioninge of Henry Hudson, master of the* Discovery, *out of the same shipp with VIII more of his company into a shallop in America without meate, drink, clothes, or other provision, whereby they died.* They pleaded Non Culp, and being so found, they were freed, and it may well be that the finding was good. Henry and those VIII may still be alive. Who knows?

PASSENGERS ON THE *MAYFLOWER*

> *Aboute a hundred sowls, came over in
> this first ship.*
>
> —Bradford: *History*

Among those sowls, by God's blessing the beginners and the foundation of all the Plantations in New England, there were these

> *Mr. Stephen Hopkins, and Elizabeth, his wife, and 2. children,
> caled Giles, and Constanta, a doughter, both by a former wife;
> and 2. more by this wife, caled Damaris and Oceanus; the last
> was borne at sea; and 2. servants, called Edward Doty and
> Edward Litster.*

For all that's known of Doty and Litster (mayhap Leicester was the way to spell the name), they too might've come into being on the voyage: each, like the daughter of their master, might've been christened Oceanus, each seaborne, each put ashore near the Rock. They seem, that pair of Edwards, to have had no terrestrial origin; they arose on the stream that flows around the world.

Servants, they were styled in the History, yeomen bound and therefore low, menials, they must've been, sellers of their hands, and holding no coat of arms, they were entitled not to the title Gent. nor the right to wear a sword. Doty and Litster (or was it Leicester?), servants equal to each other and other servants, but not to Mr. Hopkins, nor to Elizabeth his wife, not to Constanta or goodson Giles, nor to Damaris were they equal, nor to the daughter born at sea.

In the History, all Massachusetts passes through the pages before they're mentioned again. By then, the life of one has been spent

> *Litster, after he was at liberty, went to Virginia, and ther
> dyed,*

and that of the other can be told in sixteen words

> *Edward Doty by a second wife hath 7. children, and both
> he and they are living.*

They came over in that first ship, then, two servants that never got to be Gents., and for all that appears, they simply *were* and in the course of time were not. But once, as the story goes, once in those two mortal ages, they sought a little more than their portions gave them: it's merely rumor now, a whisper somewhere written down, but the prenticed Edwards, baseborn and unescutcheoned, fought a duel!

Their Triall by Battel took place on a summer's day in 1621, barely half a year after they'd waded ashore in Plymouth Bay — why, their buskins were hardly dry before they were at it with sword and dagger somewhere in the woods in the dark green shade, or it may've been full and flashing in the sun, or was it over the stumbling stones on the beach that the bladed hirelings tried for blood? And they drew it too, liquor of no particular quality, true enough, but red it flowed from every prick and thick from every slash, and each had wounded the other sorely before a hue and cry was raised.

The Colony made much exercise over their passage at arms: it was a great evil that minion had maimed minion to the hurt of a master, but it was an evil even greater that neither was patrician, no, nor cavalier. Wound in bandages, they were tried and found guilty of mutual injury with weapons unsuited to their station. The punishment meted was more in keeping with greasy hair and buckskin jerkins: tight bound hand and foot, they were made to lie thus through a day and a night. Doty and Litster (or Leicester), the lowly brought lower, the mean demeaned, your obed't. servants serve forever while lying on the ground. But in all that copious chronicle of the Governor's, no word is writ of the quarrel's cause.

> *Mr. Hopkins and his wife are now both dead. His sone Giles is maried, and hath 4. children. His doughter Constanta is also maried, and hath 12. children.*

Nor is there further mention of Oceanus, the child brought forth at sea. For aught one knows, she may have lived to land and lasted but a day. So too Damaris, named for her that in Athens clave to Paul. But did she rise to him or fall to someone else — Litster? Doty? both? — and was it thence their duel arose? None can say now. No one knows.

I AM, SIR, yr. MOST OBEDt. SERVt.

*March 5 1644—One Franklin had taken to apprentice
Nathanael Sewell, one of those children sent over for
the country. His master used him with rigor, and the
boy being very poor and weak, died. . . .*

—Winthrop's Journal

He swung for it in the end, Franklin did, but there were some on
the Court who thought him ill-used: they doubted the justice in giving him death for murder when murder had not been proved. Intent
to harm did not appear, they said, and where that was wanting, the
charge must fall. As against the master here, what had been shown
but zeal, a sincere desire to redeem a scurvied noisome boy? In exposing him to cold and wet in the winter season, where was the
dark and heartless heart, and where, in hanging the boy in a chimney,
was the malice in fact or the malice in law, and was it not a licit
thing to lash him upside-down to a horse and drive the two to Boston,
to deny him water along the way, though water lay by the road?
These were but corrective measures, they said, and if bane had been
shown, none had been meant, and through no fault but his own,
a froward boy was dead and gone. Why the hue, why the cry? There
were many such in England, and more would soon be sent. . . .

*Sept 7 1639—One Marmaduke Percy, of Salem, was arraigned
for the death of one (blank), his apprentice. The cause was this:
the boy was ill-disposed, and his master gave him unreasonable
correction, and used him ill in his diet. . . .*

(blank) hadn't died of hunger, nor, overtaxed, had he died of work:
he went to hell with a broken pate. This, he deposed as he lay with
it dying, derived from his master's blows, fetched, he'd sworn, with
meteyard and broomstaff, and upon dissection, fancy became actual,
the fracture became a fact. Another testimony was found, however,
according to which (blank) had spoken of a falling bough that struck
his head, whereupon the master, though not denying that he'd
cudgelled the boy, was held to be acquit. His new apprentice, when

he came, would be a kinsman of the old—his name too would be (blank). . . .

> *August 6 1633—Two men servants to one Moodye, of Roxbury, went out to gather oysters, and they were both drowned, an evident judgment of God upon them, for they were wicked persons. One of them, a little before, being reproved for his lewdness, answered that if hell were ten times hotter, he had rather be there than serve his master, etc. . . .*

Well, the fellow had his way, and to hell he went, and who should greet him at the door but Moodye!, the master he'd cursed a day or two before. He was in disguise, of course, all dressed in red, but the servant knew him none the less for that satin cape and body-coat and the cock-feather aslant in his hat, knew him even with the limp he affected and the sagittary tail he'd affixed to his back—that was Master Moodye, and he too had gone to hell! The place wasn't hot enough for him, though; he was feeding the fire. . . .

> *April 13 1645—A master, being forced to sell a pair of his oxen to pay wages, told his servant he could keep him no longer, not knowing how to pay him the next year. The servant answered, he would serve him for more of his cattle. But how shall I do (saith the master) when all my cattle are gone? The servant replied, you shall then serve me, and so have your cattle again. . . .*

Insolent, Winthrop noted in the margin, but it was rather more than that. *Seditious*, he might've said, and for its hint of rouge, he could've written it in red. The ominous day, when servant ruled and master served, when the foot became he head! A chill was felt by the Governor, as if a wind were on the way. . . .

THE TROUBLES IN NEW-ENGLAND

by Reasons of the Indians there
— Increase Mather

All the sore afflictions of that country
stemm'd from ship-master Hunt
that was with capt Jno Smith
on his voyage,
this unworthy adventurer
having by divers wiles
entic'd some four-and-twenty
savages
on board of his vessell at Patuxet,
or Plimmoth,
and carrying them off
beyond the Streights of Gibraltar
to Maligo
and there chaffering them to Spaniards
for Rials of eight,
a most infamouse act
for which many not yet arriv'd
in the colony
nor even on the way
were to pay with all their treasure,
nay, even with their lives

This unhappy broil with the savages
came to pass some years
before the coming of the first planters,
but, *manet alta mente repostum,*
the Indians were not wont to forget
an injury,
and when, thinking peace prevail'd,

a certain Mr Dermer found port in a ship
(Darmer, some have it, and some Dirmire),
they gain'd the deck treacherously
and gave him fourteen Woundes,
of which he later died in Virginia,
nor was this melancholy event
the last of such
betwixt savages and Englishmen
whose onely aim
was to worship God in Purity,
and ever and everywhere in the Collony
disaster impended,
requiring vigilance of all
in their comings and goings,
and they were rash in the extream
that stray'd from field and fire,
nor were souldiers, arm'd and armour'd,
safe,
for even in open places,
where naught seem'd inimical,
the savages would materialize
from the very grasses
and shower them with arrowes,
all the while yelling
in a manner most barbarouse
until musket and pistole drave them off

Two savages that were very bolde,
one Picksuot and one Wittawamat,
came to the Collony
and behav'd insolentlie,
casting out bloudy Expressions
whilst one of them shew'd a knife
with a woman's face on the handle,
saying he had kill'd with it
and would do so againe,
and having another with a man's face,
he said the twain
would marry in some one's boddy,
whereupon capt Standish
snatch'd one of the knives

and slew the savage with his owne weapon,
and for good measure
the other was slain
and his brother as well

And there came to the Plantation
a certain Sachem
with a large Companye of men,
and with great gravitie he spake,
saying
he would know if he or his
had wrought harme upon the Collony,
and if none,
why had his Corne been stolen away
after notice of such theft
had been given times without number
with neither satisfaction nor reformation?,
and he was answer'd thus,
that but one man had been the thiefe,
and he had oft been whipt for it
in the presence of the Indians,
and now here he was, bound,
and they might have him
to do with as they pleas'd,
but the Sachem demurr'd,
calling it unjust dealing,
for when his people or any of them
wronged a neighbor Sachem,
worde was sent him
and he,
not the one offended,
meted out the proper punishment,
all justice being done by one's owne,
and where not so done,
then it became knowne
that all were leagued with the offender,
as now,
and therefore it was all the English
that had stolen his Corne,
and despite that the thiefe

was then and there kill'd,
the Indians departed
enrag'd and dissatisfied

There follow'd upon this Quarrell
three severall Skirmishes with the heathen,
one at Weseguset,
one at Mattapanock,
and one at the bay of Agawam,
in all of which they were notably beaten,
and it was about this time
that Thos Morton,
the Lord of Mis-Rule,
a drunken and riotous man,
saw fitte
to teach the savages the use of Gunns,
how they should be charg'd and discharg'd,
how to imploye them in the hunt,
and,
worst of all,
how to obtain them,
for which irresponsible acte
he was seiz'd and sent over to England
there to be punish'd as seem'd meete,
but the Damage had been done,
and there began,
or,
since they were constant,
there continued,
those Insolencies,
those treacherouse Ambuscades,
those disturbances in the night
(thirty murthers were suffer'd!)
that cullminated in a warre
to end them,
an enterprize in which they were aided
by Uncas,
or Onkos,
a Mohegan lately renegaded from the Pequots,
a self destructive Propensitie,

true,
but one most wellcome to the Collonists,
for to the wayes of God
it added Indians wayes
to defeate the Indian

Under capt Mason,
ninety souldiers were sent
against the Pequots,
who were arm'd with sixteen Gunns
beside their usuall Artillerie,
arrowes,
and when the forces met at Mistick,
bloud began to flow,
Thos Hurlbut being shott
almost through the Thigh,
Jno Spencer in the back
and into his kidneys,
and lieutt Gardner near the groyne,
two others being shott dead,
and afterward,
through the offices of Uncas
or Onkos,
Mason and his men
were able to force the Indians' palisado,
and, once within,
they fell to with blade and Musket,
determin'd to kill to the last man
and very narrowlie miss'd,
not above five
of the four hundred in the fort
escaping their hands,
and great and doleful was the sight
of so many upon the grounde,
in places so thicklie
as to barre the waye,
and as for losses of their owne,
Master Hedge was shott through both Armes,
capt Mason rec'd many arrowes
against his headpiece,

and capt Gardiner was wounded in the hipp,
and many others were wounded too,
some through the shoulders,
some in their Face,
and some in the legs,
twenty in all being struck,
and then fire was put to the inclosure,
in which many savages died,
or,
if not there,
then in the burning fields of grayne
that grew outside

These and the like
were the Troubles in New-England
by Reasons of the Indians there

VOYAGE OF THE *JAMES*, 1675-76

Monday 6th August . . . a neaggerman
dep'ted this life whoe died suddenly. . . .
—Journal of Peter Blake, Commander

His company, the Royal African, was chartered for trade along the western shores of the continent from Tangier to the Cape of Good Hope, and royally did they work it for gold, beeswax, ivory, and slaves. These last, of course, never saw England; they went to the Barbadoes. . . .

Monday 10th January . . . came to anchor in Wyemba road.
. . . The slaves were at the old Factory house, very thin ordinary
slaves. . . .

They cost too much, those thin and ordinary slaves, they weren't worth the scarlet cloth they brought, the false crystal, the worsted sash and fustian fringe. They fetched too high, those scrags that cast a peaked shadow, overprized against such prime things as trumpets, such plums as padlocks, glass beads, callicoes and taffeties, shells, basons, bells and rings of brass. They must've been Jews, the neagger kings that got such coin for weazened trash. . . .

Wednesday 8th March . . . sett saile from Dickey's road bound
for the Barbadoes. . . .

They were seventy-four days to Kerley Bay, and all along the way, dead neaggers were thrown to sharks that crossed the ocean in their wake. They made a great commotion over thin and ordinary slaves; one would've thought them well-fed, such was the daily thrashing that took place astern. They died from 8th March to 21st May. . . .

dyed of a flux, he wrote in his Journal
departed this life suddenly
departed this life of Convulsion Fitts
departed this life of a Feavour

consumed to nothing and so dyed
very thin and dropsicall and so departed
this life
departed this life of a Consumption
and Wormes
thin and so Continued Untill Death
miscarryed and the Child dead within her and Rotten
and dyed 2 days after delivery
fell into a flux and soe continued
until death
fell into a Consumption and dep'ted
this life
continued Wasting untill death
very sick and fell overboard
dyed of a Great Swelling of face and
head
thin and dyed of a flux
would not eat nor take anything
leaped overboard and drowned
departed this life of a flux
departed this life of a flux
dep'ted this life of a Dropsy
dyed of a feavour by Lying in the
long boat in the rain
thin and old and dep'ted this life
of the flux
consumed away untill life dep'ted
dyed of the Cramp in all Joints
dep'ted this life of Convulsions
dyed of a flux. . . .

All for naught, the gifts of goods and, by way of dashee, the anchors
of brandy. Lost, the ginghams and the chints, the printed lynens,
like unto Birds eye, lost as well the Dammasques, the cowries, the
Blew Perpetanoes, gone all such to hell. . . !

dyed of a flux
dyed of a feavour
dyed of a dropsy
dep'ted this life
dyed
dyed

BACON'S REBELLION

If the redskins meddle with me, damn
my blood, but I'll harry them!
— Nathaniel Bacon

They were fire, those Susquehannocks, they ate at the fringes of Virginia like fire, and they had to be beaten out, wherefore he hated even more the whites that smelt no smoke, the Cavaliers, safe in the Tidewater while the frontiers burned from the Pamunkey to the James. *I hould them our irreconsileable enimies,* he said, but it was hard to tell which race he meant. To the Royal Commissioners, he appeared thus: *Pestilent in discourse, tending to atheisme, in most companyes not much given to talke or to the makeing of suddain replyes, and of a dangerous hidden Pride of Heart.* They might've added this to that, *a slaughterous man, very gorye.*

In his time, it was a crime by statute to entertain or parley with the naturals, to admit more than one inside a palisade, and to trade with them for arms. They'd sworn to forswear their own chiefs for Charles, to hold him alone in dread and sovereign, and each having been given fifty acres for forage and game, they'd been told to stay there and stray no more, to eat what they found, bird, beast, and wormcast, and last but not least, the ground. Small wonder, then, that blue-eyed dead came stiffly down the Pamunkey and wambling down the James, or just some staring head, or the eyes alone, bait for crabs in wait among the reeds.

Bacon owned two domains in the Old Dominion, one at Curl's Wharf and the other up the river near the Falls, and when his overseer was brained and a servant died without his hair, the master raised an army to avenge the purple-blooded pair, and they did so. They tracked down some Nanticokes, or Potomacs, or Doegs (no one seemed to care as long as they were red), caught them redhanded, so to speak, and shot them dead to a man. *Irrecosileable enimies,* he had said.

But putting forces in the field and pledging them to kill was an accroachment of the King's power—Governor Berkeley called it treason—and when a warrant issued, Bacon fled. His flight was short, however, and on being taken, he was brought in and remanded for trial and such doomages and forfeitures as the Court saw fit to impose. The burden was light—if pardon were asked, pardon would be granted—and he bore it.

Oddly now (ungodly so, Bacon thought), he, the same usurper, the same traitor, was prayed to levy and lead a force whose aim it would be to cold-cock every brave he could smell out west of the Chesapeake. Instead, he smelt fish, dead fish and one of them he, and he ran. The chances are, he never heard of Cromwell or any other regicide. He was no ragtag scum in outsize smalls, shagged or torn from some East End ditch; he was well-born, and well had he wedded, for his Suffolk-gentry wife was rich. But from that day on, he was a Roundhead, and, bent on rebellion, he found himself an army, took the capital, and sent it up in smoke—and then, alas, of a stroke or the fever, he went up himself.

He was a hundred years too early with that revolt: set it ahead a century, and it looks like the real thing. Even so, even where it was, it looked real enough to Berkeley, and if Bacon hadn't died, what the old man had in mind for him one fine day was a walk on the wind: the Puritan dog would've worn a hangdog look. As matters were, with Bacon dead, the Governnor relieved his passion by hanging thirty-seven of his men. When told, the King said *As I live, the old fool has put to death more people in that naked country than I did here for the murder of my father.*

JOURNAL OF THE *ARTHUR*, CAPT. ROB'T. DOEGOOD

Gravesend to New Callabar, thence to the Island of Barbadoes, our Portt of Discharge.

−5 Decb'r 1677

−11 Feb'y 1678

Came on Board the Kinge of New Callabarr
and came to Agreem'tt.
For negro man 36 Copper Barrs,
for negro woman 30,
for one metal ring 8 yams.

−12 Feb'y

Came on Board negroes
but nott any we did like.

−13 Feb'y

Bought 14 men 18 women,
very good and young negroes,
with some provitions for them,

−17 Feb'y

Bo't 10 men 5 women 1 Boy and 3 girles
all very likely
not one exceedinge 30 yeares.

−21 Feb'y

Bo't 9 men and 11 women
which were very stout negroes indeed
Butt nott many yames.

−24 Feb'y

Bo't 11 men 6 women and 3 girles,

finding the negroes to be very good
and Likely,
stout and young.

                         —1st March
wee Bought 13 men and 4 women
very good negroes
with some provitions.

                    —Sattday 2 March
Wee have made Choice of Negroes
to the Best of our skill and Judgm'tt
as likely as a man should see
yett wee finde that some doe decay
and grow Leane
and some are sick.

                         —3 March
about 4 in the afternoon
died one negro man:
have 5 others sick.

                         —5 March
Bought 5 men and 5 women.
As yett wee finde the women
generally Better than they men.

                         —Fryday 8
Bought 2 men and 1 woman.
Resolvinge to Buye not any Butt such
as might if Life bee permitted
Answer your hon'rs expectation and advantage.
About four in the afternoon died one woman.
Many sick Captives
Butt take the greatest Care to preserve them.

                    —Sattday 9 March
Bought 8 men and 6 women
very Likely negroes
with some provitions.

We had died this day
one man
and several others sick
notwithstandinge the Docktor's phisick.

                    —Tuesday 12 March
Att 10 in the forenoon
died one man
which
to our knowledge
had nott been sick 12 houres.

                    —Wednsday 13 March
This day died 1 man and 1 Boy.

                    —Thursday 14 March
Are very Likely to Loose more
havinge many very sick.

                    —Fryday 15
Bought 11 men 4 women 2 Boyes and 1 Girle
finding them very likely negroes
and havinge then many sick.
Died this day one man.

                    —Sattday 16
We hope to depart in few dayes
our Complement being up.
Wee have many sick and will not long live.
The reason of ouer Byinge
is bye loss of negroes.

                    —Monday 18
Expectinge the loss of some negroes
and haveinge very likely negroes
By the side
wee Bought 4 men and some provitions.
This day died 1 woman.

                    —Wedsday 20
died this day 1 man and 1 woman

        —Thursday 21
Wayd anchor for the Barbadoes.
Died one man
haveinge many more very sick.

        —Thursday 28
I caused a muster
and found to bee on Board a life
175 men 135 women 9 Boyes and 10 Girles.
This day died one man and 2 women.

        —Fryday 29
In the afternoon
we had sight of Farnandy Po.
This day died one woman.

        —Sattday 30
This day wee had died two men
haveinge att Least 30 more
very sick.

        —Sunday 31
in the afternoon died our Docktor
w'ch wee did accon'tt a great Lost. . . .

Jacob Leisler, 1640–91

LEISLER'S REBELLION

*I do declare before god & the world that what I
have done was for king William & Queen Mary,
for the defence of the protestand Religion & the
Good of the Country.*

—Leisler, on the scaffold

I do declare, he said, but they hanged him anyway. They let him
have his say from up there in the May rain to the crowd in City
Hall Park below, and he was still at it when they tied his eyes, still
speaking *before god & the world,* as they let the trap go. *I am ready,
I am ready,* he was saying, and when they kicked the prop away,
the drop scragged him. The sound of his breaking neck carried despite
the weather and over the groans and the catcalls, and there were
some who heard it afresh whenever they passed Park Row.

By those of another day, he goes unremembered. In the half-paved
park, there's no statue to mark where the gallows stood, no bas-relief
in a wall, and the crowds that cross the place are dead to all but
the small concerns of the hour, dead to his bewildered ghost, lost
now in noise, smoke, and motion. They know nothing of the palatine
Dutchman, nor, knowing, would they care that they were walking
through the space where once he'd walked on air. He was a fool
they'd've said, to buck the rule of the few, and though he thought
he died a martyr, he became no more than meat. To the rich, he
was merely game, prey, something to kill on a rainy day in May.

What I have done, he said, *was for the protestand Religion,* but
what was protestand about summoning an assembly and taxing the
patroons? *What I have done was for the Good of the Country,* he
said, but to the Van Cortlandts and the Schuylers, there was nothing
worse in Rome. *What I have done,* he said, *was for king William
& Queen Mary,* but had James fled the Boyne beaten and come to
haunt us here? To be for the people was to be for the Pope—spit
when you say the word!—and for such the Dutch had rope.

Leisler got a length of it, and at one end he died. There's some uncertainty about where his bones lie now, his skull, his knees, his broken spine, but few inquire these days, only those who can still hear the sound that was made by his neck.

ON THE CARE AND FEEDING OF SLAVES

> *We had aboard four hundred seventeen*
> *men women boys and girls.*
> —James Barbot's Journal

Our passage from Guinea to America, he wrote, *may reasonably be perform'd in fifty days,* and he wrote further that the great mortality on such a Voiage deriv'd from two causes in the main, viz., taking too many slaves in a Cargoe and knowing not how to manage the complement once the shippe had sayl'd. Putting to one side the prolonging of the passage by failure to steer a proper course and by omitting to allowe for the strenth of the currents, these two things, mishandling and overcrouding, were the chiefest fatal mischiefs to be wrought against the slaves.

We lodge the two sexes apart, he wrote, the which was accomplish't by a strong partition at the mainmast, with males forward and females abaft. Very requisite as well was a deck lofty enough to ensure the slaves a goodly supplye of air, five foot high at the least, for they lie below in rows, one above the other, and so that they are kept sweet and cleanly, they are happy and thus the easier to treat.

Slovingly, foul, and stinking, he wrote, were the Dutch shippes and the French, indeed, were some of the English too, not having a sufficiency of coarse thick mats to serve as bedding for the slaves. These, for want of which they must couch upon the bare deals or decks, fended off the distempers of cholick and the bloody flux brought on by the damp of rain and their very owne sweat. Thereto the prudent Captaine would thrice a week add a perfuming of the hold with a quantity of hot vinegar followed by cold, all being well-wash't and scrubb'd with brooms.

Some commanders of a morose and peevish temper, he wrote, would perpetually beat and curb their slaves, but we us'd them with more tenderness, allowing them to be much of the time on deck till evening fell, whereupon the males were sent below. The females, many of them young and sprightly maidens, afforded us abundance of recreation, as did several little fine boyes. We took care that they did wash from time to time to prevent vermin, which they are very subject to.

We mess'd the slaves twice a day, he wrote, the first meal being of beans boil'd with Muscovy lard, whilst the other was of pease, Indian wheat, or the flour of Mandioca, this too with suet and sometimes palm-oil and the Guinea grains called malaguette. Beans we found to be the best food for the slaves, fleshing them far more than wheat or yams, though that root was much prized by such as came from Calabar. These victuals were served out in small flat tubs, each slave being given a little wooden spoon wherewith to feed himself handsomely, and they were well pleased with it. From time to time, we allow'd them a dram of brandy to give strenth to their stommicks.

As for the sick or wounded or out of order, he wrote, our surgions daily went below, and finding any indispos'd, caus'd them to be borne to the Lazaretto where in a sort of hospital they were carefully look'd after. Being there out of the croud, the surgions had more conveniency and time to administer proper remedies, which they could not do between decks, the heat there being so excessive that candles would not burn, and the surgions would faint away.

And he wrote *Much more might be said relating to the preservation and maintenance of slaves in such voyages*, but before saying it, he was compelled to enter a note bearing date of 5 January 1701:

> At about one of the clock in the afternoon, with many of the shippe's company weakened by sickness, the slaves broke their shackles in some fashion and swarmed the decks. Armed with billets, knives, pieces of iron torn from the hatches, and whatsoever else they could lay hands upon, they fell in crouds and parcels on the crew, stabbing the stoutest of all with fourteen wounds so that he expir'd. Next they assaulted our boatswain and cut one of his legs quite round the bone, so that he could not move, the nerves being sever'd. Others cut our cook's throat to the pipe, and still more wounded three sailors and threw one such overboard, who, however, getting hold of the bowlin of the foresail, contriv'd to save himself. Along the lower wale of the quarterdeck, we stood in arms, firing on the revolted slaves, killing some and wounding many. Several, showing no manner of concern for their lives, leapt into the sea and drown'd themselves with much resolution. We lost in that day's work

twenty-eight slaves. The rest were most severely whipt by all our men still capable of that office.

True it was, even as he had written, *much more might be said, much more.* . . .

LIVINGSTON MANOR

he had Rather Bee Call'd Knave Levingston
than poore Levingston
                    — Gov. Benj. Fletcher, of New York

His father, a Scot, was a Calvinist minister who fared poorly under the first Charles and not a little worse under the second, and having nothing at all of the martyr's blood, he fled the Restoration for Holland. Such blood as he did have bred him fourteen children, the first of these begot only after a month of prayer had passed (the flesh!) and the last the son Robert, born at Ancrum somewhere along the Teviot and taken to Rotterdam at the age of nine. There, barely fifteen, he became a merchant, trading in Bordeaux wine, pepper, rye, tobacco, and herring, and in his first full year of venturing, he did quite well, netting some 8,000 florins, a persuasive number whatever the coin was worth. His greatest gain, though he knew it not at the time, was a knowledge of Dutch, and so it proved when, after the death of his father, he turned up on the wild edge of America with his modest sack of chink. Albany, the place was called, for the dukedom of the Stuarts.

When first beheld by Livingston, it was hardly more than a fort on the west shore of the Hudson, a score or so of houses within a palisade. But to his trader eye, its image was that of a door from which the treasure of a continent could be descried, the furs, the timber, the minerals, the land itself and the waters that ranged it. The door, he learned, was one that none could use save by the leave of them that owned the circumjacent world, some seven hundred thousand acres that began at the Mohawk and ran, forty-eight miles broad, down twenty-four miles of the Hudson — the wyck of the Rensselaers. *Rather Knave Levingston than poor Levingston*, he may have thought, and finding one of their widows willing, he wed her, it's said, for her name.

The door opened at once, and through it went his duffels and his stroudwaters, those coarse cloths that the Indians prized, and back they sent the peltries of the wilderness, the otter, the fox, the beaver—and he thrived. Duns now ceased to plague him, indeed, when they came at all, it was to grant him still more goods and still more time, and where he walked, there heads were bared, and few dared speak until he'd spoken. There were some, though, who swore that he knaved it to the end, and in the fifty years left of his life, much appears to bear them out.

Item: He was a partner of Capt. Kidd in a privateer sent out to rid the Red Sea of pirates. The venture itself became piracy when prizes were made of merchant ships, and Kidd, being taken, was held to his trial. Against Livingston, there were charges of *Imbezzelments and concealments*, and while these were being explained away, Kidd, misfortunate fellow, danced on air at Scrag-'em Fair.

Item: By royal appointment, he became Victualer to Crown troops in the colony of New York. He was free, as such, to spend up to 5d. a day per man, profiting only if he could feed them for less. Being a pinchgut with the best, he cheesepared much, and during his tenure, it was short commons for the scarlet regiments. What stick-shanked starvelings they must've seemed, what bones in belts and brass! They were there to hold back the French, but it was all they could do to stave off hunger, and to still its pangs, they stole from the roost, the sty, and the vine, from the steaming pot, the teeming hand, and yet for all they found to eat, they stayed leaner than the shadows they cast on the ground. He made great gain in the sutling trade, but it was said that he billed Whitehall for feeding fictive soldiers and even soldiers dead.

Item: In that time and place, it was land alone that measured fortunes, and Livingston had little enough of that, a lot or two in Albany, to show for his aptitude in Dutch. He did, however, possess a warrant to treat with the Mohicans for a tract *lying upon Roeloff Jensen's kill or Creeke upon the East side of hudsons River, near Cats kill*. For a certain number of hatchets, knives, and cooking vessels, he obtained title to a parcel rather uncertainly described as *the place the Indians call Sa-as-ka-hampka* and meted by such features as *the thicket Ma-ha-aka-kock*. Even so, with his grasp thus scarcely restricted, he could seize no more than six hundred acres, far too few to rival a Beekman, a Cortlandt, a van Rensselaer. He complained to the Governor that the purchase he'd made was paltry, being *much Contrare to Expectations*, wherefore he prayed for leave to purchase more, the area adjacent to the east. In truth, the two plats were fourteen miles apart, one lying near the Hudson and the other in the hills on the Massachusetts line. Still, when the patent was later surveyed, somehow they'd grown together, absorbed what lay between, become, by virtue of those vague descriptions (*the 5 Lime Trees, the rock named A-ca-wanuk*) a manor of 160,000 acres. He was no longer poore Levingston, he may have thought.

If so, there were others who thought otherwise: he was still poore Levingston, and now he was knave as well.

VOODOO ON BROADWAY

Fire! fire! Scorch! scorch!
A little damn by and by!
—a Negro, overheard by Mrs. Earle

There were three such, and they were witchmen, she must've thought, and what they wrought was incantation. *Fire! fire!*, they cried, and then, she said, they laughed. She must've remembered the late conflagration at the Battery, where the fort had been consumed, and the King's chapel (*Scorch! scorch!*), and the barracks, and the stables, and the Governor's house, for all these too the torch—and suddenly she imagined, nay, she knew what was afoot, a plot black and fell to burn the city down, turn the town to ash. *A little damn by and by!*

When the words were reported to the Justices, other prodigies were brought to mind, the finding of coals in a cow-stall, flames in a room where a Negro had slept, the smell of smoke in the night, and they found Mrs. Earle as right as rain—a criminal plot is what it came to, and the name they gave it was Incendium. *Fire! fire! Scorch! scorch! A little damn. . . .*, and even as whites took flight to Bloemendael and Jersey, the jails began to fill with blacks, free and slave alike, men, women, children of every age.

The prisoners were entreated to confess—weeks were spent on such beseechment, and in golden silence the weeks all went. In the end, money was offered for speech, a hundred pounds!, and from Mary Burton a sterling stream of secrets flowed. She was a white indentured servant—some say black and an Indies slave—but black or white, she was the property of John Hughson who with his wife ran a lowlife dive near the Hudson docks. There the bilge of both races mingled, and there, she said, three Negroes (those of Mrs. Earle?) had spoken of burnings and murder, of making Hughson the governor and Cuffy Phillipse king. She declared too that no small part in the conspiracy was played by Peggy Carey, known as the New-foundland Beauty, at once a white strumpet who sold her favors to the blacks and a mistress to Caesar Varick, a fractious Negro bold as brass.

These revelations gave profound appall to the magistrates and the crowd attending Court, and it was no long while until all the island was fraught with fear, and many fled who'd tarried before. The Carey woman was straightway seized, and at her trial, she made a joint and several denial of the charges—they were false, she vowed, false each one and false in sum. Her word, however, was held to be unworthy of belief, and having been found guilty, she was condemned to die. What money had done for Mary Burton doom now did for the dockside jade: it tripped her tongue, and from her mouth a cascade fell.

Under oath, she avouched that there was indeed a conspiracy to kill every white in the city, to strike them down in the streets or drown them in the rivers when they sought to slip away. She further deposed that there was a master head behind the uprising, that on his orders the dead were to be plundered, and that in return for the spoils, the blacks were to be carried to a far country and there made free. She spoke in fine detail, giving names and descriptions and even, due to her trade, the odd scar, the telltale nevus. All thus implicated were laid by the heels and brought before her, a long black procession, a very parade, and though terror shook them, she shook not nor did her story: these were they, she said, theirs the dark hands for the dire deeds of fire and murder.

If she hoped to save herself, the hope was vain: the rope was meant for her as well. She thereupon recanted, swore that she'd been lying, tried to rescue those she'd just now sent to hell. Alas, nothing served her

The executions began with two blacks,
Caesar being one of them,
bold and desperate Caesar,
and Prince the other,
abandoned men, they say,
and both died recklessly,
and Peggy the Newfoundland Beauty
wept at the scaffold,
and weeping
went.

And then it was Hughson's turn,
and all the way to the Battery,
where the gallows were,
he stood pale and proud
in the cart,
holding high a fettered hand
(at what and why?),
and those that saw him
spoke of bright red spots
on either cheek,
a mystery,
for they knew not what such things
might mean,
nor did he say a word.

He was hung in his chains
side by side with a slave,
and together in the April air
they swung
where they could be seen
from ship and shallop in the bay,
and some
who'd come to watch them dangle
said that day by day
their color turned
till Hughson became a Negro
and the slave became a white—
they more than said,
they swore,
and the crowds grew,
marvelling at the change,
thinking it something sent
from the damned world
by the dead.
And as time wore on,
the bodies decayed
in the heat of the sun,
and they began to drip dreadful drops
of matter,
and at last Hughson burst,

a bag of pus,
and so stenchful was the air
that many stayed away,
but not all.

And the bowling green
was thronged
for the burning of the blacks,
these going to the stake
laughing,
buffooning for the multitude,
mocking them
to the end.

In all,
fourteen blacks were burned alive,
eighteen were hanged,
and seventy-one sent to the Indies.
Only four whites were killed,
one a Catholic priest.

Fire! fire!

Scorch! scorch!

. . . by and by!

IT BEING A PLEASENT CUNTRY

the land so good that the weeds hided me when on horse
from seeing the men march at twenty yards distance
—Journal of Capt. Cholmley's batman

It was less than Pleasent for Cholmley, who, unaware that he was due to die in an hour, had for his breakfast on the 9th of July *a little Ham and a Bit of gloster Shire Cheese and a milk punch of which he drank a little.* The repast was taken at nine in the morning, after he had forded the Monongahela with two companies of Foot in advance of the main force. As the Grand Army began the knee-deep crossing, the vanguard moved on toward Fort Duquesne, eight miles distant. Having met with no resistance at the river, the men were quite free from care about this final stage of their traverse of the wilderness: *There Never was an Army in the World in more spirits*, the batman wrote, and the Grenadiers March was playing *Never Seasing.*

And they had reason to rejoice, being but a day's journey from the campaign's end. They'd come far, from Cove near Kinsale to Hampton Roads and from there still further to here—he was right, the Captain's batman, never were spirits higher, and the men went as if on parade while the band played *Never Seasing.* Their woodsmen had hewn them an aisle in the forest four yards wide, and brushing the trees on either side, the two-mile column snaked, the guns, the baggage train, the scarlet body of grenadiers. The very leaves were shaken by martial airs—hearts were high and the music *Never Seasing*—and in fear and fascination birds forgot to fly.

Barely an hour beyond the ford, the guides ran into a lunette of Indians and opened fire. There was no surprise: the savages, sometimes on their own and sometimes with the French, were a presence always, and they'd been sighted often and more than once engaged. But on this occasion and at that particular place, they were no small party sent out to maraud and harass, to try the nerves and pick off stragglers—here was Beaujeu's host from Fort Duquesne, and in two long lines it lay on the hills that flanked the road. Threading it below them came a red and glinting serpentine, Braddock's battalions of Coldstream Grenadiers, thirteen hundred men in embroidered mitres, in gaiters that reached the thigh, in sabretache and bandolier, a glide of red and metal, a reptile four yards wide.

The Indians, and the French who were dressed as Indians, could hardly miss their marks that day: it was two miles in length and twelve feet broad, and after a while they stopped taking aim, forgot the separate soldiers, and popped away at the mass. *My Master,* wrote the batman, *died before we was ten Minuits Ingaged,* and he cited five hundred dead before and after and four more hundred winged and wounded. *Such was ye confusion,* said an officer, *that ye men were sometimies 20 or 30 deep, & he thought himself securest who was in the Center,* but with the enemy firing downward, death found the center too. It hit those pointed caps and bored through the peaks and flaps of embroidered cloth, it hit collars, epaulettes, and frogging, and it struck as well the unobstructed face, and the dead at the core stood as if still living till the outer edges fled. *I Expected Nothing but death for Every Oone of us,* wrote the batman when the flight became general. Abandoned then were the twelve- and six-pounders, the howitzers, the coehorns, left behind the wagons, the gear, the food, the flags, the musical instruments that had Seased to play the Grenadiers March.

Braddock had four horses shot under him, and he was in the act of mounting the fifth when a chewed ball tore through the back of his arm and wore its way down to his lung. *We was Oblig'd to carry him on two long poals,* the batman wrote, but other officers, a score or more from colonel to ensign, were suffered to lie where fallen and die when the Mohawks came. The General was buried in the road, scalp and all, and those who'd put him away cut and ran for it over his grave. They forgot the place, and he's there yet.

A fine level Cuntry, the batman wrote. *Plenty of fruit, both Peaches and Apples.*

IMPRESSMENT, 1769

*No Mariner on board any trading ship imployed in any
part of America shall be impressed or taken away by
any officer belonging to her Majesty's ships of war.*
— Statute 6 Anne (1707)

In the early morning hours of 22nd April, at which time the brig
Pitt Packet, Cadiz to Boston, was still some leagues off Nantasket
Roads, she was hailed by H. M. frigate *Rose,* 20 guns, and directed
to lay to. This done, she was boarded by a small party under the
command of Lieutenant Henry Panton, and, upon his inquiry, her
burden was found to be a quantity of salt, certain wines and spirits,
and some few crates of citrus fruit. Much less interest was shown
in the vessel's cargo, however, than in her complement, and on being queried, her master Thomas Power declared that save for himself
and the mate Hugh Hill, she carried a crew of but six. Not at all
beguiled by this avouchment, Panton cautioned Power that matters
would go ill with him should more be found than the six he had
named over, but if the master was shaken by the admonition, he
gave no sign of disquiet. Less steadfast the mate, and coming un-
done, he was heard to cry a warning down a companionway to a
person or persons below, whereupon Panton charged him with summoning the person or persons aforesaid or himself suffer the pain
of impressment. His threat producing nothing further from the mate,
Panton resorted to action.

Two members of the boarding party were placed in the charge of
Midshipman Bowen, and being ordered to search the *Pitt Packet,*
they forthwith descended into the hold, showing their way with
lighted candles. In the gloom, they came upon nothing but the
cargo specified until, in the planking of a lower deck, a scuttle was
descried. This, on the removal of its cover, proved to be the subter-
fuge of four seamen, all of whom were armed, one with a musket
and the others with a hatchet, a harpoon, and a fizgig, which is to
say a spear tipped with fishhook tines.

Panton was now sent for, and with sword drawn, he went down into the hold and called on those who were lying perdu to discover themselves and surrender. By way of reply, they swore to cut the legs from whosoever should attempt a passage through the scuttle to the forepeak. Having little relish for any such encounter, Panton requested aid from the *Rose,* whereat its cutter was dispatched to him with a press-gang of sailors and marines. Pending its arrival, he sought to parley with the cribbed seamen in an endeavor to persuade them that their plight was hopeless—but they would not have it his way, they said, though he and half a hundred more assailed them. Still, they did agree to let him see their lair, in pursuance of which they accepted a candle from him and passed it about among the recesses of the forepeak, yet when he essayed to set foot in the scuttle the better to view its interiors, a musket was presented to the space between his facings, and he felt constrained to withdraw.

By then, his reinforcements had been delivered by the cutter from the *Rose,* and certain of their number were put to the work of breaking into the forepeak. When those within became aware of what was abroach, they called out that they would fire through the first aperture made in the bulkhead. It befell instead that one of the marines fired first, he discharging a pistol at random into the crepuscular forepeak, with the result that a seaman named Corbet was seared on the lips by the powder-flash.

Once again Panton besought the four seamen to give themselves up, but their response was the same as before: they would not be pressed, they vowed, they would not be made to serve the Crown. Corbet cautioned Panton that he would be the death of him if he failed to stand aside, at which Panton warranted him that should he chance to kill anyone, he would surely dance the gibbet jig. As the demolition of the bulkhead continued, the naval officer, in order to observe the progress of the work, seated himself close by upon a mound of salt. Alas, he did not live to find his feet again, for suddenly a harpoon was thrust through the riven wood, gashing his throat and severing a carotid artery: he bled to death in half an hour, his slayer being the seaman Corbet.

Thereafter the men began to surrender, a certain John Ryan first, his arm broken by a stray shot, then a pair together, and lastly Corbet, all blood about the face. They were at once transferred to the *Rose,* which, in company with the brig, spread sail for Boston. Upon arrival, Panton's body was removed from the *Pitt Packet,* prepared for burial, and interred in the presence of Commodore Hood and a great congress of officers in full array. Only then did attention turn to Corbet and his fellows and their Felony upon the Sea.

With John Adams and James Otis of counsel, the four were tried before a commission of judges without a jury, and after proceedings that consumed several days, the case against the seamen was halted during summation, and to the astonishment of many, the charges were dismissed. It was held, per Francis Bernard, justice and royal governor of the province of Massachusetts, that Lieutenant Panton had met his death during the commission of an illegal act, viz., the search of a trading vessel, not for dutiable goods, but for able-bodied men with intent to impress them, contrary to the statute of Anne; the taking of his life by Corbet had therefore been a justifiable act.

THE BOSTON MASSACRE, 1770

He has plundered our Seas, ravaged our Coasts, burnt
our towns, and destroyed the Lives of our People.
—Declaration of Independence, 1775

They were a sorry lot, the 29th Grenadiers, micks in the main, trotters of the bog, foul, witless, full of snot, and, Lord, how they did long to down their dram and skin the snake! God's truth, they were good for little else but grog and dice and sniffing quim. As soldiers, the sonsofbitches didn't cut much feather, being as near to scum as one could skim from Queenstown's ditches. Only Tories found a boon in the shabberoon regiment: it was a cure, they thought, for Adams (Sam) and his Sons of Liberty. They were taught otherwise as soon as the Lobsters were quartered on Boston.

There was the devil and all to pay when they began to parade around, the men in their blood-red coats and their mitred caps of bearskin, the officers crimson-sashed, with espontoons and silver gorgets. They flashed in the winter sun, and as they strode the wharves and streets, they made drab New England bright. But they were sheen and shade and nothing more, and where they went, there the cold shoulder, the smolder and spite, and boys came japing in their train, taking off their way of walking, disdainful, vain, and now and again one would toss a horse-turd, make the long nose, and speed away.

For the most part, they'd frequent the rum-shops of Castle William and the cribs along the docks, and there, on drink and bobtail, they'd spend their slender pay. And then, hard up for one more wet, one more sight of the upright grin, they'd traipse the town for a job of work, whatever would fund them for sluts and stingo. A place sometimes good for a shilling or two was John Gray's ropewalk, a long walled-in shed that housed the gear for making cordage, the spinners, the hackles that combed the flax. There, they'd heard, a man might find what he sought, a day's char for the odd stiver.

One such Queer Street grenadier was Patrick Walker, and around noon of a certain day, he betook himself from Murray's Barracks to the ropewalk, where a cable-layer named William Green asked him if he was there to hire out. Upon his reply of an oath and an aye, Private Walker was invited to clean out the ropewalk shithouse, at which witful sally a horselaugh ran through the shed. Walker, swearing by the Holy Ghost that he would have his quittance, attempted to assault the ropers without the Paraclete's aid, whereat he was given his bastings and driven away. He soon returned, abetted by some ten or a dozen of his fellow grenadiers, but the workers, armed with clubs and wouldring sticks, beat the attackers off. Once more came the soldiers, forty-odd in number now and stiff with bludgeons, and there ensued another passage at arms with the same result as before, the citizens holding the field, the soldiers put to rout. But the Ropewalk War was not yet over. During the next two days, there were further affrays between the people and the regiment. In one such, someone broke a grenadier's crown. In another, when a soldier was challenged for lurking in the dark, he said he was pumping shit, and if true, so sore was he beset that erelong he had to pump it from his pants.

The town was quiet all through the following day, but something quite as sensible as sound was in the air, and as though by a general clairaudience, everyone seemed to know that the night would never pass without a flow of blood. When evening came, it was clear and cold, and a quarter-moon shone on the foot-deep snow in King Street. A few small parties were abroad, some made up of soldiers and some of townsmen, and these met in chance collisions that at first ran only from lurid curse to vivid gesture. But their appetites merely fed on feeding, and presently it was not enough for a redcoat to cry *Scabby colonial knave!* in return for *Son of a whore in a ditch!* More was needed, and more was found when Captain Goldfinch was clapper-clawed for failing to pay his debts. The impeachment was made in the presence of a sentry posted before the Custom House, and it was hardly more than spoken when his musket struck the accuser's jaw. Dazed, he crept away—a small fire, but in no long time all Boston blazed. Strays fell in with strays, twos and threes grew to dozens, and these, swarming in Dock Square, in Cornhill, in Brattle Street, became too numerous to tell, and the bells began to ring, and there were cries of *Fire! Fire!*, and soon no one knew the real from the fire in the mind. Now, as though the very stones were burning, people ran through the streets, men, boys, servants black, and sailors white, but there were no red skies to be seen that night, no reddened streaks of snow. There were only ever more people, and many (all, some swore) were armed with staves, cordwood, hangers, tip-cat sticks.

The flow was toward the Custom House, or, more narrowly, toward the sentry, a soldier by the name of White. With a liver to match, he'd taken refuge inside, where, shielded only by the King's money, he stood in fear of his life. No less fearful was Captain Preston, who ordered a squad of soldiers from the guardhouse, tall men all and all of them taller for their bearskin caps, and with bayonets fixed they were marched through the crowd in King Street and drawn up before the empty sentry-box. White was then called out, and he was allowed to come, but when Preston attempted to pass back through the crowd, they would none of them give way for him, one of them crying *Fire, you sonsofbitches! You can't kill us all!* The officer commanded them to disperse, but they pressed in all the more, jeering the while and filling the air with curses, chunks of ice, and double-daring: *Fire!* they cried, *Why do you not fire!,* and they rapped on outthrust muskets with their scantlings and their strakes.

Further taunting led to further menace from the flintlocks, half-cocked and presented low, and now, flung by an unknown hand, a bludgeon fetched one of the grenadiers a blow that put him ass-down in the snow. Rising, he recovered his fusil and fired into the crowd around him, most wonderfully hitting nothing. Thinking therefore that the guns were charged with powder only, the people closed in on the soldiers with the patent purpose of doing for them all. The guns, alas for a random five, were also loaded with ball.

The first to fall was Samuel Gray, one of the ropemakers and possibly a kinsman of the owner of the walk. He died of a bullet through the head that made a hole as broad as his hand. A soldier then shoved his bayonet into the skull, picked out the brains, and scattered them on the snow.

Next to be hit was Crispus Attucks, thought by some to be a mulatto and by others a half- or even a fullblooded Natick Indian. He was shot in both the right and left breasts just below the paps, and he lay gurgling blood for a moment or two and died.

James Caldwell, reputed to be a mariner, was killed by a ball through the body.

Patrick Carr, a maker of leather breeches, was shot twice, once in the hip and once in the spine, and after lingering for six days, he died.

Samuel Maverick, a youth apprenticed to an ivory-turner, was found by a ricochet while running from the scene, and he died on the following day.

In addition, Edward Payne, a merchant, was struck by a bullet in the right arm, and Robert Paterson, a sailor, by a bullet in the right wrist; as for Kit or Christopher Monk, John Green, John Clark, and David Parker, they were said only to have been dangerously wounded.

Captain Preston and a dozen grenadiers of the 29th Regiment were tried for murder, and all but two were acquitted. These, privates Mathew Kilroy and Hugh Montgomery, having been found guilty, were sentenced to be branded on the right thumb, and this being then and there done, they were released. . . .

THE BOSTON TEA PARTY, 1773

tea — that bainfull weed
— Abigail Adams

Sam Adams had his hand in that stunt, Sam and his Sons of Liberty, which to cousins John and Abigail made Liberty a bitch. Depend on it, Sam was somewhere in that night's work: he was in on any game going, or, better put, he'd often set the game afoot and send his Sons to play it. Those wipe-noses of his, pocked, pustulent, and saber-shinned, they'd come when called and go where told. Doubt not, then, that Sam was in the wind that night, that it smelled of Sam and rebellion before it smelled of tea.

Tea, tea—how the people did long for the fragrant infusion! God knows in what ways it wondered them, that brown decoction with its shy perfume, but whatever it did when downed, they were its creatures all, and many ran to buy it with holes in both of their shoes. They would have it, the hyson, the bohea, the smoky souchong, come what might, they would drink the essence of the delicate leaf—but when, as a royal right, the Crown dutied it at 3d. a pound, they denied their desire and turned to other things. They tried Labradore, which they made from the red-root bush, and they steeped sage and camomile, which tasted of apples, and they used spearmint too and wintergreen, and valerian, celery seed, and vervain blue. But it was all a brave show, and in the end they turned back to darjeeling, to singlo, twankey, and black congou: they were slaves, no less, of the bainfull weed.

For which great was the joy in the counting-rooms of London, in the auction-halls, in the distended warehouses—one could almost see the walls subside! From the East India docks, four tea-ships sailed, the *Dartmouth*, a three-masted constant trader, the brigs *Eleanor* and *William*, and the *Beaver*, a brigantine; among them, they carried seventeen hundred chests valued at £18,000. The *William* was driven aground somewhere along the Cape Cod shore, but the other three made a safe arrival at Boston and docked at Griffin's Wharf.

It was then that Sam and his Sons made the stair creak in the night, made curtains ripple though the air stayed still. Warnings were sent to the consignors: refuse the tea, they were told, *fail not, upon thy peril* to ship it back to where it came from. On the town, a squall of handbills fell, and there were tumultuous assemblies and torch-light parades, and toughs were suffered to roam the streets, to fill the dark with fearsome roaring, to destroy at will what took their fancy, and well might they do what they'd done before. In the Stamp Act blow-up of '65, plug-uglies—Mackintosh's Chickens, they were called—had sacked the house of the Governor. In a reverse Crea-tion, they'd reduced a whole to a pile of parts: they'd pulled the siding off, exposing the studs, and then, having ripped up the floors and torn out the paneling, they'd fallen to work on the roof, and slate by slate they'd trepanned it down to the rafters. Small wonder, then, that the nip-cheese tea-merchants felt safe from the Sons only at Castle William, under the guns of the Crown.

At an eruptive session in Old South Meeting House, someone shouted from the crowd *Who knows how tea will mingle with sea water!*

And someone else cried *Boston harbor a teapot tonight!*

And from a third there came a cheer—*Hurrah for Griffin's Wharf!*—and the mob was on its way.

An outpour of people flowed from Old South and ran down Milk Street toward the bay, but, strange to say, those in the lead were led themselves—ahead of them, they found a howling band of In-dians, feathers aflutter and fringes flying. Narragansets, an observer later said, but at this turning or that, as all had done that night, he'd lost or suppressed the faculty of recognition. The daubed figures he saw before him were no more savage than he: they were near neighbors, they were kinsmen and friends, they were buyers of his wares and sellers to him, they were pranksome boys, tipplers, tapsters, drovers, and -wrights, they were the riff and raff of Boston, dense, rancid, base, and (quite as stupid, rank, and low) some of them were gents. Whooping as they went, they streamed off Milk and across Cow Lane, and brands were burned to light their way, fire that seemed to float on the night, and from the warped-in ships at the wharf, their coming was seen and heard, a thousand or more on a roaring run.

Reaching the waterfront, they boarded the vessels at once, and challenged by their captains, the mob put them aside, bawling

The tea we want, and the tea we'll have! — and they straightway had it. With block and tackle, the chests were hoisted from the holds, smashed open with axes, and emptied by the board, dozens thus, scores, and in the end hundreds went, by which time, with the tide ebbing, the bay was too shallow to carry off the leaves, and they lay where poured, saturate and swelling, growing up alongside the hulls like new land, and they grew until they began to spill back onto the decks. Men were put upon the tea-islands to shovel them away, but by then the tide was at the turn, and what they sought to send was brought right back, and soon, from Fort Hill to Dorchester Neck, the bay was a swamp of astringent steepings.

No injury was worked on the *Dartmouth*, the *Beaver*, or the *Eleanor*, and when the exploit ended, they were left as they'd been before: ropes were recoiled, lifting-gear was trimmed, and bulwarks and hatches were swept clear of tea and tea-dust. Two sneaks, caught trying to pinch some of the jetsam, were given their comings, after which the ruddied whites, the white Narragansets, marched away from the wharf to the knife-like note of a fife.

Names were rarely mentioned at the time, nor even when the deed was a crime no longer, and therefore none can say now who took part and who did not. Still, as the years went, a list seemed to lengthen, as though a sense of history had made men decide to hide less closely, lest they die and go unknown. And so hints fell and rumor was sown, and one day the register came to embrace many, some of whom were there that night, some who'd merely dreamt of being, and some who, asleep or waking, never were at all. Only these, in Heaven now, are privy to the truth:

Major Nathaniel Barber: a Whig merchant
Captain Thomas Bolter: a housewright
Adam Collson: a leather-dresser, said to have been the person who shouted *Boston harbor a teapot tonight!*
Samuel Cooper: an inspector of pot and pearl ashes
John Crane: a carpenter, who suffered the only harm of the night, having been struck on the head by a derrick-boom and left for dead under a pile of shavings
Captain Joseph Eaton: an eccentric hatter, who wore a tricorne and called himself General
——Eckley: a barber, who, on being informed against, was sent to prison

Nathaniel Frothingham: a coachmaker

John Hicks: a printer, later killed by the British at Lexington

John Hooton: an apprentice, who on seeing a tea-thief in a canoe, leaped overboard and beat the boat from under him with an oar

Matthew Loring: a cordwainer

Ebenezer Mackintosh: a tradesman, reputed to have been the instigator of many violent disturbances

Major Thomas Melvill: a man of business, known as the last to wear small clothes in Boston, grandfather of Herman, who attained some popularity as an author

Thomas Moore: a wharfinger

John Pearse Palmer: a dealer in West Indian goods

John Peters: born at Lisbon, Portugal, fought at Lexington, Bunker Hill, Princeton, Monmouth, and Trenton, was in at the surrender of both Burgoyne and Cornwallis, died at the age of 100

Dr. John Prince: a pastor from Salem

Paul Revere: a metalsmith

Robert Sessions: a justice of the peace

Samuel Sloper: said to have been one of the party, but nothing further known

Thomas Urann: a shipjoiner

David Kinnison: a farmer, fought in the War of the Revolution and the War of 1812, both legs shattered in a gun-burst at Sackett's Harbor, learned to read at the age of sixty, father of twenty-two children, moved to Chicago at the age of 109, died there six years later

Lendall Pitts: a clerk of the market

William Hendley: a mason

Moses Grant: an upholsterer

and there were these too, an importer of wines, a house painter, a dyer, a surveyor, a teacher and usher, a publisher, a native of Malta, more, more, always more, as if none could bear to have been in Boston that night without having been *there* . . .!

A MARTIAL AIR AT A HANGING

> *Your music is excellent.*
> —Major Andre, to his guards

John Andre, Esq.,
Major, Fifty-fourth Foot,
Royal Fusiliers
at Tappan, in New York state.

Sir:

To be addressed by a stranger at a time such as this will doubtless seem to you a most unwarrantable intrusion, bold, gross, cold even to the point of cruelty, wherefore I beg leave to say that erelong we shall meet face to face, on which occasion what satisfaction you may require I shall readily accord. For all that, sir, I venture to suggest that upon our thus coming together, you will demand no *amende honorable* for my conduct. Nay, rather will you have come to feel that in accosting you as you went toward extinction—in plucking your sleeve, if you will, on the road to the grave—I was chargeable only with a wish to pave your way. Would that as much had been done for me when, four years gone, I trod that road myself.

Ah, but yes, my dear Major, he who indites these lines to the rope's next victim was once its victim too. Small wonder, then, that at this juncture my mind should be drawn to you, but be assured, sir, that I hold you to be more than a mere gallows-bird, more than my fellow following four years behind. Since my hanging, many another has swung for a crime, but until now none I know of has paid for one so very like my own: you spied for your country, I spied for mine. I feel, therefore, that we stand, you and I, in a quite special relation, more apposite than opposed, more like than not, indeed, more the self-same thing.

Being there still, being still alive, you may doubt the comparison, deny the alliance, but I urge you to remember that I am *here*, where the sole denial is the denial of doubt: here there are only meanings;

here, sir, we see what you fail to see, the conjunctions you are unaware of, the presences that have you by the hand. Thus, I say that if we differ at all, it is simply in the respect that we each served our own—you the King, and I—well, I another George. Beyond that, like our deaths, our lives lie very near.

We began neither in the glare of wealth nor the glow of purple: we sprang from less well-lit loins, a merchant's you, a yeoman's I. Our early learning came from pastors, our later from within the walls, mine Yale's, Geneva's yours, and even as my *amorosa* would have none of me (marvel not that I know these things), no more would your Honora, blue and blonde, honor you. To our like annals, add that final correspondence, our melancholy fate on the gibbet, and, A to izzard, what you have, dear sir, is the illusion realized: parallels that meet, or, rather, parallels due to meet within the hour.

I know that hour well: I have endured it. Mine ended at daybreak, when the Provost sent his men to fetch me from the gaol. Some say I was then borne away to a place in mid-Manhattan, near a tavern named The Dove, but no such journey can I recall, nor do I remember my hangman as a beast. He did not deny me a Bible, he did not destroy my last letters, curse me coarsely, taunt me as a traitor to the Crown. He merely hanged me, as General Howe had ordered, and then he lived on, as your topping-cove will do—and my General.

Soon you will join me here, and then that which is now dim will clear, the presences you now but feel will grow, and you will know them to be real: in an hour, sir, you will be admitted to the mysteries of the future and the past. I learned them four years ago, but you will not share their meaning for yet another hour. Alas, and I tell you this with rue, it was a sell, our dying as we did, you for England old and I for England new—a sell, sir, and we were sold.

I changed nothing when I danced the Tyburn jig for Captain Cunningham, nor will you for Colonel Scammel. Our real hangman is the world, and it will make its round of itself and the sun never knowing we are gone since it never knew we were there. The same sovereign, your George or mine, will rule it forever, and the same rag-tag will be forever ruled. We spied each of us for his own side, thinking there were two, but here we know the tristful truth: there really is but one. I entered the British lines to learn how their forces were disposed, and you conspired with Arnold for the betrayal of the Point, but had we both achieved our aims, neither the King nor the people would have feasted: the fruits are for the few.

Go, therefore, on your morning's walk from Tappan. Go arm in arm with your guards while fife and drum play you *Roslin Castle,* and say, as I know you will, *Your music is excellent.* Go now a mile or so to the gallows—go, my friend, and we shall meet within the hour. . . .

Valley Forge, 1777–78

OF THE GOINGS ON OF THAT WINTER

Cold Weather
Nasty Cloaths
Vomit half my time
smoak'd out of my senses
No Whiskey
No Forage
hard lodging
                The Devil's in't
Lord
        Lord
                Lord
— diary of Surgeon Albigence Waldo

As winters went, it wasn't the worst those parts had known. There'd been colder days in other seasons, and more snow had fallen, lain longer, grown grayer in the rain, there'd been thicker ice on the Schuylkill, and in memorial years there'd been twice the wind and half the sun. Still, it *was* winter, and snow did fall and water freeze, and for eleven thousand men, fed ill and poorly housed, it was small assuagement to be told of snows of the past, of bygone rains.

The ground lay well enough, being much of it bluff and vale, rather like redans and lunettes, which they quite became when the guns arrived from Gulph Mills and Whitemarsh — a good lie, the land had, and along the rises tents arose, dingy little clouds discarded by the sky. Greenwood fires warmed little but the air above them and the earth beneath, sentries used their hats for shoes, made leggins of straw and paper hose, and some wore borrowed small clothes or froze in none at all.

Of those in camp, one in three was unfit for duty, what with blueballs, rheum, and putrid fevers, and there were itches too and the breast complaint, and what soldier was free from the trots? The smell was intolerable *oweing to the want of necessaries, or the neglect of them* — the neglect, meaning that eleven thousand men pretty much stooled where they stood and pissed where they pleased,

until an order was issued to shoot any who eased outside the Vaults.
For one infraction or another, a Court Martial sat nearly every day.

Capt. Lambert
of the 14th Virginia Regt.
was found guilty of stealing a Hatt
from Capt. Allis
and sentenc'd to be Cashier'd,
and it was stipulated
that his Name & his Crime
be publish'd in every State,
most espetially in his own,
and that he pay 30 dollars
to Capt. Allis
for the stolen Hatt

and Wm. McIntire
of the 7th Pennsylvania Battn.
was tried for robbing
a load of wheat &c.
from Colo. Spencer's Waggoners,
and being found guilty,
was sentenc'd to receive
30 lashes on his bare back
well laid on
in the presence of his entire Regt.

and Wm. McMarsh
of Capt. Lee's Artillery Compy.
was tried on two counts,
stealing a Horse & Deserting,
and though acquit of the desertion,
he was found guilty of the Theft
and Sentenc'd to 100 lashes
and to have half his pay stopt,
but having had a Good Character
theretofore,
the Lashes were remitted
but the pay was lost

From Philadelphia, twenty-some miles away, stories came to

the camp, and they went from fire to fire, passed as the smoke did, swirled with the wind, and in tent and hut men spoke of their own, prisoners now of the Enemy and starved in the midst of glut. One, they heard, driven by hunger's rage, had devoured his own fingers, others had eaten lime dug from the prison walls, and dead had been found with bark in their mouths, with bits of wood, aye, not with bread but stones.

and Lt. Guy
of Colo. Lamb's regt. of Artillery
was found guilty of
unGentlemanly and unOfficerlike behavior
in committing Robbery and Infamous stealing,
and he was sentenc'd
to have his sword broke over his Head
on the grand parade
and to be discharg'd from the regt.,
and the Court decreed
it wd. be deem'd a Crime
of the blackest Die
to associate with him thereafter

and Joseph Edwards, drover,
inhabitant of Pennsylvania,
being tried for attempting to sell Cattle
to the Enemy,
was found guilty and sentenc'd
to pay the sum of £100,
of which 20 dollars
should go to each of the Light Horse
that apprehended him
and the rest to the Sick in Camp

and Capt. Zane
of the 13th Virginia Regt.
was tried for Acting in a Cowardly manner
when sent out with a scouting party,
in that he order'd his men to retreat
when advantag'd over the Enemy,

and being found guilty,
he was sentenc'd to be discharg'd
from the Service

For eating fire-cake and beef so thin they could see the butcher through it, for going without women, soap, stockings, mittens, boots, bedding, hope, for wading through shit to take a shit, for pissing yellow ice not seldom streaked with red, for drowning in their own snot, for being high enough to stink a dog off a gut-wagon, for freezing, scratching, puking, coughing, and standing for guff from commissioned poltroons—for all that and more, the soldiers were occasionally paid, but always in Continentals

private	6 2/3 dollars	per mo
fifer	7 1/3	do
cannoneer	8 1/3	do
dragoon	8 1/3	do
bombardier	9	do
trumpeter	10	do
drum major	10	do
farrier	10	do
saddler	10	do
corporal	9	do
sergeant	10	do
executioner	10	do

It was directed, and so entered in the Orderly Book, that no furloughs were to be granted above the rank of Captain, but there were two other ways of leaving the camp. One was resignation, which, Washington wrote, had become truly epidemical, the Virginia line alone having in that manner lost ninety officers, among them *Six Colonels as good as any in the Service.* The second way was desertion.

and John Reily
of the 2nd Virginia Regt.
was convicted of deserting
while on guard
and taking two prisoners with him,
and being sentenc'd to death,

he was respited one day
and hang'd the next,
and Francis Morris
of the 1st Pennsylvania Regt.
for repeated desertions,
was given death by the Court
& hang'd,
and Thos. Hartnet
of the 2d Pennsylvania Regt.
was found guilty of deserting
to the Enemy,
and he was hang'd,
and John Morrel
of the 16th Massachusetts
was found guilty of deserting his post
while on Sentry
and sentenc'd to be hang'd,
but the Commdr. in Chief
remitted his punishment,
and Thomas Shanks, ensign
of the 10th Pennsylvania,
for offering to serve the Enemy
in bitterness over a conviction
for stealing his Captain's shoes,
was found guilty on being retaken
and sentenc'd to hang

And many fled who went uncaught, men who shed their regiment-
als and walked a winter's walk at night and wide of villages and
always through the woods, and when they reached a certain dooryard
somewhere in Jersey, Carolina, Maine, tried to live there till they
died, and some did, but not all; and there were officers who, if apprehended, would've been cashiered and ever after held to be in-
capable of holding a commission in the Continental service, and
across their files the Court would've written that it would be scan-
dalous for any other officer to hold friendly correspondence with
them, and those that lived long would long have been scorned.

and Lt. John Rust
of the 10th Virginia Regt.

was found guilty
of abusive aggravation,
of being drunk & playing at Cards,
and of striking Capt. Laird
on the Sabbath day,
and though he had borne a Good Character
in earlier times,
he was dismiss'd the Service,
nor wd. the Commdr. in Chief
reinstate him,
his gameing alone being held
to exclude him
from all Indulgence

and Lt. Frederick Enslin
of Colo. Marcum's company,
charg'd with attempting to commit Sodomy
with Jno. Monhart a soldier,
was found guilty
and sentenc'd to be dismist the Service
with Infamy,
and such being the Abhorrence & Detestation
of the Commdr. in Chief
that Lt. Enslin was order'd
drumm'd out of Camp
by all the Drums & Fifes in the army,
mounted backwards on a horse,
without a saddle,
and his Coat turn'd wrongside out,
and he was warn'd nevermore to Return

   In truth, there was much to run from, and when untold numbers
did so, no one marveled, least of all the Commdr. in Chief. The
wonder was that so many stayed, vomiting half their time, smoak'd
out of their senses, verminous, full of wind and void of food, eating,
sleeping, drilling, living, all on those fifteen hundred acres along the
Schuylkill, the biggest open shithouse in the New World. Those that
stayed, the General must've thought, Lord, Lord, Lord, they were
the ones!

THE BRITISH PRISON-SHIP *JERSEY*

Rebels, turn out your dead!
— morning-call of the guard

She was moored on the Brooklyn side of East River in the chan-
nel of Wallabout Bay—an old 60-gun frigate of the fourth-rate that
in a better day had split the wind with a lion on her stem. A long
time gone the figurehead and the guns, and with them the masts,
the spars, and the rigging: there was no more need for such things.
Chained among the mud-flats, she'd never know sail again, never
give chase, never be fought; she'd die where she rode, on a tide running out or one running in. But before her end came, she'd be the
death of many in the dark hollows of her hull. Daily there'd be the
samesome cry of *Rebels, turn out your dead!* and daily hands would
would pass them up to hands reaching down from a square of sky.

They say eleven thousand died in the hold of the *Jersey*. They tell
of six, eight, ten each night, stiff where they lay when day flowed
in over Paumonok. And this too was told, that they were stacked
in a skiff and rowed ashore, where, between high and low water,
they were barely buried in the sand. And as time went by, so said
all, tides washed the fill away, and bones began to show, skulls,
scapulae, a kneepan, a femur, and in fleshless fists wicks of sedge
could be seen, like nosegays offered from another world. At evening,
as many attested, lights seemed to drift on the meadows and the
marshes—it was the will-o-the-wisp, they swore, the sprite seduc-
ing the wanderer astray.

The sickness that seized every prisoner,
                    Christopher Hawkins said,
was *dyssenterry.*
All suffered from the bloody flux,
that violent and constant call of the bowels,
and there being too few tubs below
to hold the void,

and but two at a time being allowed on deck,
it followed that the rest
relieved themselves where they stood or lay,
and soon each was bedaubed with stool,
his own and that of others.

To John Van Dyk,
the *Jersey* was a jakes.
The very air was emulsified shit,
and umber its hue in the gloom.
I thought it would soon kill me, he said.

As for Andrew Sherburne,
he suffered severely from the cold,
toiling much of the winter nights
at the chafing of his extremities,
and while engaged with one, he said,
another would numb with freeze,
and thus the hours would pass
in thawing chill with chilly hands.
A man lying next to him,
being too sick to do likewise,
had his feet frozen
so that the soles were cleft from the bone
and hung down hinged at the heel.

On coming aboard the *Jersey*,
Alexander Coffin said,
he found there about eleven hundred prisoners
of from three to six months' duration,
few lasting longer if they failed to get away.
The living were merely bones in rags,
and so laced were these with lice
that they all but rippled.
For the use of the guards, he said,
there were hogs that were kept in pens,
and he saw men steal mash from the troughs
and partake of it as of savory soup.

And what's-his-name said

On the *Jersey*, all was filth.
Every prisoner was infested with vermin,
on his body and in his clothes,
and there were many observed
with their shirts in their hands,
picking for lice in the plaits
and for want of meat
eating the creatures when found.

          And Ebenezer Fox wrote
that each prisoner got this food and no more:
Sun.—1 lb biscuit, 1 lb pork, 1 lb pease
Mon.—1 lb biscuit, 1 lb meal
Tues.—1 lb biscuit, 2 lbs beef, 2 oz butter
Wedn.—1½ lbs flour, 2 oz suet
Thurs.—same as Sun.
Fri.—same as Mon.
Sat.—same as Tues.

          And someone else said
the butter was a sweet oil,
so rancid,
so putrid,
that its stench, even to those
who would eat the pickings of a nose,
was more than they could endure—
and yet there were some,
though few,
that would receive it most gratefully
and with a pinch of salt to season it
contrive to keep it down.

          And another said
all the food was damaged.
The bread was mouldy and shot with worms
that would not be dislodged
save by a sharp rapping on the deck.
As for the pork, so spoiled was it
that its color was motley,
like variegated soap,

and the flour was so much soured
that it might be smelled
for half the length of the ship.
The beef,
if beef it was,
was a phenomenon in that
it could not be cut across the grain,
though lengthwise it would pull apart
like rope-yarn,
like oakum
but not like meat,
and it could not be eaten
unless boiled well in salt water,
this having to be recovered from overside,
where the filth of thousands was poured
and lay till carried off by the tide.

       And another said
the bread had been so gnawed by weevils
that it could be crushed in the hand
to dust
and huffed
like dust
away.

       And another said
that at evening,
all prisoners were ordered below—
Down, rebels, down! was the cry,
whereupon down they would go
into the hot or cold stink,
there to lie in their sweat
or under the blown-in snow.

      And yet another summed it,
saying
the whole ship
from keel to tafferel
contained pestilence
sufficient to desolate the world—

disease and death
were part of her very timbers.

                                 To which someone added this,
that the atmosphere below
was so mephitic
that a candle would not burn.

    Rebels, cried the guards at morning, *turn out your dead!*
    They tried, all through those four years, to make the rebels rebel
no more, they let them perish to keep them loyal: few to save their
lives would swear away their reason for living, and there in the *Jersey,*
eleven thousand died. The ship died too, slowly settling in the
Wallabout mud, decaying, dead before she drowned, and long later,
bones would be collected from the beach, twenty hogshead, and sold
for a penny a pound.

THE LAST GENTLEMAN

His integrity was most pure, his
justice the most inflexible.
— Thomas Jefferson

He knew, when the ague shook him in the night, that the way would not be long: the winter without had come within, entered the room, entered him, and soon now he'd be one with the season, die of cold that had become his own. He knew, even as Mister Lear was sent for, Lear his aide and very near his son, that all the small and useful things would be done for him, that a fire would be lit and a linctus brewed, that someone would be summoned to open a vein—and indeed it was so. His blood did flow, and syrups were tried, and the hearth was made to glow, and still he knew that death alone would end what chill had begun. When physicians came, he suffered their auscultations, and he let them bind his throat and bathe his feet—as if remedy lay in some affinity of extremes—but never was he beguiled by their calomel, or their sal volatile, or their cataplasms of wheat: they were trying to treat what was almost a corpse.

He let his mind float from the faces roundabout, from hands doing futile this and needless that, from the aroma of sage tea, the mordancy of embrocations, let his attention wisp and wander, go as smoke and fray away. It was as though he were being borne on some current as gentle as time, but not for very far, for he had not far to go, a day's drift at most, and even now, not yet there at the end, he could see what lay beyond. He wondered as he neared it why it was known as the great unknown. Had not he soon in life seen the coming of the only death he feared, the end of order?, and had not he so lived as to fend the change, the winter on the way?, and, sad to say, had not he no more done so than if he'd never lived at all?

They wrapped his neck in flannels, and there were vapors of vinegar that they caused him to breathe, and he heard them say *quinsy*, and they bled him thrice, turned him to ease his pain, and twice he was dressed and placed in a chair. But through all the send-and-fetch, all the vain ado, he was most aware of Toby, tender Toby Lear: he could sense his nearby presence, hear his voice through other voices, feel the warmth of his furthersome hands. How lonely going, had he not been there!

The end of order, he thought, and what came to mind was the nation as a river, and powerless to stop it or change its course, he watched it join the sea's commotion. Order lost in disorder, and he rued it that he'd failed—and yet how should he not have failed when from the far first days he'd known that forces were stronger than men? His *Rules of Civility* recalled themselves, and a smile briefly marred him like a grimace. What did civility mean to the uncivil many or even the civil few—and for the matter of that, what now marked the few from the many, who now knew a *Superiour* from *One of Low Degree?*

It was hard to breathe, and what breath he drew seemed drained, as if used before, and it left him with little more than the will to breathe again. He was well on the way by then, but someone was still trying to stay him, someone was still raising his head, salving his throat, sponging his mouth. Lear, it must've been, and he wanted to speak of many things: had more snow fallen, he wondered, and had the creeks begun to freeze, Little Hunting above the Mansion and Dogue Run beyond the trees? were the Quarters snug, were My People well, were the horses being walked each day and the dogs allowed to run? The dogs, he thought, Taster, Cloe, Captain, Mopsey—Mopsey the bitch, he thought, and it was as though her feel were in his hand. Mopsey, he said.

The end of order was what he saw, and he'd helped to bring it on—who, indeed, had done so more? He'd written his Rules and lived them all, set them down by number and let them guide his life, and then—for what reason?—he'd put them all aside. It was the day of Rules abandoned now, of craft and chicane, the day of the blow-horn, the plebe, the pig in clover. All men equal? In what these days but this—that none rose higher than low? But if all were low, some were lower (among the less, the least), and to such lords would go this land. Of what use then to say *Labour to keep alive in your Breast that Little Spark of Celestial fire called Conscience?* The fire would be out.

It was going out now. *I am just going,* he said to Toby Lear, and then, though none could hear him, he called to Mopsey, but she could not come, being thirty years dead. And yet in another moment he saw her find at Muddy Hole Farm, and he followed her baying a long way through the woods. . . .

THE LONGEST SUMMER'S DAY

The first strike occurred among the carpenters.
How this ended we do not know.
—Bimba: *Hist. of the American Working Class*

In its issue for 11 May 1791, Dunlap's *American Daily Advertiser* printed a resolution passed by the Journeymen Carpenters of Philadelphia. They said, in one of its several clauses, that theretofore they had been obliged to toil through the whole course of *the longest summer's day* without the consolation of added reward. For which aggrievement, they continued, they now bound themselves to deem that a day's work should commence at six of the clock in the morning and at six of the evening end. The strike was on for the twelve-hour day!

Sad to say, though, no records remain of the carpenters' fate: none saw fit, when they hit the bricks, to note their gain or loss. And yet, how can they have fared better than The Master did, how can they have missed the Cross? Were they not mocked as Jesus was, spurned, spat on, smitten, was their blood not drawn by the thorn? Were they not, in the minds of all, given vinegar to drink and gall? And were they not made to die deaths derived from their very own trade—the hammer applied to the nail?

ALL BUT ONE OF THEM

Tracts of 50,000 acres each were distributed to
members of the legislature who voted for the
grants, all but one of them having thus been
bribed.
—T. P. Abernethy, *The South in the New Nation*

The land at issue came to 35,000,000 acres, or, so near as to never mind, 55,000 square miles. It lay in what was Georgia then, and it ran westward from the Chattahoochee River, taking in the states-to-come of Alabama and Mississippi. As land, it wasn't such a much, being for the most part sandy barrens where, a traveler said, all that could be heard was *the aerial moaning of the lordly pines.* It was the land of the salamander, of wiregrass and game and hunters just as wild, but it was no great shakes to grow on unless the crop was weeds. All the same, there were those who saw in that Creek country a chance to make a fortune cheap—by acquiring for a pistareen what they could sell to gulls for gold. The greeners were to come from across the sea, and by the time they found their holdings on the Tombigbee, the Yazoo, the Pearl, the sellers would be far away and not to be found at all. By *atrocious fpeculation, corruption, and collufion,* the Legislature of the state of Georgia was persuaded to cede a fief a fourth the size of France to a group of promoters for half a million dollars, which cast up to $9 a square mile, a figure that would've been low had they gotten no land, just the salamanders. The legislators were paid off in spoil, 50,000 acres to one and all—or all but one.

All but one. Would careful search turn up his name? Would some antiquary come across it in a gnawed liber, an old set of minutes, stringtied and friable, or somewhere on a grave? And if the name became known, what of the wearer—his schooling and temper, his place of birth? What did he look like—scars, wens, shade of skin? Was he young at the time in question, did he glow like a house at night, or had age dimmed him, drawn his blinds? From whom was he descended—the gentry or the herd? Why was he the only one to refuse his 50,000 acres of wildwood, *sad with perpetual verdure, with streaming ever-gray moss?* Did he hold that they belonged to the Indians, that they couldn't be sold or given away? Did he scorn such things as subornation, was he above the use of soap and grease, was he too high up for the low-down kind? Did he cast the first and only stone—did he, damn him!, snitch, the impeccable son-of-a-bitch?

All but one. Was he rich, that he could afford to spit on the bribe, or would twice the offer have hit his price? Did he care more about the Chickasaws than he did about gain, or hadn't he been bid for, had he been left in the rain? Was he, then, not the one just denizen of a den of thieves, but a thief at heart as yet untried? Was he not what he let on to be, the one among many that evil could not reach? And therefore was he not aspersed from the floor for what he was, a pretender, and did he not send a card by a friend, and was he not one morning shot dead somewhere under *streaming ever-gray moss,* to lie forgot save for this notation: *all but one?*

A LETTER TO CAPT. LAWRENCE

Sir: As the Chesapeake *appears now ready for sea,
I request you will do me the favor to meet the*
Shannon *with her, ship to ship, to try the for-
tunes of our respective flags . . .*
                    —Capt. Broke, the *Shannon* off Boston

Even then, on that June day, no one knew, not Broke, surely,
whether the challenge would reach the *Chesapeake* before the ship
got under way. Some say the frigate was well down-bay when the
cartel was brought ashore, and some maintain it came to hand—it
was seen, they claim, and read. But scanned or not, the writing remains, and on a reversed occasion, Lawrence might've penned it
himself and sent it to Broke, laid down the same conditions, made
the same avowal of cannon and complement, closed in the same
seemly idiom: *I have the honor to be, sir,* he might've said, *your
obedient humble servant. . . .*

It was as if they meant to arrange a game, something for a court,
perhaps, or a stately sport for field or lawn, a set of measures, really,
chaste and graceful, cousin-german to a dance. All Boston turned
out for the whirl: the hills were awave with people, the roofs, the
spires, the windows that gave on the sea, and pleasure-craft sailed
when the *Chesapeake* did, cygnets, they seemed to be, and a long
way out they swam with the swan. For the entertainment—the game,
the dance—the weather promised fine.

But when the ships closed to within forty yards, only the water
between them was seen to dance, and no game was played with car-
ronade and musket, no ground was gained, no points were made,
no count was kept except of lives. At their ghastly pastime off Cape
Ann, one hundred died in eleven minutes

G.T.L Watt died, and Wm. Birbles, and Neil Gilchrist, and Thos.
Selby, and Dominique Sader, and W. Morrisay, and James Jaynes,
and G. Hill, and John Samwell, and Francis Alberte, and Samuel

Millard, and others were dead or dying by the time the firing ceased, thus

grape carried away part of head
grape lodged in lower abdomen
cut across abdomen and hips by grape
star shot through middle
cut in two by 32 pdr. shot
head shot off
musket ball through abdomen
shot through neck
grape shot in head
cut in two by star shot
grape shot in body
shot from below while standing on grating
grape shot in belly
struck by wad in lower abdomen
musket ball through left side of belly
pistol ball through integuments of head
musket ball through hip cutting urethra
both patellae shattered by round shot
concussion of brain from blow of wad
sabre wound on head
canister above knee pan
bayonet wound in abdomen
musket ball wound on chin
musket ball through right thigh
splinter wound left breast
sabre wounds, bayonet through belly
musket ball through right humerus
musket ball inside right thigh
musket shot in ear
splinter wound in mouth
splinter wound in right eye
dislocation left humerus, gun recoil

and John German died, and Pollard Hopewell, and Courtlandt Livingston, and Alexander Marino, and Josiah Shatfield, and Benjamin Edsay, and Samuel M. Perkins, and Joseph Judith, and John Huntress, and John Reed 2d, and Abraham Cox

Chain shot killed them, and small-arm balls, and falls from rigging, and gun-burst killed them, and buckshot and crushing killed them, and cutlass-slash, and amputation, and there was something (where?) about fingers being driven through a wall. Lawrence was among the dead, hit in the groin and bled till dry. And it might be said that Broke too was killed: an axe, a pike, a sabre blade cracked his skull and laid open a part of his brain, and though he stayed alive for twenty-eight years, never did he command again nor ever did he thrive.

Aye, death came to both captains in the game, the dance, at Cape Ann. . . .

Mike Fink, c.1770–c.1823

I DIDN'T MEAN TO KILL MY BOY

*A fundamental requirement of heroic legend is
some means of terminating the career of the uncon-
querable hero in a way that crowns rather than
mars his record.*
                                                    —Richard M. Dorson

There were no auguries of his advent. No omen was found in the
lie of cards, in the color of rain, snow, sky, in fowls pecking grain.
No blood lay on the moon, nothing odd was noted in the behavior
of birds, nor did they cry in a bodeful way, and if dreams be the
visits of the gods, the sleep of all was deep, serene. Nay, he came
quietly into the world at a place, they say, where two waters meet
in the wilderness, and it was hard by these that he lived so much
of his day. But if no signs were seen of his coming, his very life
portended its end: murder marred it, murder took it away.

Of his fifty-some years on the Ohio and the Mississip, nothing
remains that floats—none of his companions, none of his boats,
women, whiskey-cans, not even Bang-all, his rifle, or Old Bets, as
he'd call her now and then. All such are lost in the flow of the
seasons, snagged somewhere in time, sunk, buried in a silt of later
things, themselves now bygones too. What survives him is only the
wind he raised in passing by, an aeolian commotion of trifles—
filaments, fumes, spores, dust—rumor, all of it, whirling air, but to
many it casts a shadow, and to them it seems to be real.

Mike was a sovereign
drinking-man, no mistake, but from Cave-in-Rock to Natchez-
under-the-hill, nary a pissen river dog ever seen him tie-tongued
or tangle-foot, and him good for a gallon a day—Monongahela,
mostly, and brandy of peach if he run out of t'other. But if it
didn't go to either end of him, all that wring-jaw and craw-bane,
truth to tell it went to his middle. It worn the nap clean off
of his gullet and gizzard, rotted the shag right out at the root,
and there he was, with his entrals so red and raw and fevierish,
it must've felt like he was scalped in there. It was plain to all

he'd have to grow more hair on his vitals, or he'd soon be fart-
ing smoke—and what he done, he et a buffalo-robe. Taken him
near about a day to do it, but it worked wonders. The fur caught
holt in his burnt-over bowels, and it grew like it did outside.
The ardent spirit give him no more trouble till the day he died,
but he did strain some at the stool.

What's known of Mike is a long they-say: they-say, all the stories
start with, and it's they-say this and they-say that as the stories roll
onward like the river he knew from the Gulf to Cairo. Aye, he knew
every bend in it, every bar and chute and stranded sawyer, every
house of joy along its green-brown way, and wherever boatmen cor-
delled a broadhorn, Mike was the boon-fellow of all who love a brag,
a prank, a shooting-match, and a good long snatch at the can.

Mike was ownwayish
from the day he was borned. Some say he was so optionary coming out of his mama's belly, there wouldn't no tittiloo hush his
roaring, and what they had to do, they give him that Kentucky
rifle to quile him down. He wasn't hardly dry before he could
make a coon climb down just by pointing the piece at him, like
Davy Crockett. Only difference being, Davy's gun was loaded.
By the time he was ten, he could drive nails at forty yards, and
at fifty, he could trim a canlewick and hardly fan the flame.
Best trick of all, though, was where who paid for the corn-mule
was settled by drilling a cup on someone's head at a hunderd
paces: Mike never missed.

Did he live, the wonder is, could the yarns they tell be true? Was
it so, as said, that he shot a spur from a darky's heel, a scalp-lock
from an Injun's head? Did he, as the gossip goes, dock the tails of
seven pigs with seven shots, did he kill a wolf with a single blow,
did he make a bear walk off quiet as a Quaker, did creatures cry
Oh, don't! when he aimed Old Bets their way? Was it a they-say
too, his place of birth—was it at Fort Pitt he was born or somewhere
else, or did he never come forth at all? If he lived, did he do the
things they-say he did, did he wrestle the Preacher Cartwright and
ride the brindle bull? And if he lived, when did he die, and where,
and of what, and who has seen his grave?

Ah, well, if Mike lived, he grew older, and if he lived long enough,
he grew old, and in a hundred different tales, that's what happened
to him who was half horse and half alligator with something extra
in between: he grew old and one day died. He didn't die on Big River,

though, which would've been fitting for one who'd dwelt in its bosom for fifty-and-then-some years: no, he came to an end far away and on dry land near a fort at the mouth of the Yellowstone. He was wintering there with a youth named Carpenter, living in a hole they'd dug in the bluffs along the stream. Well-supplied with liquid fire, they passed the time in drinking, feats of skill, shooting for the pot, and what-not else—or so rumor went at the fort. *I didn't mean to kill my boy*, Mike said, and, who knows?, his boy the boy might've been.

Confined as they were, there was no little quarreling—there always is in the cave of winter—and some of it was so wild and passionate that those in the fort, when the weather mildened, sought to rouse them out with a frolic. They entertained the pair with wrestling, nigger dancing, yarn-spinning, and a sing of boatmen's songs, all as the can was passed from hand to hand, and for a while things seemed well betweeen Mike and the boy. So much so that to show good will, Mike challenged his companion to a shoot, and the boy accepted. At a distance of forty paces, they put cups on their heads, and when someone skied a copper, Carpenter called and won the toss. The first shot being his, he took aim—unsteadily, it was noted—and fired. He must've elevated his piece a little too low, for though the cup fell, the ball also creased Mike's head, and he bled from a groove through his hair. For a moment, all was quiet there at the river's edge—no one spoke or made a move, but there could've been cries and tumult, and nothing would've changed. It was Mike's turn now, and saying *I learned you to shoot different, son. You missed, but you won't miss again*, he fired. As said, Mike never missed. He hit Carpenter between the eyes, and the boy fell dead where he stood, forty strides away.

The jamboree ended then and there, of course, but the mutterings, it seemed, had only just begun, and as time wore on, sides were taken, some opining that Mike too had missed the mark, while others held that he'd hit what he shot at, a spot between the eyes. One of the latter was a man named Talbott, the gunsmith at the fort, and he was open and staunch in his belief that Mike was a murderer. When word of this was conveyed to the boatman, he came from his cave and straightway made for Talbott's shop.

Those who watched him go said they saw no rage in him, but all agreed that he was carrying Old Bets, a fact that might've signified nothing, for Old Bets was with him wherever he went. This time, though, it got him killed: he never quite entered the gunsmith's door. Talbott, seeing his approach, had taken up a pair of pistols, and as Mike drew near, he warned him off—he was a dead man if he stepped inside. But Mike spoke sadly, they-say, with anguish, even: he hadn't come in anger, he said, but only to explain. He'd loved Carpenter, he protested, he'd loved the boy, and now that he was dead, he could hardly bear to live himself: he *couldn't've* murdered him, he insisted; it would've been an unnatural thing, like taking the life of a son. And so speaking, he made as if to enter, whereupon Talbott fired, and Mike fell. His last words, his only words, were *I didn't mean to kill my boy.*

Well, no one knows now, and maybe no one ever knew. Maybe Mike was never born, or maybe he was and never died.

THE INVENTOR

> *An invention can be so valuable as to be worthless to the inventor.*
> —Eli Whitney

They were the familiar traits of his kind, that he was deft with his fingers and nimble in the mind. As in others, there seemed to be a conjunction in him of head and hand, and let him merely perceive a need, a use, or even a possibility, and something of lead, leather, iron would evolve from the air and begin to take shape on his bench. The tools he used were few and rude (*I could make tools, he said, if I had tools to make them with*), but they answered for the simple engines of his day, the churns, the cistern pumps, the wheels that water turned, and with them he wrought new simplicities and minor refinements of the old. He took apart a watch, they say, and then caused it to run as before, and at the age of twelve, though he could not play, he fashioned a violin.

But as said, these were things that many might've done, given the knack and a flight of fancy, and had he gone on so, with no broader learning, he'd've ended a mender of harness, locks, and pocket-knives, he'd've withered away at a forge. He was twenty-three now, and still making hat-pins, nails, and walking-sticks what time he was not teaching school. *A person of good Sober life & conversation*, wrote a neighboring squire, but his aim was higher than local fame, and a degree from Yale was his heart's desire. That took the needful, which came to a thousand a year, and it was sprung for by his father, who must've put the farm in soak. It was money well spent, though. It bought his son the lore of the ages: a library containing Newton's *Principia* (a library in itself); a museum boasting a theodolite, a quadrant, and a centrifuge, all his to use; and his too a telescope, a micrometer, and an orrery. There were, moreover, lectures in Philology and the Nature of Vision, in Geometry and Conic Sections, in Hydrostatics, Hydraulics, and the laws of Simple and Compound Motion, and along with these came the courtly graces, how to dress and discourse, how to be at perfect ease. Yes, that annual thousand bought him much—all, in fact, but common sense.

His degree was conferred in his twenty-ninth year. He was no mere artificer now, fixer of buckles, hinges, broken felloes: he was an engineer, suave, well-dressed, at home with the elite, and damned hard-pressed to meet his bills, a gentleman engineer. They were tinless times, though, and when he fell in with a certain Mrs. Greene, widow of General Nathanael (Guilford Court House, Eutaw Springs), he became at her request a guest at Mulberry Grove, a plantation on the Savannah River in Georgia. There, on pillared porches, screened by the bright red bracts of the bougainvillea, he and Widow Greene spent the endless hours, sipping now and supping then and conversing softly while slaves came and slaves went.

He might've been there yet, and still bemused, if she hadn't broken the frame she used for making lace. A tambour, it was called, and in no time at all he made her one of novel design, stronger than her own and more pleasing to the eye. The Widow was quite carried away, and to many, to cousins and friends, to travelers stopping by, she lauded him for his skill and his visionary mind: *he can do anything*, she'd say, and she said it where it mattered, to the planting gentry roundabout. *He can do anything*, she told them, and under their oaks and mosses, they began to muse on the Yank whose hands were fly. Could he, they wondered, devise a machine to clean the seed from their upland cotton, a need that, filled, would make them rich? Could he contrive of wood, wire, brass, something that would do in an hour what it took their darkies a day? *He could do anything*, the Widow had claimed—was this too much, this little convenience?

Nay, it was not too much: he built the engine (gin for short) in six months' time. In six months, on a table in the cellar at Mulberry Grove, stood the realization of the plantocratic dream—a thingamadoo of rollers, teeth, and brushes that would reel in cotton bolls, and roll out cotton bales, a thingamading that would crown the cotton staple king! *'Tis generally said that I shall make a Fortune by it*, he wrote to his father, but that thousand a year, though it'd bought him knowledge of Optics, Central Forces, and the Astronomy of Comets, had brought him no wisdom in the ways of the world: he showed his creation to the cream of the crème, the planting gents.

They stole it—not the model, of course, because they didn't require it. Once its principles were known, anybody with an anvil and a swage could make one for himself, and while a patent was being sought, anybody grew to be all and sundry. Cotton was sown from the sea to the Smokies, wherever it'd grow and even where not, and slavery, lately as good as dead, was risen again, this time never to end, for how should the fruit of the cotton shrub end? That little jigamaree of combs and cylinders, it did the work that black fingers bungled: it carded out the clinging seed, it freed the nigras for another crop, it let them go—as far as the fields. Ah, but there was a great rondelle of growth, harvest, and growth again, and under the oaks and the mosses, the Massas smoked and rummed and summed up gains.

The inventor sued, certainly, and he did so until he was blue in the face and blued in spirit too. When his patent was issued (*I shall make a Fortune by it*), he went to law with all of Georgia and half of Carolina, but so far from making the fortune, he spent his little and squandered himself as well. It was a quest with him, and he pressed it as if what he sought were the Cup that had caught the blood of Christ. In truth, it held his own, and he meant to have it back. He was at the work for a dozen years, but he got next to nothing from his betters, the flora of the South: they fought his suits and writs, his pleas and petitions, they even demurred to his letters patent: what was his gin, they said, but the *churka* known to Ind? Truly, quite as he'd rued, his invention, beyond all price to others, was good for naught to him.

His way thereafter was rarely upward. He ventured in this and that, he engaged in the China trade, he made muskets for the army, but his efforts came to little while he came to less: he was always strapped and always dunned, he was ailing often, and what hopes he had were due to be dashed, nor did he ever win the widow Greene, and at fifty-two, when she'd gone to join her general (Hobkirk's Hill, the Cowpens), he married someone else.

Wedlock, however sweet, was short. Hardly had it begun than it began to reveal its end—a prostate growing, growing, until his bladder's flow was all but blocked. From this, there followed virulent retention of urine, phosphatic stone, and pain. For these things then, leeches were applied to the perineum, a dozen at a time, and when they drew his blood and his torment not, doses of morphia were tried, and they gave him one numb hour out of the twenty-four. When he could bear no more physicking and chirurgery, he put his brain to work, and his wizard hands, and from poring over books, medical journals, drawings, and even cadavers, he was able to make a pliable, smooth, small-calibre tube (of what?), and with it, self-introduced, he drew off his stagnant fluids. Alas, though, it did not shrink the gland, and in time all micturition ceased, and, poisoned from within, he died.

He never patented the tube—or catheter, as it came to be called—and perhaps it was just as well. Someone would've stolen it, not the thing, naturally, but the idea.

I HAVE MADE MY WAY ALONE

*with means gained from my nurse,
the sea.*
— Stephen Girard

He was fond of the maritime allusion: it was vivid, and largely
it was true. From the deep, he drew his substance; the mere was
his *mère*, and on her blue-green milk he grew. At eight, he lost the
sight of an eye, and at fourteen, he left his Bordeaux home to roam
where the *Pélerin* (the pilgrim!) did, and before he saw the Garonne
again, he'd been ten months on the main, his many-titted bitch.
Thereafter, he voyaged often, and all through the roll and pitch of
the next nine years, he studied and stored away the stars, mastered
the art of navigation, conned books by day with his one good eye,
and in time to come, ships of his own would blazon what his missing eye had missed — *Rousseau*, some nameboard would say,
Helvetius, or *Voltaire*. . . .

First, though, he had to get up in the baser skills. There were tricks
of the trade to fix in the mind — how to find the eager buyer, the
seller who was pressed, where the shortage was or the glut, when
war was still afar but already on the way. He had to learn such things
and learn these too, that there were some whose word would pass
for coin and some whose coin was brass, that there were short-
weighters and those who watered rum, that mungo might be
sometimes dealt and shoddy not at all. Aye, long before his house
flag flew from *Montesquieu*, he had a body of beguilers to leave in
the lurch. A good scholar in a stringent school, he got his ships, and
he got much more: lands and tenements, coal mines, a freight service on the Delaware, and the Bank of the United States. His purse
held thirty millions that smelled of Lapsang, China's smoky tea. *My
nurse, the sea,* he said.

What was the cut of the one-eyed suckling? Were they like, the
portraits that showed him squat? was he whey-faced, as some say,
was he a bugbear cold and quiet, a sight for *good* eyes, a unioptic

fright? Was it true and tried the ruin he wrought on foe and friend, as when his cashier died and he turned the widow out? And how of his wife, the servant Mary Lum, did he flout her with his appetite, not for naked her so much as naked money? Was she really beautiful, did she have black hair long and lovely? Was she ill-bred, unrefined, beneath him in station as well as in his bed? Did she die insane, confined in some hell in Philadelphia, and did he say at her grave *It is well*—is that what he said of their forty wedded years?

His ships sailed, his ships sailed—along with the literary others, it was the *Flora* now, the *Good Friends*, the *Two Brothers*, eighteen in all, his fleet, and all eighteen returned—and in his counting-house on Water Street, the counting never ceased. There was no end, it seemed, to his appetite, no draining dry the tit. . . . Ah, but there was an end, and it came upon him suddenly. A dray ran him down from his blind side, and he lay blind then on both sides, and he died without again seeing his many ships, his many mines, the Corinthian capitals and entablature, the pillars of his bank.

He left his leavings to a school for orphans, stipulating that no man of the cloth could set foot on the grounds. None ever has.

A SERVILE REBELLION

I was intended for some great purpose.
— Nat Turner

She was a wild one, his mother. They say that for fear she'd kill him, they tied her down the day he was born—a feral and outrageous thing, she must've been, fauna that'd suffer no young to live in a cage. She grew calmer, though, as her belly fell, and the boy passed into the world. She may have seen ahead, may have read, though she'd never learn to read, what he'd grow to be in one-and-thirty years:

> *bright complexion, but not a mulatto, broad shoulders, large flat nose, large eyes, broad flat feet, rather knock-kneed, walks brisk and active, hair thin, no beard except on the upper lip and the top of the chin, scar on one of his temples, also one on the back of his neck, a large knot on his right arm, produced by a blow. . . .*

A blow from whom, she may have wondered, and, wondering, she may have missed the rest, that he was six inches shy of being six feet high, and that he was vermin to be taken alive (Reward 500$) so that all Virginia might watch him die. A blow?, she may have thought, a blow from a white . . .?

The son, *bright complexion, but not a mulatto*, the son was tamer, or, due to some frailty, so at first he seemed to the eye, a tractable black with a thirst for learning. As a child, he was given a book to stop his crying, a toy to play with, to thumb and tumble and wear on his head; instead, as his mother might've done, he read it without knowing how to read. A Bible, the book could've been, and if so, it became the drink he was dry for, and it entered him, went down deep to dormant memories, bequests from the past, sources, and they drew on its minerals until he knew he was meant for *some great purpose*, and at last he knew the purpose too.

While working in the fields, he found drops of blood on the corn, and there came to him from the heavens the sound of thunder, and out of the thunder the voice of the Spirit spoke to him, saying that Christ had laid down the burden He had borne for the sins of men, whereat once again the Serpent had been loosed to corrupt the world with his subtil poisons, even as in the Garden. The day of judgment being nigh, he was told, he had been chosen to take up the yoke of Jesus and do the Savior's work—aye, to become the Savior himself.

For three years, he awaited a sign, and one day the sun was seen to come up green instead of gold, the green giving way to blue, and the blue at length to silver. A plate, a salver of silver, passed all morning long across the sky, and there was much amaze among the people, but when a spot began to appear, black on the argent white, there was fear. The sign had been given.

The insurrection started with the murder of the Savior's master and that of the master's wife. Only a few were in the uprising—Nat, Will, Hark, and Jack, and another three or four—but along their way, they picked up more, and they numbered some say sixty before being done with two days and nights of doing in whites. From Cross Keys, they took a zigzag course to and through Jerusalem, thirty crooked miles, and there was death wherever they'd been and death in store where they went. They wore feathers in their hats and bloody sashes, and drunk on brandy, they roved the woods and roads in search of game to be killed and killing all they found. They drilled at times, as though they were soldiers, marched and made formations, and they sang what songs they knew, they bragged and laughed and stopped to sleep, and some, poor Solomons, broke off to go home in a victim's gory clothes. But those that went on slew all they caught in a two-day slaughter—fifty-seven dead, they left behind them, men, women, youths, and children, and here and there a head was nowhere near a headless body.

And then, with the coming of the militia, the killing of whites ended, and the killing of blacks began. For a while, anything of color was shot where it stood, kneeled, or lay on the ground, but when it was remembered that some of them were prime, *likely, young, good with animals,* only those were doomed who'd taken up arms. After fair trials that often consumed as much as an hour, seventeen were hanged, one the woman Lucy, who rode to her tree on her own particular coffin.

All but Nat the Savior were buried in a decent and becoming manner. He, on being cut loose, was skinned and boiled down to blubber—Nat's grease, the darkies called it, and ever thereafter they fled from castor oil. His skeleton was long in the possession of Dr. Massenberg, but it became misplaced and was deemed to be lost. Many, however, claim to have seen the skull, and they have said that it was of a most peculiar shape, resembling that of a sheep. It was that of a man, though, one that his mother had tried to keep from a cage.

THE STAIN OF SETTLEMENT

*The Indians used to say that a white settlement was
like a spot of raccoon grease on a new blanket . . . you
did not realize how wide and how far it would spread.*
—Donald Jackson

He was born, Black Hawk said, in a Sauk village along the Rock,
no great way from where it joined the Big River, and he claimed
descent from an early chief of his people, Na-na-ma-kee, meaning
Thunder. But beyond these things, he could remember nothing of
his younger years save that he was permitted neither paint nor
feathers until, at fifteen, on wounding an enemy, he was given the
rank of brave. Thenceforward, there was much to remember, the first
Osage he killed and the lance and axe with which he killed him,
the bleeding swatch of scalp he took, his father's look of pleasure.
In those youthful days, the Osage were always there, and he recalled
many killings, once, with a party of only seven, attacking a hundred and coming off with scalps to show for it and never the loss
of a man, and there'd been a great raid he made with high numbers
against even higher, and he'd killed five Osage and a squaw, he said.
The Osage! ever the Osage!, and when they'd grown too few to kill,
their forces being so weak, I thought it cowardly to kill them, he'd
fallen on the Chippewas and the Kaskaskias and the Cherokees: *I
killed thirteen of their bravest warriors with my own hand,* he said.
Campaign followed campaign, and then he was no longer young,
being in the thirty-fifth year of his age, and still it was only Indians
that he'd slain, never yet a white. But the stain was about to
spread. . . .

In the spring of 1804, a Sauk Indian, not without grave provoca-
tion, killed a white man in a French settlement on the Cuivre, or
Quiver, River, but when he fled to his own people, it was they, his
own, who yielded him up to the law. They believed, though, for it
was the Indian way in such matters, that they could pay for the dead
man, that is to say, requite his wife and children with suitable gifts

and seemly ceremony, but when a deputation was sent to St. Louis for that purpose, it was informed that the murderer would surely be tried and no less surely hanged. Cast down by this dictum, the Sauk remained in the village, hoping to persuade the whites to their view, and whilst there, they were made abundantly welcome by the trader Pierre Chouteau, who, knowing of their lands that began and never ended, let them buy on tick, and what they bought was tanglefoot, and it likewise tripped their brains. High-wined by the settlers, they were led to believe that their Indian would be freed if they signed a treaty, and eagerly they did so, hardly aware that they were ceding fifty-one million acres in return for a thousand dollars yearly in tools and goods. The lie-treaty, the wringjawed fools would one day call it, a flim of paper that flammed them out of Illinois. And the murderer they'd come to get, what of him? Oh, they got him, or what was left: the whites turned him loose and then shot him dead. . . .

They were now beyond the Big River in a country not their own, and from there they looked back, Black Hawk and his people, and they watched the stain begin to spread: it was small at first, a mere blot on the blanket of the prairie, but the spot grew, and it grew toward them. They could see it from the far side of the Big River, roads, fences, smokes in the sky, and all were running westward over the mounds and the swales of the blanket, the haws and hazel of Illinois, and one day soon they'd arrive at the stream, and then— what then? would they stop there? would the stain end? But Black Hawk had used sixty of his years, and more, and he knew his life might sooner end.

There were whites to be killed, and the Sauk went back across the river to their own country. *My reason teaches me that land cannot be sold,* Black Hawk said, and whites died because they thought otherwise. They'd bought those fifty-one million acres, or so the lie-paper told them, and they died all over the breasts and between the thighs of the woman Illinois. Their bodies were found everywhere, though not their heads of hair, yet down deep under the rage of the Indians, there lay regret, and deeper still despair. Despair, because where one white went, two more seemed to come from an endless store of numbers—all could not be killed, indeed, they should not, for would they not then double?—but the Sauk tried, as if bent on killing themselves.

They fought and won at Sycamore Creek and Stillman's Run, and they came off well in many a place that bore no name, but they were always on the move, always going, and their women and children were growing leaner, eating bark, bitter roots and berries, and anything green that came within their reach, and on such thin fare they warred as far as the Bad Axe River, and there they knew they could fight no more.

They sought now to surrender, tying a white rag to a stick and trying to show it as a flag of truce. But no truce was granted, and they were hunted down to the river's edge, and when they swam for their lives, they lost them: they were bagged by the sportsmen who were sitting, standing, kneeling on the shore. When the shooting stopped, the Bad Axe was a flow of blood, and squaws and children bobbed on its red waves, and dead scrags too, and, bellies up, scores of feathered braves. The war's end had come, the Sauk's war was over. *My reason teaches me that land cannot be sold*, Black Hawk said, but was not his reasoning wrong?

THE *AMISTAD*, FORMERLY THE *FRIENDSHIP*

> *a Baltimore-built schooner of about 150 tons,*
> *painted black with a white streak*
> —New York Globe, Aug. 1839

When first sighted off the Jersey woodlands, she was sixty-three days out of Havana with a cargo of fancy merchandise—crockery, silks and satins, and four dozen Mendi slaves. On being taken in tow by a government brig, it was seen that much of the ware lay about broken, its shards in the scuppers or rocking on the decks, and the fine and sibilant stuffs were streamers in the rigging or wound around the blacks. The Captain, Ramon Ferrer, was eight weeks dead by then, slain with a swipe of a sugar-cane knife and tossed to the deep with his mulatto cook to keep him company. The schooner itself was sea-bitten and now in need of a full refit. Her sides and hull were breaded with barnacles, and weed that hung from her cables seemed to curtsy with the ship. Torn and tattered all her sail, the fore, the main, the jibs, and from rail and gunwale, the paint had peeled away. Also in poor condition were two white and frightened Latin swells: one had owned the crockery, silks, and satins, and both had owned the slaves.

Arrived at New London, the two spics lodged a complaint alleging mutiny and murder against the blacks, and those that were left of them, only nine-and-thirty now, found themselves in the clink along with their leader

Cinque,
or Cinquez,
or Cingue,

a Mendi from Mani in Dzhopoa,
which is to say *the open land*,
ten suns away from the waters of the sea,
seized, taken hold of in a road,

and sold, and sold again, and sent
many suns west on the waters of the sea
(The phrenologist Mr. Fletcher
has expressed the opinion that Cinque
                              or Sinko,
                              or Singbe,
is of a bilious and sanguine temperament,
the bilious predominating)

On being sworn, the Cuban dons produced licenses from their
Gobernador permitting them to transport the slaves from Havana
to Puerto Principe, and they deposed that said lawful purpose was
precluded by an act of piracy, to their grievous loss. They demanded,
therefore, the return of the *Amistad*, repossession of the slaves and
the cargo, and compensation for the merchandise destroyed. In their
list of these, they itemized 40,000 needles, 48 rolls of wire, 45 bottles of essence, 500 pounds of jerked beef, sundries such as glass
knobs, raisins, and 50 pairs of pantaloons—and of course the cam-
bric and Canton crepe, the shawls of gauze and bombazine.

and from Fulu
two moons away from the waters of the sea
                              Grabeau,
                              or Gilabaru,
meaning in Mendi *have mercy on me*,
caught at Taurang on the way to buy clothes,
sold to a Spaniard in Lomboko, and shipped in a hold on
the waters of the sea,
speaks Vai, Konno, and Gissi,
four feet eleven inches in height,
very active, especially in turning somersets

Aside from those relating to the rights of salvage, doubts arose
as to the propriety of a slave escaping slavery *vi et armis*, to wit,
by inflicting death on his owner. It was urged that the black pirates
of the *Amistad* were merely runaways, in no better case than their
like in the States. Argument was offered that were the law to
distinguish between domestic and foreign ownership, the entire in-
stitution of slavery would be open to question.

by Kimbo, meaning *cricket*,
born at Mawkoba in the Mendi country
far from the waters of the sea,
knows numbers
                              one *eta*
                              two *fili*

                                              five *loelu*
                                              six *weta*
his father was a gentleman

Per contra, it was maintained that the slaves so libeled were not
fugitives within the meaning of the Federal Constitution. They were
not, it was claimed, persons held to service in one state who had
sought to escape such service by fleeing to another. Cuba was no
part of the Union: the decks of a ship lay outside its jurisdiction,
which did not extend to the waters of the sea.

      that was what Bartu would have said,
                                    or Gbatu
      meaning *a club or a sword*,
                                    and Kwong,
      who was sold for crim. con.,
                                    and Fuliwa
                                    and Pungwuni,
      who was sold by his uncle for a coat,
                                    and Moru
      would have said the same when sold
      to Belawa, which meant *great whiskers*,
      the Bandi name for Spaniard,
                                    and Fuliwulu,
      who had a depression in his skull,
      would have said it too,
                                    and Bau
      from the Wowa River would have said it,
      he who paid a goat for his wife
      and plenty mats and a gun—
      ah, they all would have said it,
                                    Faginna,
                                    and Bagna,
                                    and Shuma,
      who also said *No one can die but once*

In the end, the case reached the Supreme Court, where John Q.
Adams, in a two-day speech, spoke a hundred thousand words for
the blacks. He talked one judge to death (he died at fifty thousand),
and he made the others find that the slaves were slaves no longer:
they were free.

They were sent back to Africa on the waters of the sea, and there
they shed their clothes, the God of the whites, the manners learned

in Connecticut, forgot the words of J. Q. Adams, the verdict of the Bench. It is said that in 1879, Cinque, or Cinquez, or Sinko, died at a mission, in Freetown, it may have been, or along Boom River a hundred miles away. Some say he had become a trader, a bandit, a dealer in slaves, but such things may not be true.

A PLACE OF FLOWERS

The United States must have Florida.
—James Madison

It was no isle, no spit of sand, but a vast and well-favored land, as one could discern even from the sea, whence mile on mile it ran toward the sky, a great plain whereon flamed a smokeless fire of flowers—and for flowers it was named. But for those that went ashore, it was more than a savanna, for a variety of marvels were found there, swamps where cypresses grew, and papaw trees, and oaks that sported moss, and lakes of sweet water made a stained glass window of the earth, and there were caves, and springs, and indigo, and the grass was dense in the densest shade.

Amid these pleasures of nature, there dwelt a certain people known as Seminoles, a name meaning *runaways*, and such in all truth they were, having fled the tribes of their fathers, the Muskogees, otherwise called the Creeks. They were a hot and high-blooded strain, those that had broken with their folk and strayed to the hammock country and the everglade—and, killing and being killed, they fought no matter whom for such places, their own at times and at other times the whites. But always, win or lose, they were forced to fight some more, until, their numbers few and these starving, they made their mark upon a treaty under which they agreed to give thought to relinquishing Florida and removing to a country that lay beyond the Great River a thousand miles away.

In conformity with the agreement, seven of their chiefs were sent to inspect the proposed new home, and under the escort of Major John Phagan, they journeyed far upon the waters, and then when the waters ended, they went some mounted and some afoot to the site selected by the whites for their exile. It was small, hardly the hundredth part of Florida, but it seemed fairly featured, being prairie-like, and there were woods within its compass and also many springs. A paper was there put before them by Major Phagan, he representing that it merely certified the land to be good, and in this he was confirmed by Abraham, the Negro interpreter, whereupon the chiefs one by one made their mark. What they had thus been induced to sign, however, was a cession of all Florida to the white man.

On their return, the truth was revealed to the Seminoles, and there was deep disquiet among them, for they had empowered the seven chiefs only to report to them on the new territory, not to surrender the old. To persuade them from their agitation, a council was convoked at the Fort King Indian Agency, and ranged with the whites at the table were General Duncan Clinch, commander of the United States forces in Florida, the Indian agent Wiley Thompson, himself a general, their several aides and subordinates, and a Mr. David Levy, a gentleman from St. Augustine, who was charged with taking notes. For the Indians, many of their chiefs appeared, along with many braves, and there were some who had brought their wives and children, but these of course remained outside

                                          yes,
        many chiefs were there,
        some who had gone with Major Phagan
        and some who had stayed at home.
        Micanopy,
        the governor of the Seminole Nation,
        was there,
        and Yaha Hajo,
        a war chief
        whose name meant *mad wolf*,
        and Hitchiti Mico,
        meaning *broken stick*,
        and Assiola,
        whom some called Osceola,
        and Moke Is She Larni,
        meaning *one that sleeps*,
        these too were there,
        and Topalargee *the wonder* was there,
        and Powhaila *the dwarf*,
        and Charley Amathla of Wetumpky,
        and Jumper too,
        Jumper was there,
        for he was the Sense-keeper of the Nation,
        and when he spoke
        he was heard,

                              and Jumper said

I speak now saying
I was one of the seven that went
to see the land beyond the Big River
where my people were asked to live,
and I will tell you in truth
that it was good
a good place to be,
and its fruits smelled sweet to me,
a good place,
I thought,
one where men might live in health
and hunt in contentment,
but I tell you also
that it had bad neighbors,
the Cherokees and the Chickasaws
and more especially the Creeks,
our great and hated enemy,
and the harvest of a bad neighborhood
is blood,
and blood
spoils the land and dries the brook,
wherefore,
never having signed our hands
to more than a promise
to look at that faraway country
and then say what we had shown
to our eyes,
we will not go there,
we will stay here,
we will live where our home is
forever

                                    and Charley Amathla said
I am not a warrior,
I am a farmer,
and my farm is at Wetumpky
very near where I now stand
and speak to you,
and I say that when a man
has a country in which he was born
and has his house there
and his home
and where his children play

and he delights in watching them play,
that place becomes sacred to his heart,
and it is hard to leave it,
it is like leaving the heart itself,
and therefore,
not being hungry for other lands,
why should I go and hunt for them
in the distance

These orations were little to the taste of those that sat on the white side of the table, and the Seminole spokesmen were still on their feet, still trying to explain the Indians' infrangible attachment to the land of their people, when they were treated to such grave discourtesies as anger, mutterings, and, worst of all, motion. At length, unable to wait for Charley Amathla to finish speaking and resume his seat, the agent Thompson rose and spoke through his speech, saying that he would hear no more of refusal. Under the treaty of Payne's Landing, he said, the Indians had agreed to sell Florida and remove to the West, and having seen the western lands, they had ratified the treaty, put their hands upon it pledging honor, and now they must talk no more—they must go!

They went, but not yet to the West: they went quietly from the presence of the whites to where their wives and children waited and made known to them the doings of the day, after which there was much discussion, each that chose being given a say. On the morrow, the chiefs returned to the council to disclose the decision of the people. Holata Mico, the *blue king*, introduced Micanopy, the chief of chiefs, and

Micanopy said

we cannot go from our homes,
the strings of our hearts
are twined about them,
and were we to leave
they would snap,
we cannot pluck them off
and they not break

And then Jumper, the Sense-keeper, spoke again, he being married to Micanopy's sister, and he said what he had said before, and he was heard, and then

Charley Amathla said
why quarrel about dividing the hind quarter

when we are not going to hunt,
why strain water
when no man thirsts,
why talk of the West
when we intend to stay in Florida

And then there stood up to speak the Indian Assiola, or, as some knew him, Osceola, and he spoke last, as if he had reserved the place for himself by right, though, being half-white, he held no rank through blood among the Seminoles

                                        and what he said was this,
when I make up my mind
I act,
what I say
I will do,
and what I resolve
that I execute

                                        and no more

And now on the white side of the table, they knew that the Indians would never surrender Florida without a fight: they would have to be killed. To strengthen the garrison at Fort King, soldiers were sent for from Fort Brooke far to the south on Tampa Bay, and in response soon thereafter a force of some five score men under Major Francis Dade set out for the agency a little more than a hundred miles away. Their route lay along the Hillsborough River and then the Withlacoochee and past the Wahoo Swamp, the stronghold of the Seminoles, and they were six days on the road when a single shot was fired at the column from somewhere near the swamp. A ball struck Dade in the chest, perforating his heart, and he died while still astride his horse.

Now Indians appeared, or smoke from their guns appeared, through every shrub, every palmetto frond, every clump of grass — a hundred and eight guns, almost all unseen, were firing from close range, and at the first volley, half the waylaid soldiers lay singly dead, like Dade, or dead in twos and threes

Lt Mudge,
          hit,
sat against a tree
with blood on his coat

and his head sunk against his chest,
and Lt Henderson,
his left arm broken by a ball,
held his musket in his right,
but he could not load
once he fired,
and as for Lt Keais,
both his arms were broken,
and he was unable to defend himself,
and well into the fight
Dr Gatlin loaded both his weapons,
saying,
well I've got four barrels for them,
but he was killed before he could fire
one,
and Capt Gardiner,
already four times hit,
was hit a fifth time
and died,
and Lt Basinger,
shot through both thighs,
died too
and the musician Joseph Wilson,
playing possum,
sprang up and brained Jumper's cousin
with a gun barrel
and ran away,
but two Indians followed
and shot him down

Very few whites were still alive when the Indians withdrew, four
at most, and one of the four was caught and killed in the Fort Brooke
road. Somehow a drummer got away, crawling in days later with
a ball in his groin, one lung left, and a shoulder so cruelly smashed
that ever after the wound discharged matter and bits of broken bone;
and a wheelwright too came back living, but he'd been hurt before
the fight began and never saw the battleground; and a third survivor
was Private Sprague, who with a shattered arm lay a day and a night
in a pond, showing only his nose among the reeds.

It was many a week before a force could be assembled and sent
to the scene. Fifty-four days went by in preparations and in the march

itself, and only then, when the company came to the strewn clearing in the pines and palmettos, did eyes see what minds had missed. None in that party of eleven hundred could have imagined the flapping canopy of vultures that overhung the trees, the pond, the clearing in the grass: it was as if pieces of night were falling, drifting down in great black flakes, and, once fallen, never lying still but milling around the corpses and dining on the go. For fifty-four days and more, they'd been flying in from everywhere to feast there in the road. . . .

These things that happened brought on a seven-year war, and when the war ended, the Seminoles were seven years worse off than before: they were removed then instead of earlier to the prairie country beyond the Great River. *The United States must have Florida*, James Madison had said. Well, now she had Florida.

POOR MEXICO, SO FAR FROM GOD

and so near the United States.
— old saying

They were nearer than near: they touched. They lay side by side along the *filum aquae* of the Rio Grande, the middle line, the thread of a stream that in certain seasons sank from sight, became a bed of silt, a dry and winding band of gravel, sand, and stranded reeds. They verged there, the two, in a concurrence of curves that was very like an embrace, but alas the day for poor Mexico!— the *abrazo* cost her Texas, and still more would be lost, twice Texas, before the gringos were through.

Her army was a press-gang army, indios and peons dragged or driven to some regiment, scrags even in uniform, for their officers sutled the mess. Thin men made thin soldiers, and when they were killed for running away, the ranks were filled with picaroons, assassins, and (far, far from God!) ravishers of boys. Their muskets were the discards of the British, and the French had cast their cannon for some long-forgotten war, but their lancers—ah, their lancers would ride through hell, and their bands would play them back! An army of put-upons, those mix-bloods and Yaquis, sad, hopeless, strange to Christ, but they tired never, like burros, and always they were brave.

On their north, the South—and having taken Texas, she looked beyond to what Texas led to, a bigger Dixie for her nigger slaves. And there it was, from the rise of the Colorado to Califa's paradise—a million square miles! If all went well, they'd make five more states for cotton, and well it went indeed. At Resaca de la Palma, with their secondhand guns and their know-nothing generals, the Mexicans fought for two days before being driven back against the river, leaving twelve hundred dead on the field, little piles of regimentals, rather like fallen flags, and then, *mala suerte,* three hundred more in water that was deep for the time of year aye

                              it went well there for the gringos
and well at Monterrey,
where you would think the Citadel
might have stopped them,
the Black Fort, we called it,
with guns commanding two approaches,
the Monclova road and the road from Marin,
and we had much faith also
in the redoubts
that were placed about the city
and in the high hills that walled it
and the walls within,
and there was a river to be crossed,
a gorge to take in single file,
after which the massed houses
in the narrow streets—
you would think these things enough
to turn them away
and send them back the long march
to Port Isabel,
but they were not enough,
no, nor would more have been enough
and all the things that had to fall
before they gained the day
fell, and sad to say,
not even the lancers
with their red and green pennons,
their gold frogging,
and their bridles that seemed all silver
could keep the white flag
from being raised
above the Black Fort

                              it went well there for them,
and at Agua Nueva,
where they were outnumbered
four or five to one,
and we were so positioned
as to be able to take them in rear
unless they fell back on the sheep ranch
at Buena Vista,
and burning their stores,
they ran for it,

and we pressed after with twenty thousand,
a third of whom were cavalry,
our best arm,
and our General,
the Lame Man we called him,
sent a flag to inform them
that he would grant a surrender
on liberal terms,
and their General
(may he be forgiven)
told him to go pull his popish pud,
and the attack began—
but it was the same as before,
it was all the same,
and a sad sight it was to see
our cavalry beaten again,
six thousand plumed horsemen
stopped by buckshot,
torn from their saddles,
fallen upon with knives,
and slashed to rags,
sad to see them so closely lying
as to interlace,
supplying missing parts for each other,
a head where a head was gone,
a leg for a blown-off leg,
and to see our eighteen hundred dead

                              it went well there for the gringos,
and well at Cerro Gordo too,
and at Churubusco,
and at Chapultepec,
and in the end over all Mexico
the white flag flew

it went well, that war, but not for us,
poor Mexico
we lost Califa and her paradise
and San Francisco Bay,
poor Mexico,
so far from God
and so near the United States

A BOOK FOR KNOW-NOTHINGS

It is hoped that the reader of the ensuing narrative will not suppose that it is fiction, that the scenes and persons that I have delineated had not a real existence. . . .

—preface, *The Awful Disclosures*

There were too God damn many foreigners here, and more were on the way—micks, spics, wops, all the Old World sprue was coming to the New. Bad enough the nigger and even worse the Jew, but worst by far the prone at the feet of Peter, the idolists of Rome. Popish paupers, they were, starvelings of the facing shore, clannish and clandestine, sanguinary, base, and their church was a rubied Whore. Beware their coming, the lighters of candles, the hugger-muggers of the eastern shore, beware their sly ways, their spurious relics, their god on a greasy cross. . . .

    She was born at St. Johns,
she wrote,
a port on the river Richelieu
in the province of Quebec,
and there she knew her youngest years,
a lone lass amidst the French
            une seule Écossaise
wherefore it was small wonder
that she fell,
spellbound by roman splendor

    A child beguiled, she was,
and with a child's artless ease,
she lent herself to the enchantments
of the purple woman and scarlet,
l'église, mother of abominations,
lost herself,
sat through masses and missal music,
dipped her fingers in the stoup,

signed the crucial invocation,
and hailed the graceful Mary

From there it ws no great way
to a nunnery

She was a postulant for five years,
she wrote,
during which, for some mild displeasure
hardly worth recall or mention,
she fled the convent
and reentered the world,
marrying the first to find her favored,
but soon enough repentance came,
and then it was him she forsook,
and again the cloister claimed her,
nor did she, when confirmed,
reveal her fall from grace,
thus being guilty of mortal sin
and hazarding hell
if death should come before confession,
hell,
where her sin would blaze from her brow
and bring down torment all the more

Still, she ran the risk and took the veil,
made her vows and lay down
in a coffin engraved with her nun name
                    Saint Eustace
and under a pall
                    un Drap Mortel
she heard hymns sung,
smelled incense, which sickened her,
she said,
and recalled another novice
who, when the cloth was removed
was found to be dead

She lived, though,
and lived to rue the day

Being a nun now,
she was told of her claustral duties,
among which the one she owed to priests,

obedience in all things,
including the unresisted use of her body,
an abhorrent sin in the world outside
but not in the world within,
for priests were holy men,
leading arduous and abstinent lives
for the salvation of others,
saviors, they might be called,
as without them there was no pardon,
thus permitting them her flesh
was pleasing in the sight of God,
and on that very day,
she said,
she was called out by Father Dufrene,
who, in a private apartment,
treated her in a most brutal manner,
after which two other priests
gave her similar usage,
and then again Dufrene,
who made her stay till morning

And in the days and nights to come,
she said,
she learned of other dark things
that were done at the Hotel Dieu,
as, what became of the issue
of priest and nun
born of such illicit commerce

The practice was to baptize the infant
and then strangle it at once,
thus securing it eternal happiness,
since the chrism cleansed its brief past,
and death prevented future sin,
for the which
how gladsome
those little souls must have been,
sent thus straight to blessed bliss
from this,
the infernal world

It was unwise to oppose such ways,
she said,
and told of seeing the fate

of a restive nun,
nay, being a part of it,
for when ordered to drag the sister
before the Bishop,
a dire word, *drag*, and the tone direr,
she was one of those who did the dragging,
who seized limb and hair and clothes
and dragged *Saint Francis* up the stair,
though more gently than the rest,
or so she claimed,
but nonetheless her hand was raised

   The little nun,
barely twenty and very fair,
was gagged,
thrown upon a bed,
and bound,
and then a pad or *matelas*
was placed across her face,
and Father Benin first,
following whom all,
climbed atop the pile,
taking turns, as it were,
at jumping and stamping thereon
in order to press the breath
from the youthsome nun
and crush her to death,
and in no great while
this was done

   Laughter began when her life ended,
and there was much rallying,
one of another,
someone saying
the dead sister would have made a good martyr,
so steadfast was she, so resigned,
and then her body was taken below,
dragged
to the cellar,
where it was flung into a pit
and sprinkled with lime
and a particular liquid,
its name known in France,

there being sovereign in cemeteries
for suppressing effluvium

    Not long later,
friends came to inquire of *Saint Francis*
and were told
that she had died gloriously,
uttering heavenly expressions,
and these being recited to them,
they departed
satisfied

    And she wrote this too,
that not even the ceremony of confession
made the priests put aside
their abandoned nature,
each of them receiving penitents
not behind a chapel lattice
but openly in a private apartment,
oftentime the Mother Superior's
and there, asprawl on her furniture,
hearing tell of peccadilloes
and pronouncing absolution
only when a coif came off,
and a habit slid to the floor

    And she wrote
that being sent one day to the cellar
on some errand,
she tripped and fell and,
rising,
found what had caused the fall,
an iron ring
fastened to a trap door
which,
she said,
she had the curiosity to raise,
whereat she saw four or five steps
leading downward into the darkness

    She pondered much on the subterrane way,
at first unable to imagine its purpose,
but at length it came to her,
she said,

it led to the Seminary,
thus accounting for the presence of priests
in the Nunnery
when the Nunnery gates were closed,
and thereafter,
by pacing distances and noting direction,
she ascertained
that her conjecture had been correct

And she wrote
of the child of a rich old Canadian,
a young lady of seventeen
remarkable in little
but her sprightly disposition
and yet quite the object
of the Superior's desire,   .
who hoped,
should the girl take the veil,
to be ever so dowered by her doting sire

She inclined not at all toward the cloister,
though,
had no vocation,
no intention,
indeed, no wish whatever for convent life,
and the less she leaned
the more the Mother yearned for her,
yearned too for her sweet endowment,
and so vast was her need
that she resorted at last to *tromperie*,
and the trick was this,
that the girl be induced,
in sport only, of course,
to don the splendid robes of the order,
recite a few prayers,
and act out part of a ceremonial,
a game,
a lark,
but having done these things,
she learned
that it was play no more but earnest,
that she had entered the convent in fact

and would never be suffered to leave it,
and no tears that she wept,
no repugnance shown or expressed
served her,
and she gained nothing
save that no crime was attempted
against her person
for a time,
and her father,
believing that the event
had found him peculiar favor in Heaven,
was prodigal in his gifts

And she wrote, did *Saint Eustace,*
about the priests in great detail,
expatiating on their character,
their numbers,
their nightly presence
in the halls and chambers of the nunnery,
saying they were greasy and degraded,
licentious without exception,
none possessing the least virtue
required by their callng,
corrupters all,
tempters of the spirit and the flesh,
lost to God,
and loathed by those they forced to submit,
mon père, they were ever addressed,
but their Christian names were known
to the nuns
and whispered with their unchristian ways,
and other things passed current too,
that some suffered from disease,
that when said to be in Retreat,
as they claimed,
they lay instead in the hospital,
stranguried
exempli gratia, Father Tombeau
beside whose bed
bloody instruments of surgery
had been seen

And she wrote of penances
that the nuns were made to perform,
mentioning those only that might be named
without offense to the virtuous ear,
among such kissing the floor
or the feet of other *religieuses*,
also kneeling hourlong on dried peas
or walking with these in their shoes,
and some were made to eat
with ropes around their necks
and then of foods they found repugnant,
such as eels,
which were said to feed on the dead,
and she recounted this too,
that they were constrained
to brand themselves with hot irons
and to stand with arms extended
for extended lengths of time
in imitation of the Savior on the cross,
and there was a certain solemnity
called *Chemin de la Croix*,
a falling before many stations or chapels,
a variety of prostrations
such as were suffered by the Lord
on the way to the Hill,
and there were other mortifications,
as,
in the presence of the Superior,
chewing a piece of window-glass
until it became a powder,
and often they wore studded belts
that drew blood,
and there were bindings
and gaggings
and confinements in the dark,
and, cruelest of all,
the leathern cap
which when fastened on the head
and buckled to the chin
could scarcely be worn for a moment
without causing such pain
as to bring on convulsions

    And she wrote
of something in a glass box
shown her by the Superior,
a waxen disc called an *Agnus Dei*,
an object worthy of the highest reverence,
to be gazed upon only in a state of grace,
it having been blessed
in a dish eaten from by Jesus,
a marvel, it was,
and if kissed
or even merely looked at,
it would give a hundred days' release
from purgatory
to all but Protestants

    And she wrote,
finally,
after years of immurement,
years of lickerish life,
false prayer,
self-abuse,
and participation in the crime of
murder,
at last and *enfin*, wrote she,
she made her escape from the Hotel Dieu
thusly,
she opened a door and walked away,
walked without let or hindrance,
walked, it seems,
to the city of New York,
there to pen her awful disclosures,
beginning with this from the Revelation
Come out of her,
meaning the Roman Catholic Church,
come out of her,
my people,
that ye be not partakers
of her sins
and that ye receive not of her plagues.

When the book appeared, dark fears grew darker, and there were
new forms of old aversion, and a humming could be heard, as from
demonkind on the wing and hidden behind the air. Here and there,
a riot began, a sanctuary went up in smoke, and they were shunned

who believed in a three-in-one God, in the death and resurrection of the Savior, in the seven sacraments. The book was widely read and widely credited by those who thought there were too God damn many foreigners here. It contained no reference to the writer's arrest in a whorehouse for picking the pockets of a customer.

THE DORR REBELLION

in Rhode Island and Providence Plantations

The swells had owned the place since the Charter days, owned the rivers and bays and beaches, *the bogges and Firme Landes, the Soyles, Groundes, and Havens, the Royall Mynerals, among which Gould and Silver, and the Mynes of pretious Stones* — all these they'd owned from the beginning, and they'd own it, they swore, to the last, when God frowned on the world, and the *Trompe la Mort* was wound. Till then, the Best would ride, and the Beast would bear them.

Tom Dorr was made for equitation. His father was in the China trade, and his mother's side had blood, and, given the tin and the lineage, he needed only Harvard to fit his hand for the whip. He was sent there at fourteen, small for his age, retiring, they say, studious, free from pranksome ways and superfluities, and it came as no surprise that his senior thesis was The *Calculation and Projection of a Lunar Eclipse in 1825*. It was merely an exercise, of course. His bent was toward the Law, which he learned from Chancellor Kent, and after that he was ready to join the gents in the seats above the salt.

There must've been something wrong with him, though, because he didn't seem to belong there: his mind was on the ruffraff at the lower end of the board. Something must've gone bad in his head: it was beclouded, many thought, by his father's money or by the moon in his mother's blood, but whatever had caused it, they'd bred themselves a sport, a freak, quiet, small, and portly, but a rum one nonetheless. He simply wasn't right, he wasn't right at all.

He believed in the Invisible Hand of the people, the -wrights and -smiths and -makers, the tinkers, the tanners, the blowers of glass. He believed that the people were sovereign, the tapsters, the coopers, the chandlers and spinners, the pickers-up and layers-down. He believed that government was the people's creature, the potter's, the founder's, the steeple's jack, and he believed that its power, when necessary to their happiness, could be taken back by the plodders, the lifters of weight, the work horses, the many-assed Beast. He was wrong in the head, that Tom, a fool at least and maybe even a Tom o' Bedlam.

Under the Charter of '63 (meaning 1663), the people couldn't vote without proving title to $134 worth of Rhode Island earth. They could pay taxes and fight fire, they could serve in the Militia, they could hew and draw and do as told, fetch when a finger pointed and bob if thrown a bone, they could eat crow, lick spit, sing small, and stand aside as the Lords of the Land went by—but they couldn't vote without those chattels real, and the only earth they owned was the dab between their toes. They weren't freemen, that sort; they were chattels themselves.

Being daft, Dorr thought that to be contrary to what they'd fought for in the war against George. Distraught fellow, he fancied that when the King went, the Charter went with him, and the Colony became in fact what it was by Nature's law—the property of the people, serf and squire, lower-down and higher-up, Beast and burden both. That was rough enough, but rougher was coming: all men were free, he said, and each had the right to vote. It was plain—he wasn't quite sound of mind, there was something the matter with his head.

The people found him sensible enough. The stonecutters and millworkers, the artisans and casuals, all those hired hands—the people saw no Simple Simon, and when he called for a Constitution, they gave him one that read so: *this government shall be a democracy.* The trouble with that was this—the other government was still there. It didn't blow away on the new wind, it wasn't smoke that ravelled, thinned, and disappeared. It stayed, it spoke, it made a shadow, as black now as in Charles's time, and when it fell on Dorr and the demos, their only hope was rebellion.

It wasn't even touch-and-go. The march against the arsenal was a cap-and-bell parade of brewers, painters, seamen, bakers, cobblers (4), farmers (5), and the solo lawyer Dorr. Under a flag of truce, he demanded surrender, and on being refused, he aimed a pair of cannon and tried to touch them off. No one knows whether they hung fire or blew up, but they laid a dreadful stroke on the air and ear, and the rebels—butchers, bakers, harnessmakers—fled the field and ran for home.

Dorr was taken in hand and made to stand his trial for treason against the state of Rhode Island. Upon conviction, he was sentenced to imprisonment for life, but he only served a year. A year was enough, though: when he came out, he was no longer sane; now he really did have a bubble in his brain.

A ROPE WITH TWO ENDS*

*This is a beautiful country. I never had the
pleasure of seeing it before.*
—John Brown, on the scaffold

They think I thought the slaves would rise when I rose, they think I heard black cries in my head, my crazy head, heard chains cast off in my mind, they think I hoped to live if caught. With my two-and-twenty men, I sought to take the world, they think, best it with sabers, fowling-pieces, pikes (pikes, for God's sake!) — and when I was pent up there in that engine-house, down to a dozen and some of those dying, even then they think I thought I'd prevail.

In my head, my crazy head, I never dreamed of winning. I never saw past where I presently stand, on the trapdoor of this platform. I never desired more than this endmost pleasure, a long view of my country, a vista of blue distances. But goodly though it be, still it is a sinful nation, and to purge it, to save it from the cormorant and the bittern, blood must be shed — a little, I once supposed, but as now I know, much.

Soon the axe will fall this vale from my feet, and I'll depend in space for thirty-seven minutes (why thirty-seven?) before I'm taken down thirty-six minutes dead, an enemy of Virginia, they'll have said of me, an enemy of the Union. Not so, not so: I am an enemy only of slavery, and when my neck breaks, its neck will be broken — but in between, blood. With the last of sight, I see the Blue Ridge redden and the Shenandoah drown, I see a rain of blood on the Old Dominion, I see the gaps fill with it, the sunken roads, the runs, the fords, and seasonal streams will flow all year. A great storm is coming, and its color is crimson — I can see it from here, I can see it in my crazy head. . . .

---

* "one around the neck of a man, the other around the system of slavery" — George William Curtis

Dan Decatur Emmett, 1815–1904

IN DIXIE'S LAND

I'll take my stand.
—Dan Decatur Emmett

   In '59, when he wrote the song, a walk-around, a cornshucking tune, he was forty-and-some, and he still had some forty to go. Till then, he'd had fair skies, favoring winds, but with his *Dixie*, the airs seemed to die, and in the deadness, headway ended, and though his life was hardly half over, his living ended. In '59, John Brown too took a stand and died. He said *Had I so interfered in behalf of the rich,* and he was dead, but he left nothing behind, no time unspent. It all went with him: he died lived out, at the end of living.

THE CONSCRIPTION ACT

*The Congress shall have the power
to raise and support armies. . . .*
   —U. S. Constitution

*You who do not wish to be soldiers
do not like this law.*
   —Abraham Lincoln

It was the poor who rose, but not against the law: what they sought to oppose was poverty, and they did so dumbly, out of squalor and hunger and the long disease of despair. They were barely aware of what they were doing—it was merely an act of riddance, a throwing off of cover, sad rags shucked for a Sunday suit of clothes. They cared little about whether their names were drawn or not—with their rotten teeth and rosé blood, their blains and rachitic bones, they had nothing to fear from the lottery drum. Nor were they enraged because some, the rich, could buy them for beans to die in their stead: poor sons-of-bitches, all they'd fetch was three hundred Ones. And their minds were free of this as well, the need to be on the winning side—to hell with the Blue, and this, Kiss my Ass!, to the Gray. What they strove against, though very few could spell its name, was their own kind of servitude, a bondage hard to tell from that of the coon. When, therefore, the day of the drawing dawned, their myriads emerged, as though by some supersensual knowing that the time to act had come.

From holes in the wall, from slum and stable, from such rookeries as Sweeney's Shambles and Brickbat Mansion, from Cow Bay and Five Points and Paradise Square, they flowed over the cobbles of New York as if the date, the very hour, had been determined by some power of the air. Welled up and ran, a fluid horde that filled the city's grill of mews and lanes, flooded the streets and ditches—an army of ants, they must've seemed, the *Anomma!*

In an instant, hundreds become thousands, rise out of the earth
and spread in all directions, and all live things flee as though

demented, and every creature that moves and has a heart that beats is attacked with blind impassioned gluttony . . . true, for the *Anomma* are actually blind. . . .

No one led them, those guttersnipes, those waifs and strays and tatterdemalions, no one told them where to go, those wives and doxies, dips and lowlives, louts and loons, no one took them by the hand or nose. They went, as surely as the sightless ant, to where the blood was fluent.

The lottery was held at the Provost Marshal's office in the Ninth District. There, on a dais in the middle of a room, stood the cylinder of chance: within it, on little rolls of paper, were the names (in advance!) of those due to stop a ball in the Wilderness or to be squandered at Cold Harbor and those who'd live till old age killed them. It was all there on the little furls of paper, and only time would tell who fell and where.

Where the human eye encounters them, it sees a torrent without bounds. . . .

The hosts came together where their lots were being drawn, at Third Avenue and Forty-sixth, and the first name they heard was *Jones, William.* But as if awaiting some signless signal, they merely jeered him and joshed him, cheered him, laughed, though who he was, or what he said, or whether he'd keep on living or soon be dead, no one knew and no one cared save William Jones. By evening, when the office closed, twelve hundred and thirty-six scrolls had been unrolled, Joneses all, and still little had occurred, nor did much occur through the night. There were the usual fires and the usual brawls, but nothing to cause disquiet—except, perhaps, a certain burden under the humming of the city, a sound as of something still afar but coming. Ants, it might've been, or the poor, *a torrent without bounds,* but though sleepers may have stirred, they slept the night away.

Whatever it was, a torrent of people or torrential ants, it knew no bounds by the following day. Many, watching the way things simply *began,* put it down to some call that came from within, a flare sent up in the mind. All at once, they said, there were headlong flights and pursuits, shots, cries, and the everywhere chime of breaking glass, and the air, a criss-cross of missiles, seemed filled with birds—pots, tins, books, pictures, stones, bottles, shutters, food, and niggers swinging from gas-lamp poles. They went for the niggers, the rioters did, sought them out, killed them when caught, and milled around for more—they even burned down the nigger orphan asylum, and if they'd gotten hold of the niggers' toes, they'd've burned the orphans too. They looted homes, stores, arsenals, stole suits, booze, guns, stoves, and shoes for two left feet. They killed cops, bystanders, children, invalid soldiers, and troops rushed back from Gettysburg, and of course, as aforesaid, a slew of blackface bastards. In all, during those three or four days, by rifle and bludgeon, by fire, knife, and rope, twelve hundred died in the streets. But when it was over, when the torrent had passed, only the dead poor might've become richer; for the living poor, there'd been no change.

THE PRINCE OF CINCINNATI

No one has ever written a book about him—a sketch for a genealogy, yes, for some dictionary of biography, yes, but a book, no, and so the leaves of his life have largely blown away. What's known, though, points to something more than one of the rich who'd grown richer, an eight-figure son-of-a-bitch. He left fifteen millions when he died, a mort of green for a horticulturist, or even, if property is theft, for a thief—but his story doesn't quite end with his fortune.

Not from his Catawba wines nor his hermaphroditic berry vines did those fifteen millions spring. They came from land, from the lots he got for two secondhand stills, and what he'd bought by the acre, he sold by the pinch, retiring at the age of thirty-seven to cover the hills of Ohio in grapes. He didn't let his strongbox rust, though. The lid was always creaking open and shut as cash went out and promises in—sight drafts, bills of exchange, notes, leases, forfeits, mortgages chattel, and mortgages real—and it wasn't long before he needed another strongbox. A quick forecloser, Nick was: you paid on the tick, or you went to the wall.

There were forty years of all such ahead of him, and if it hadn't been for one of his quirks, there'd be nothing but numbers to remember him for, and the kink in his horn was this: he hated his own class. None of them could touch him for so little as a dollar, and when pressed for some donation, he'd jeer well-dressed beggars from his door. He gave nothing to the church, nothing to the genteel cause, and satin ladies sent to dun him said they'd sooner walk the streets.

They'd've had better luck if they *had* been on the town. That was the sort he was drawn to, the pickup at the corner, the souse, the stiff, the on-their-uppers, the down-and-damn-near-out—there was a soft spot in him for that type, a ripe place, and what sweetness he had to give he gave to them. It didn't amount to much—a bone is all it came to—but it was thrown with what looked a little like love.

A queer cove, he must've been, to embrace only the roughscuff of the world—a traitor, many thought, for he betrayed the top for the bottom dogs, and some were so sore that they said so.

ALLONS, ENFANTS DE LA PATRIE

Le jour de gloire est arrivé.

The day of glory was the morrow of the fall of Fort Sumter, and in all the northern journals, a call appeared for volunteers — seventy-five thousand of them, to serve for three months and preserve the Union. Thus far, there'd been but one casualty — a gunner killed when his cannon burst — and therefore the streets were filled with hotspurs, and the air was flown with flags. Seventy-five thousand had been asked for, and that number came, and more. Drilled, paraded, cosseted, huzzaed, they were marched off into Virginia, wherefrom rumors soon blew in of action at Sudley Spring (where was Sudley Spring?), at Cub Run and Blackburn's Ford. Gunfire, a summer storm, could be heard at the bottom of the sky, and watching clouds form over fields afar, the Capital awaited the outcome in the open, stood about, spoke little, peered at empty roads, wondered. And then in the distance dust, and, still a long way off, a cannonade of feet in flight, and all night long they fled from roiled springs and reddened fords, ran in rout from the dams of dead in the runs, and well into the next day they were still coming back across the Potomac to fall down fagged out and sleep in the gutters of Washington.

When word spread of Federal losses, of the abandoned wounded, of the gear flung away, the rations, the pride — when ninety-day soldiers carried the battle home to wherever they hailed from, Rhode Island, Indiana, few came forward to take their place. High hearts lowered with the tales that were told of the Henry House hill, of the Stone Bridge and Centerville, of the sounds, the smoke and commotion, the fallen and how they lay: before the rack and smash of battle, the blood, the beshat pants, the hallucination, not long did ardor last in Maine and Minnesota. The season for camping out was over, the spell under the stars, the camaraderie of sport and story. *Le jour de* glory had come and gone, and with it went a skin-deep love of *la patrie*. Thenceforth, it would take more than a notice in a paper, more than a poster on a wall, to call *les citoyens* to arms.

That was block-letter bombast for the fools of April. From then on, money was the music that made men martial. It was useless to cry *Aux armes!*—after Bull Run, Simple Simons were hard to find. Bounties were offered now for volunteers—soon enough, the figure grew from fifty dollars to a thousand—but when the pay ran out, few were they who gave themselves away. Let impure blood fill the furrows—what did it matter?

Well, it did matter. To some, it mattered much that slavery end and the Union last, wherefore a law was passed under which service became mandatory for all—for all, that is, who couldn't buy some whey-faced dunce to fill their shoes or pony up the price of safety—three hundred dollars to stay at home. That made it a rich man's war and a poor man's fight. Those with funds spent four years far from the sunken roads and bloody angles, far from the peach orchards, the wheatfields, the churches white against darksome woods; those without the long green went, and many of them are there yet, chemicals in the earth now, bones and buttons in a stream, a rag still snagged on a tree.

Small wonder, then, that what the well-off bought for cash, the hard-up sought with guile. To win exemption, what would not a conscript do? what sham and deceit would he stop at, what ruse was too bald, what claim too bold? what would misgive him, what minim of honor would hold him back? None, nothing, nix! . . . At stake was life itself. Death lay in every field, lurked in every thicket, commanded every road, and to cheat it, subornation became the game for knaves. How they lied, the shysters, how they shunned their Chickamaugas, how they tried to let George do it!

And George did do it, because George was true, George was on the square. The draft was drawn before his eyes—he saw the wheel, saw it turn and tumble the lottery slips, saw the blind man called from the crowd. He never knew the slips differed, some of them smooth and some sanded, and therefore he never learned why his name came up and his neighbor's not. Poor innocent, he was blinder than the blind man, who saw by touch, and without much fuss, he let himself be sent to some faraway junction, some mill or courthouse, and there he stopped a ball from killing someone else. George was artless, George was fair.

During the four drafts of the war, seven hundred and seventy-six thousand men were drawn, of whom three hundred and sixteen thousand were declared exempt for one reason (afflicted with a peculiar malady) or another (subject to fits), and there were these reasons too

    sole support of a crippled mother,
    widower with minor children,
    deafness,
    contracted mouth,
                  (what was contracted mouth?)
    missing fingers, toes, teeth,
    debililty due to masturbation,
    cousin-marriage,
    eating too much grease and saleratus,
    night sweats, palpitations, scrofula,
    these last due to masturbation,
    and to produce conjunctivitis,
    they rubbed sand into their eyes,
    and they ulcerated their feet
    by soaking them in fomentations of lye,
    and to simulate asthma,
    they inhaled the fumes of burning matches,
    and with caustic substances,
    with splintered wood and crooked wire,
    they worked up artificial hemorrhoids,
    and to trump up inguinal hernia,
    they blew air into their scrotums
    through a pipe.

They didn't seem to care what they said or did or swore to. They were in a stew to stay alive, and they did, three hundred and sixteen thousand of them. The dying was for George. That was the name for all those at Shiloh, and in the bloody lanes through the Wilderness — George.

TURN RIGHT ON A DIRT ROAD

*At Chivington (inquire directions locally), turn right
on a dirt road 10 miles to Sand Creek. The site is
unmarked.*
— Tour 8 Colorado, Amer. Guide Series

And when you ask the way, they say you can hardly miss it. Take
the road to the right, they say, and make for that smear at the bottom of the sky. It's a range of bluffs, where the creek bends when
running and the bed when dry. It's a scanty stream, you're told, rarely
full and never deep, enough and no more to keep the willows alive.
And they say this too, that when the rains are over, a meander of
wet sand is nearly all you'll find, but if you don't mind the taste
of the plains, look for a pool in the shade: it'll be cool enough to drink.

Inquire locally, the guide-books read, proceed from here ten miles
to there, ride those ups and downs of grama grass, proceed, proceed
ten miles on a fine-dust road, wind with its wends and leave behind
a flight of birds, go, go through ghostly herds of game, turn right
and go, proceed ten miles. At the base of the bluffs, a village of Indians died, but they say no plaque shows the place, no sign, no pile
of stone, only Cheyenne shades and Arapahoes, and they live there
still, they say, they hunt the hills, their ponies graze, their dogs and
children play. . . .

They were asleep, most of them, that winter's morning. In a hundred lodges, hundreds lay in buffalo robes, and embers in the open
sent up smokes that went unread — a squaw, foraging for wood, saw
dust in the south distance, antelope running or mounted men, but
by then it was too late to learn what the live coals said. The dust
had been raised by the 1st and 3rd Regiments of Colorado Cavalry,
who, all night long, had been riding hard with their only baggage,
four pieces of field artillery. The stars were gone or going when they
spotted the encampment, the picketed ponies, the smoke that
might've told what else was in the air.

The Indians, assured by the Army that they would be safe from harm on the Big Sandy, were given no more warning of the attack than they got from their dogs. It was the baying of dogs that gave the whites away, and then from higher ground around the village, fire poured down from seven hundred carbines and four twelve-pound mountain howitzers. Braves, squaws, children, and barking narks, their dogs, were shot. Those that fought were shot, along with those that sought to surrender, that threw away their bows, held up their hands, waved white rags and a flag they'd been given to show they were friends. They were shot, those that stayed to fight and those that fled, they were shot from first light to halfway through the afternoon, by which time so many were dead that firing ended. . . .

An Indian Agent said the command, under Colonel John Chivington, left Fort Lyon around eight in the evening and rode all night to the encampment on Sand creek, thirty miles away. They got there at daylight and opened fire at once despite an American flag shown by Chief Black Kettle and a white flag as well. The Indians were either killed where they stood or shot on the run, and all bodies, men, women, and children alike, were cut to pieces, as if they were meat the soldiers meant to eat then and there and raw. . . .

An interpreter said the soldiers scalped the men and then knocked their brains out with gun-butts. The women were ripped open with knives, and children were clubbed dead, sucking infants. The creek ran blood. The bed was a red streak in the sand, there were red stones, red reeds. . . .

A First Lieutenant said there were five hundred souls in the lodges, mostly women and children, and going over the battlefield, he did not see a body but was scalped, and a large number had their privates cut out. He saw a soldier with a woman's private parts speared on a stick, and some were stretched on saddle-bows or worn around a hat. Colonel Chivington knew of those atrocities and did not take any measures to prevent them. One man told of hacking a squaw's heart out of her body, and he had the heart to show for it. . . .

A soldier said he could not say how many were killed. He kept count up to eight, but he could not stand it any more, they were cut up

too much. Standing-in-the-Water was killed in the creek, a bad
name to have that day, and White Antelope was killed there
too, and his nose and ears and privates were cut off. A papoose
was carried in the feed-box of a wagon for a day and a half and
then thrown out to perish on the plains. The Indians of the
village were considered to be friendlies. . . .

A First Lieutenant said
eight Indians, three women and five children, were being
guarded by a detail of soldiers. An officer came along and killed
all the prisoners, though they screamed for mercy. . . .

A Major said
the bodies of females were profaned in such a manner that the
recital was sickening. . . .

A Captain said
the privities of White Antelope were cut off to make a tobacco
sack. . . .

A Surgeon said
he did not see any Indians scalped, but he saw scalped bodies
afterward, and Colonel Chivington was so placed that he could
not help but know that scalping was going on. . . .

A soldier said
he judged that about four-five hundred Indians were killed. He
counted as many as three hundred and fifty in the creek alone.
Nearly all were scalped. . . .

A Sergeant said
he counted up to a hundred and thirty bodies, and he did not
see any but what was scalped. Saw fingers cut off, saw privates
cut out, saw a Major scalp an Indian to get a scalp-lock or-
namented with silver, there was a long tail of silver hanging
from it. . . .

A Corporal said
he saw a little boy still alive in a trench dug by the Indians,
and a Major drew his pistol and blew the top of his head off.
He saw soldiers unjointing fingers to get the rings. . . .

Colonel Chivington said
he knew nothing about the Indians being under the protection

of the Government. No one told him that when he arrived at Fort Lyon, neither Major Anthony commanding the post nor Major Colley, the Indian agent. . . .

A Major said
he saw a man dismount right alongside Colonel Chivington and scalp a squaw who had already been scalped. And there was a little child, perfectly naked, that was running away, and two men tried to hit him from a distance of seventy-five yards and missed, and a third man said to let him try the son-of-a-bitch, and he fired, and the little fellow dropped. . . .

A Captain said
he counted sixty-nine dead Indians and a hundred live dogs. . . .

A frontiersman said
he could not guess within a hundred how many Indians were killed. . . .

A soldier said
he saw a camp of Indians, and the stars and stripes were waving over it. . . .

A soldier said
he saw a number of children shot. One of them had both ears cut off. . . .

A Sergeant said
he went over the ground the next day, acting in the capacity of clerk, and he counted four hundred and fifty dead Indians. . . .

A guide said
the colors were flying over the camp, and a white flag too, both so conspicuous that the soldiers could not help but see them. Then the firing started, the Indians ran for their guns. They might have gotten away if they had tried, but mostly they stayed to fight, and all fought well. On a visit to the camp a month later, he saw the remains of sixty-nine dead. The rest had been eaten by wolves and dogs. . . .

Turn to the right and go ten miles to the site on Sand Creek, the Big Sandy. Nothing marks the place but those that died there, and they abide yet. They dwell in the self-same lodges, the shades of braves, squaws, papooses, and still there on the plains, the shades of ponies graze, and dog-shades drowse at the remains of fire. All is as that morning saw it in '64, all save this, that what lived then is now dead. But the creek runs clear again, and it's good to drink, so turn right and go ten miles on that dirt road, proceed toward those bluffs, that smear, go, proceed. . . .

WAR MEANS FIGHTING

and fighting means killing.
— N. B. Forrest

He'd been a muleskinner once and a dealer in slaves, but that was far behind him now, and he wore two stars and a plume, and he was storied, sung of, instantly obeyed — still, the niggeryard smell stayed with him, and he made fans and kerchiefs wave. But if he stank at routs, he was sweet in the field, where only killing counted, and for that kind of work, he was surely the right kind of man. In all, he had fifteen horses shot under him, and if the war had lasted longer, he'd've had some more: he liked to be where the swarm was thickest, where he could hear death coming and go humming away. Verily, killing was work he had a fancy for, no one more so, and he found much of it in those raids he made so many of, on Paducah, on Union City, on stores, stations, weapons parks, on any point where two roads crossed, on Fort Pillow.

On Fort Pillow. The stronghold, on the bluffs above Memphis, was occupied by a battalion of white cavalry of the 13th Tennessee and a colored battalion of light and heavy artillery, and together with a number of wives and children and a score of officers, the garrison comprised some six hundred when, early one April morning, Forrest fell upon it with a force of five thousand. The defenders fought well for the better part of the day, but along toward the middle of the afternoon, they were pitched into everywhere at once, and their lines, always thin, were quickly overrun. A further stand being hopeless, firearms were thrown down, and from sticks and sabres surrender flags were flown.

But to the rebels, it was as if they were still being resisted, as if emptied hands were all the more deadly, and from their ranks a cry arose, and it was heard all along the bluffs, out on the river, and by some on the other side, watching the fight from Arkansas. *Kill 'em*, cried the rebs, *kill 'em, God damn 'em! That's Forrest's orders, not to leave one alive!* They killed about four hundred, and for the most part they were black

being sworn,
Horace Wardner, surgeon, said
the Federal dead at Fort Pillow
were the worst butchered set of men
he'd ever seen
in a life of gore and fracture,
he'd handled crow-bait often,
he said,
the torn parts, the parts of pieces,
but never was meat so mangled before,
there was a negro boy of sixteen,
he said,
and the boy was in the hospital,
sick with fever
and unable to rise and run away,
and one of the rebs broke in
and hacked at his head with a sabre,
and the boy threw up his hand
to fend off the blows,
only to lose two of his fingers trying,
and in the end he died anyway,
the outer table of his skull
being incised,
the inner table broken,
and a sliver of bone
being driven into his brain

and being sworn,
Ellis Falls, cook (colored) said
after the surrender,
the rebels came into the fort
and killed all they could find,
white and black
the one the same as the other,
they cursed the wounded boys,
he said,
and shot one in the hand,
aiming to shoot him in the head
as he lay on the ground,
and they killed two women and two children,
he said

and being sworn,

Duncan Harding, private (colored) said
he was Number 2 gunner,
and he was shot in the arm
when the fort was captured,
and while a prisoner
he was shot through the thigh,
and he saw a corporal,
Robert Winston,
shot and killed
because he would not march fast enough
to suit the rebels,
and there were officers around
at the time,
and all they said was
Kill the God damn nigger

and being sworn,
Benjamin Robinson, sergeant (colored) said
he saw the rebels
shoot two white soldiers
after they had laid down their arms,
and over by the river bank,
where he was trying to hide,
they hallooed for him to climb the bluff,
and when he did so, they said
Give us your money, you damn nigger,
or we will blow your brains out,
and what money he had he gave,
and they made him lie on his face
all night,
and come morning,
he saw them burying the dead,
black and white,
and one man his hand was still working
when they covered him

and being sworn,
Daniel Tyler, private (colored) said
he was shot after the surrender
by a reb he was so close to
he could put his hand on the gun,
and he did so,
and the reb said
Whose gun are you holding,

and when he said
Nobody's,
the reb said
I will shoot you,
and that's what he did,
not in the eye, though,
the eye was lost just before that
when someone knocked him down
and jabbed it out
with the muzzle of the gun

and being sworn,
Thomas Adison, private (colored) said
he came away from Carolina at nineteen,
and now he was forty
a gunner with Company C
when the fort was taken,
and he was shot in the face,
his jaw-bone being broken
by a rebel with a pistol
standing ten feet off,
and when he fell,
someone came by and took his money,
saying
God damn his old soul,
He is sure dead now,
He is a big fat old fellow,
and as he lay there not moving,
he heard the rebels shooting children
not more than this high
(holding his hand four feet from the floor),
heard them say
Turn around so we can shoot you good,
heard the guns go off
and the children fall

and being sworn,
Manuel Nichols, private (colored) said
after he gave up,
he was shot in the head
under the left ear,
also he was shot in the arm,
and while he was on the ground,

he saw the rebs go to a house
where a lot of soldiers were,
and the rebs said
All you damn niggers, come out,
We are going to shoot you, and
If you don't come out,
We will go in and carry you out,
It is only death anyway,
and one of their officers came along
saying
Forrest says No Quarter,
Black Flag,
Black Flag

and being sworn,
George Shaw, private (colored) said
he was shot about four o'clock
in the evening
after he had given up,
he was in the river,
he said,
close to the bank,
and a reb shot him from there
point blank,
saying
Damn you what are you doing here,
and when he said
Please don't shoot me,
the reb said
You are fighting against your master,
and shot him,
and the bullet went in his mouth
and came out the back of his head

and being sworn,
Jacob Thompson (colored) said
he was not a soldier,
but he went to Pillow
and fought with the rest,
being shot in the head and the hand
after the place fell
by a reb who said
God damn you, I will shoot you, old friend,

and he was not the only one,
he said,
there were about fifty,
he reckoned,
white and black,
and he saw some nailed to logs
and the logs set afire,
not killed first,
mind you,
but nailed through the hands,
saw the rebs do it,
saw four-five such nailed-up men,
two of them white,
saw Forrest around at the time,
a little bit of a man,
he was

and being sworn,
Ransom Anderson (colored) said
and W. P. Walker, sergeant (white) said
and James Walls (white) said
and D. W. Harrison (white) said
and Lt. McJ. Leming (white) said
and Nathan G. Fulks (white) said
and Woodford Cooksey (white) said
he saw one of the rebs
shoot a black fellow in the head
with three buckshot and a musket ball,
and when he still moved,
the white man took a sabre
and stuck it in the hole
in the black man's head
and jammed it way down,
saying
Now, God damn you, die,
but the black man still he moved some,
and the white man clubbed his carbine
and beat his head soft with it,
that was the next morning after the fight

and Mr. Lincoln said
We do not know that a colored soldier
or a white officer

commanding colored soldiers
has been massacred by the rebels
when made a prisoner,
We fear it
believe it, I may say,
but we do not know it,
If there has been
the massacre of three hundred
at Fort Pillow
or even the tenth part
of three hundred,
retribution shall surely come

In his dispatches, General Forrest said
The river was dyed with blood
for two hundred yards

Retribution shall surely come,
it was said,
and it came:
a third gold star

A MILITARY HISTORY OF SLAVERY
in nine photographs*

*Secession should be thundered forth
by the united voice of Georgia.*
— Robert Toombs

1. Muster in a Wheelbarrow
   They were Federals once, these five skulls that rest on rags, these breastbones, kneepans, clavicles in broken sizes. On the grass, a canteen lies, as if the lately dead knew thirst, and a foot still wearing a shoe seems to lie in wait.

---

* by Mathew Brady and T. H. O'Sullivan

2. Railroad Bridge at Richmond

In single file, its piers wade the river, the far ones fading into each other and the rain, but they bear no rails now, nor tie nor stringer—all such lie where sappers blew them, deep in the broad brown James. On the near abutment, though, the throws of switches lean in abandon, inviting wheels, enticing trains.

3. Union Soldiers Fishing in the Pamunkey

From a bank beside a burned-out bridge, they try with their crook-ed poles, their strings and bait, for mudcats, perch, and spotted bass. But other things, deep down, come tumbling toward them turning in the stream, an arm in a sleeve, a basket of ribs, a snarl of brain, letters in a packet, and before the living strike, these dead may take the worm.

4. In a Barn near Fredericksburg

Doctor Bunnell, for a small fee, will embalm bodies *free from odor or infection*, or so reads his sign, but nothing is said of freeing them from being dead. For all the blood he draws, they'll stay that way, and for all his proxy blood—formaldehyde. They'll reach their destination quite sanitary, but after the sunken road on Marye's Heights, none will come alive.

5. "No Two Have Fallen in the Same Position"

Eight men lie near the caisson of a fieldpiece, one of them under the limber. The gun itself is gone, drawn away to use on another day, to win or lose another Antietam. A shell having found them, the dead are where they fell, in gray among the weeds. Beyond them, white against a black wood, a church seems to hang from the trees, and before them, quite apart from all the rest, stands a pair of shoes.

6. Debris in the Wilderness

On a bed of leaves and twigs in a thicket, seven skulls stare at an empty canister—eight empty canisters in a thicket on a bed of twigs and leaves.

7. Two Days after Gettysburg

Here, near at hand, a dead man sprawls in the shot and trodden wheat, his head between his outstretched arms, his mouth a wide black ring, as though death had caught it crying out at something seen beyond, or perhaps at seeing naught.

8. The View from Cemetery Ridge

Downhill, the town the fighting flowed around, a roofed and steepled roll of ground, fences, trees in leaf, and a stone-walled road, and where the road ends or begins or bends out of sight, a blur of motion—a dustwhirl, is it, or, after a three-day stay, might it be death on the way to the next stop, a new Peach Orchard, another big or little Round Top?

9. Destroyed Ordnance Train, Atlanta
   What guns there were are gone. All that's left is a slain engine,
a slant of ties and rail, and three dim men beyond the remains—
wheels and wood and wavering track and three dim implications..

THE PERFORMANCE WILL BE HONORED

by the presence of the President
— playbill, April 14, 1865

On entering the box, he'd gone forward to bow to the audience, and then he'd retired to a chair at the rear, where, in the shadow of the curtains, he seemed to merge with the pattern of the lace, to become a darker place in its weave. On the boards below, players strode and postured, told their flimsy jokes, spoke *sotto voce* to the furthest row of seats, but he was little aware of their mimic elegance and their tricks of speech. In his mind, he was far away from Ford's, in regions so real to him that he might've been borne there in body too, set down in parts he'd never seen but somehow always known. Brandy Station, Frayser's farm, the sunken road at Shiloh, at Fredericksburg — all the sunken roads and Bloody Lanes, they ran now on his face.

On-stage, *bavardage* and plays on words, the bombast of *Asa Trenchard* and *Dundreary* the lisping Lord, but none of these lightsome things could dim the sights of Salem Church, kill the sounds of Malvern Hill. A great cyclorama quickened in his presence, and winds rose, and dust set sail, and there were shots in sprays and cannonades, and he saw gutted horses fall and thrash, dying on the run, and men ran too, and other men pursued them, and there were some, a few, who merely drifted with the smoke, smoke themselves, and expresses of canister passed, and beelines of lead stopped in heads, in tripes, in the trunks of trees. In that box at Ford's, he saw and heard these things, all seen and heard before, in dispatches, in collodion prints, in the stuttered word of the telegraph.

In that box at Ford's, he saw four years of war, saw each engagement however small, he was at all the taverns, all the mills and bridges, all the places where two roads met, and all the wounds were his, and his the lives that were lost. With no diminution, he knew again his earliest anguish: the last death, blue or gray, rent him like the first. and now the things he saw were done with, and there'd be no more women begging for their one remaining son, no more reprieves for sleeping pickets, no more boxes of john-doe bones — the death roll would show no new names, grow no longer.

The war was over, he thought, and he felt that it had been fought within and upon his person: he contained the Wheatfield, the Round Tops, the fords and junctions, in him were the armies, the guns, the wagon trains, and no shot had been fired that failed to strike him. For him, therefore, the war would last forever, and he grieved, he grieved. But in a moment, a door would open behind him, and the war would end, the grief would go. . . .

CHRISTMAS EVE IN PULASKI, TENNESSEE

ku klux, from kyklos, *meaning circle*

At the beginning, a social thing is all it was, a ring-around, no more than that, of men-at-arms come home from war. God knows where for each the shooting had ended—at Appomattox, it may have been, at Durham Station, at this church or that chimney—but it was over now for all and they with voids to fill in small-town Tennessee. At camp and bivouac, the killed had been among them yet, their faces clear, and their jokes and jeering, and they were defined and heard, and they were not yet open spaces in the mind. As with the Indians, their shades came and went at will, and the living did the same; but when the guns fell still, the dead withdrew, and then it was lonely here in the world.

In a law office on or near the courthouse square, six paroled soldiers (some say seven) met that night of the birth of the Son of Heaven, but they exchanged no gifts nor sang glad songs, nor did they gaze in wonder at the figures in a crèche. They saw not the rise of the wise men's star, no, nor did they warm in the glow of a miniature manger. Six hearts were dim and chill (seven, if the rumor is right), and they drew neither heat nor light from the luminous marvel. Instead, the young old soldiers joined cold hands in a *kyklos*, meaning circle, to keep the gloom of defeat away, and for a while they deemed they did—*old times dar am not forgotten.*

At their second meeting, they thought it might amuse to masquerade in sheets, and rather more so, they supposed, to parade Pulaski's streets. And diverting it was to whiten the night and frighten the coons: it was sport to shake their hand with a skeleton's, to take off a gourd that looked like a head, it was a lark on the darkies, pretending to be dead. There at the start, it was horseplay, high jinks to keep the lows at bay—they wore horns, some of them, they bled from bladders of blood, they were back, said they, from hell, and when they saw the fear in blacks and whites, their blues

began to go. The hoods, the horns, the robes, the hopeless tricks
of the six or so, they were drollery no more. They'd been beaten at
the fords and the angles, in the orchards, the wheat, and the sunken
roads, but what once they'd lost by day they now might win at night.
. . .

                                                                           beware

smart kikes,
brash coons,
scalawags,
and
you that come with carpetbags

                                                                           beware

the Bloody Moon
has at last arrived
some live today, tomorrow die

                                                                           beware

we the undersigned
understand
you have recommended
a big Black Nigger
for male Agent on our nu rode;
wel, sir,
if he gets on the rode,
you can make up your mind
to pull roape   *beware*

and Jasper Carter (colored) said
twenty-six men came to his house
and knocked the door down
and made him kinle a light,
and then they taken him away
about a quarter far
and whope him,
and after they had all done that
as much as they liked,
one of them tole the rest
to go stand on his head,
which they done,
making him lay on his face
while they done it,
and there are whelps on his back,
he said, thick as a finger and black as a hat,
a hundred and fifty such,
he said

and Caroline Smith (colored) said
the Klux
made a great scatterment of darkies,
coming to her house on Thursday night
in some kind of false face,
and they laid holt of her husband
and beat on him
as much as they wanted to,
and then
they made her get down on her knees
and hike up her dress,
and when she did they switched her,
and then
they made her take her body off,
which she worn under her dress,
and they give her fifty more
with hickories,
she said,
and then they beat on Sarah Ann,
her sister-in-law,
and kicked her in the back,
and she has not got over it yet,
and they hit her on the head
with a pistol,
and she has not got over that needer,
and then
they done for her husband
with rocks and pistols and sticks
of hickory,
and he said *what for you whop me,*
and they said *never mind, just so we do it,*
and after that
there was a great scatterment,
she said

and Alfred Richardson (colored) said
he was about 34 years of age,
was borned a slave,
remained so till mancipation,
being a house carpenter,
married and three children,
voted with the Republicans,
and was attackted twict,

there being a set of men
that came in disguise,
doughface, long caps, gowns,
and one thing or another,
and they got a hold of a old man,
Charles Watson,
and they swinge him good
till his family hallooed and screamed,
and when he
(meaning Alfred Richardson)
went out to see what the matter was,
the matter was this,
they was looking for Alfred Richardson
and walloped Watson to tell them,
and he must of done so,
because a man come holding a pistol,
and he
(meaning Alfred Richardson)
took his own pistol and shot him,
and then three four men shot him back,
about twenty shots in the leg and hip,
he said,
and he ran and hid in the cuddy-cole,
thinking they would not find him there,
but they did
and shot him three more times,
but he shot one of them
on the top stap of the ladder,
and the others taken him by the legs
and drug him away,
and he has not seen them since,
he said,
but he has heard talk
that they will have him
no matter where he may go

some live today, and tomorrow die

                              beware

you that come with carpetbags

                              beware

scalawags

and beware Judge Chisolm,
a Republican,

a merchant and married,
with an interesting family of four,
Cornelia, nineteen, being eldest,
and John, at thirteen, youngest,
a Republican merchant,
kind-hearted and generous,
a most likeable man
with friends wherever he went,
but having been a witness
to certain outrages in an election,
he had to be gotten rid of,
and they tried to do that
by marching to his home
with a cannon
and firing it through the doors,
and they had a band of music too,
and it played all through the bombardment,
but the Judge didn't scare,
so they went about another way,
using a numerous family
in those parts,
Gully being the name,
and when one of them,
John Gully,
was waylaid and shot,
they put the crime on Chisolm,
and he was thrown into jail
along with certain others
said to be in on the conspiracy,
one Gilmer and one McClellan,
both of whom were shot in the back
and killed
by a mob,
and having Chisolm under lock and key,
they set out to do the same for him,
but his wife and son and Cornelia
being there,
they guarded him,
but they were only three
against many,
and guns went off,
and Cornelia was hit in the face,
and John the son was hit too,

a shot tearing off his arm at the wrist,
but he stood to his father all the same
and took a bullet through the heart,
at which the Judge
in a rage
grabbed a gun and killed the killer,
scattering his brains on the wall,
and with the jail burning,
the Chisolms ran for it
with Cornelia all the while
pleading for her father's life,
but a charge of shot
shattered her arm to the elbow,
and a pellet carried away some of the Judge's nose,
and then the mob shot him front and rear
at once,
and he fell
mortally wounded,
but begging to be taken home
to die there instead of in jail,
and when Cornelia appealed for help,
someone fired sixteen duck-shots
into her leg and foot,
breaking her hip
and cutting her bonnet-strings
at the very neck,
but finally two volunteers
carried the bleeding family
home
where the Judge and Cornelia
died,
all this happened on a Sunday
that might have been
the Sunday of the Bloody Moon

but it all began to happen
on Christmas Eve
in Pulaski
Tennessee

A FLOOD UPON THE EARTH

a vast sea of animals
—a hunter, 1875

So spoke all, in infinitudes. To the eye, the creatures were more numerous than numbers, wherefore the mind abandoned figures and turned to figures of speech: where the herds grazed, it was claimed, there all the world was engulfed, as by the Waters once in the days of wrath. *A vast sea* said they that saw it, *a motionless ocean*. To the Indian, they were all his needs on the hoof—their flesh fed him, their hides robed him, their powdered horn would work his spells. They were living treasuries, and, best of many things good, though ever drawn on, they were ever full: they were killed, but still they lived; they died and were not dead. Indeed, it seemed, they multiplied.

And then, with the People from Heaven, the horse came, and the sticks-that-speak, and the Deluge began to recede. They were not the hungered that hunted now, not the naked, not the magician seeking medicine: they were the butchers, or, worse, the skinners, out for pelts alone, and a curse on what was left. And there were epicures that, from a thousand pounds of meat, would only eat the tongue. And there were toffs with their heavy Henrys, .50 calibre and deadly at a mile: they hardly had to stir from camp; they killed from a chair in the prairie shade. And there were the marksmen, the firing-squads, concerned not with food, fur, or trophies, but with scores. And back and forth across the plains, the railroads ran excursion trains

> *will leave Leavenworth for Sheridan*
> *on Tuesday,*
> *refreshments on the cars*
> *at reasonable prices,*
> *and return on Friday*

and there was shooting from the windows all the way

a large herd seemed to go wild
at the shrieking of the whistle
and the ringing of the bell,
and suddenly the animals charged,
and down on us they came,
trembling the earth
as they plunged headlong into us,
some becoming wedged between the cars
and some beneath them,
and so great was the crush
that they turned three cars over,
killing the ones
our guns had missed

And then a day came when the vast sea dried, when there were Henrys by the hundred and nary a sight of game—the herds were gone, the bands of strays, even the lone head on the ghostly ocean. And there was silence now, there were no more downwind surrounds, no more droves driven over cliffs, no more corrals of burning grass, and the Grand Duke Alexis was back at Court, all such sport forgot. There was silence and, when the bone-pickers arrived, one last to-do

along the Santa Fe right-of-way,
near Granada, Colorado
there was a rick of buffalo bones
twelve feet high,
twelve at the base,
and half a mile long,
it would fetch ten dollars a ton

It is related that one spring early in the new century, a party of Indians was preparing for a ride into the hills when a white man asked them where they were going. *To hunt the buffalo,* they told him, and he said, *But there are no more buffalo,* and they nodded, saying, *We know that, but we always look at this time of year, and maybe we will find some. . . .*

THE WORLD'S HARD EYE

Robert Owen: Do you know God?
Breaker-boy: No. He must work in some other mine.

God's first week of work was long over by then. After a day of rest, He'd rested some more, and He was still at it, still taking His ease, shooting the breeze in front of the store, when the question was put to a boy of twelve: *Do you know God?* Stooped over a bank of coal, coonblack with its dust, picking slack and slate with black and bloody hands, breathing black air and hacking up black snot, the coal-dyed boy, twelve years old, replied, and it was as though the coal itself had spoken: *No. He must work in some other mine.*

The boy was wrong. In no other mine would God be found, nay, nor at a forge or a furnace or the sley of a loom: God those days didn't work at all. Not for Him some fall from a height, the scald of steam, or death by methane gas. No scaffold knew Him, no belt or spindle, and He blew no molten glass. *He must work in some other mine*, the boy said, but God's fingers would make no meals for gears, and He'd be cut in twain by no train of wheels.

Some other mine, the boy said, and he may have supposed a boy like himself, a twelve-year-old digging duff and shale from a passing mass of broken coal. As he cast aside bits of impurity, he may have wondered whether God was a last or a Christian name, wondered too where God's mine was, why no one knew its hours of work, its rates of pay—did God earn more than he did, forty cents a day? If he thought such things, he was fooled by fancy, fancy ruled him: there was no boy called God, there was no other mine.

Do you know God?, he was asked, but he couldn't raise the face, couldn't say he'd seen Him in this or another place, in a shop or foundry or taking piecework home. There were many who'd done a shift on bread and tea alone, so famished that they puked when fed, and there were pictures of that kind, the future necrotics, the coming blind, match-packers, dyers, gilders, makers of lace and felt, but God was not among them, staring back at the world's hard eye. *He must work in some other mine*, the breaker-boy said.

[190]

IN THE SAN JOAQUIN

*Lo! to our great delight we beheld a wide valley,
and young, tender grass covered it like a field of
wheat in May*
                                        —John Bidwell, in 1841

Following the course of the Kern, he was well across Walker Pass when, far below him, he saw for the first time the great basin of California. The old sea-floor seemed to flow as if it were water still, but it was only the grass, young and tender, on the move before the wind. What water there was ran red-brown through creeks in the marshes, made channels in the bottomlands, ate at the roots of reeds. A most pleasing prospect, he thought, as did all who were with him in his emigrant train, but from where they stood, only the actual was visible, not the times to come: forty years away the sound of gunfire, the bloodstains on the wheat.

They'd be gone by then, that ancient party, dispersed and lost or dead; they'd never know that on a day in May in the year 1880, seven men would die in a wheatfield near a place called Mussel Slough. On the homestead of a Henry Brewer, the seven would be killed with navy pistols and smoothbores loaded with pistol balls, some of them falling in the grain and some crawling off to end in a ditch or a bend in a road. The seven would be farmers, the youngest aged twenty-two and the eldest forty-nine: they'd be James Henderson, who, after shooting Mills Hartt, would be shot by Walter Crow, and so would Daniel Kelly, Iver Knutson, James Harris, and Archibald McGregor; having picked off five, Crow would run for it, only to be bushwacked in a clump of willows by someone whose name would never become known. On that quarter-section, seven would be killed in an affray, each supposing his enemies to be among the other six: alas, the enemy of all would be a dozen miles away, a line of ties and track called the Southern Pacific.

[191]

Under the act of Congress authorizing the construction of the railroad, the Company was granted a right of way from San Jose to Fort Yuma, a distance of six hundred and ninety miles; in addition, upon the fulfillment of certain conditions, it was to be given title to alternate parcels of land on both sides of the track, these to be ten per mile in number and twenty miles deep. In one such plat, the Brewer homestead lay.

Lo! to our great delight a wide valley, a newcomer once had cried, but in truth what had spread away below him was an almost empty view: a few shrunken cattle grazed on last year's weed (the very birds had to bring their own rations!), and little else moved but time. Even when the railroad came, it was merely a slash through the sand and silt, a string of poles and a strand of wire, a rosary of stations called Hanford, Armona, Lemoore, Goshen Junction. *Lo! a wide valley* with grasses young and tender, but it was so only when settlers got their hands on it — only then did the vale become a field of wheat in May.

> The Company
> invites settlers to go upon its lands
> before patents are issued
> and gives them the privilege
> of purchase at a fixed price,
> which in every case
> shall be only the value of the land
> without regard to improvements

So the circulars had said that were issued in the east, and those the War had beggared read the call and went — families in box-cars bound for the Canaan of the west. Weeks on the way, they were high of heart as they wound down Cisco grade toward the new Euphrates, and they were higher still for the snows on the long Sierra — water held in waiting for their wheat!

A fixed price, the Company had pledged, *without regard to improvements,* and the people, being simple, made the promised land bloom

> We flowed the sterile plain,
> brought water there in ditches
> dug by hand,
> and acres by the hundred thousand
> glowed with snow-fed grain,
> we laid out roads

and shaded them with trees,
we built houses, churches, schools,
we put in orchards and gardens,
we draped wells and walls with vine.

A fixed price, the settlers had been told, which they took to mean the Government's price, a dollar or two an acre—*a fixed price without regard to improvements*—but when the Company perfected its title and offered the land for sale, one or two dollars grew to be forty, and the simples wouldn't pay

How, they asked,
could they be asked to pay
for what they'd made
and therefore owned,
for barns built with no man's aid,
for sluices draining sloughs,
for roads and fencing,
for grapes and figs and thrifty trees
in their dooryards,
for glinting seas of grain,
how could they be asked to pay
twentyfold
for improving a barren plain?

The Company, they learned, was a sovereign within a sovereignty—*imperium in imperio*, as the legal jargon went—and in that state contained by a state, it was imperial. There, so desiring, it could've destroyed the towns, the willowed roads, the irrigation, it could've razed the walls and filled the wells, and had it willed, it could've blazed the earth and burned the wheat away. That was what the settlers learned.

The Company, of course, did none of those wasteful things. Instead, when the settlers refused to pay or leave, it sold their land to others and sued to force them out. In every case, the courts upheld the Company: the settlers were so no more; they were squatters and must go. To Brewer's field on a day in May in the year 1880 came Mills Hartt and Walter Crow, two who'd bought what the settlers had sweat for, and with them came a sheaf of writs and a team of marshals to serve them.

They were met there by those who'd fought for a long time against something that couldn't be seen or reasoned with or taken by the hand: the Company. Now for once they were facing people, not a disembodied name, and being people themselves, they thought the enemy had materialized at last. In Brewer's field of wheat, seven were killed that day, none of them the enemy. The enemy lived on.

THE VIEW FROM MT. McGREGOR

The cannon did it! The cannon did it!

In his chair on the cottage porch, he was far above where the railroad ran, but now and then, when a train went by, he'd see its smoke, and if the wind was right, he'd hear the cylinders pound, the sound of signals made of steam. Sometimes, through a daze of pain, he'd wonder which way the cars were headed—toward Schuylerville, was it?, or north toward Hudson Falls?—but the thought would soon be shredded like the smoke and steam, and then only the pain would matter, *the endless train,* and he'd cry out through the morphia that nothing would make it pass.

The cannon did it!, he'd say, *the cannon did it!,* meaning that the guns had brought him to this wicker chair, this knitted cap and fringed lap-robe. But for the guns, he'd've still been stolid in a Galena store, slow of speech with a customer, vague about prices, quality, the stock he had on hand; he'd've been failing on some farm, peddling cordwood in the streets of St. Louis, drinking alone in a riverside dive—he'd've been Stupid Sam, who went by the name of Ulysses.

The Adirondacks were flats of scenery stacked against the sky, screens that faded from blues to greens and finally faded away. Had he sought them, he might've sighted the flash of a pond, the thread of a stream, but walled within pain, he was lost to such seeking and barely up to waving at those who waved from the road. They'd come, some of them children, to watch a General of the Army waste and wear, they'd come from afar or merely from the foot of the mountain to peer through fronds of spruce at an old man chomping a cigar, and now and again a scarf would flutter among the trees, and less and less often a hand would flutter back. Soon, at any hour of any day, a five-star commission would lapse, and word would be passed to the rubbernecks that Ulyss was dead at last. *The cannon did it! The cannon did it!*

But when had he lived?, he'd wonder—in Illinois?, in Missouri?, a nobody hauling firewood, collecting rents, swapping horses? Had he been alive then, on that no-star round of the sticks? Or was it when the honors came, the hurrahs, the gifts of money, houses, and half a million cigars? Had he been quick then, in those days of ruffles and flourishes, of spanking spans and private cars? Or, forgetting the sashes, the silver swords, the elevation, was he living now, in a cottage lent for a summer he'd never spend? Tarnish hid the luster, he'd think, the tassels were dull with disgrace.

In the distance, the slopes seemed to stand in two dimensions against a two-dimension sky. Their edges, stepped with pines, led the eye to summits and then lost them to the blue, but none of these ascensions drew the gaze of an old man smoking a gift cigar in a lent chair. He was concerned with the catastrophes of peace, harder to bear than those of war. His Shilohs he could endure, his check at Spottsylvania, his defeat at Holly Springs, even that terrible hour when six thousand fell along the Chickahominy—he could bear such things; they went with the cannon.

But what he couldn't endure was the long Black Friday of his White House reign, and when body-pain permitted, he suffered that of the mind. How in so short a time could the country have been plundered by the country's worst? How, he wondered, could the forsworn have slicked it away, how the bribers and the bribed, the elected dishonorables, the titsuckers, the silk-hat slobs of Nast? How could counties have been given to railroads along with triple the cost of a mile? How could gold have been cornered? How could posts have been bought and favors sold? How, even through clouds of Havana, could he have failed to see that what his guns had won (six thousand dead in an hour!) was being stolen by a ghoul called Gould?

And yet he hadn't really known. He'd merely been Stupid Sam to the end, lending his name to a brother-in-law and sending thirty millions up the flue. Up too went all he owned and much sent in by his trusting vets—it came from the chimney blue, like smoke from a panatella. He was broke now, except for sixty-seven dollars in cash and five stars leadened by suspicion, dim with shame. Stupid Sam, he'd be gone in four more days.

The mountains seemed to rest against a wall of sky, but he was aware only of something red waving to him from the road. He waved back once, and then he went inside. *The cannon did it!*, he thought, *the cannon did it!* But he was wrong—he was dead long before he died.

The Haymarket Bombing, 1886

HARANGUE IN DESPLAINES STREET

The best shape for a bomb is globular.
—Johann Most,
Science of Revolutionary War

When the police came, Sam Fielden was holding forth from a wagon-tail. He'd been speaking for no little while, telling a crowd of some five hundred workmen that the rich had robbed them: the many owned nothing, and the few owned all (A voice: *Right enough!*), and if matters were left to the law (Cries of *No! No!*), so they'd stay forever, with a million getting meat and fifty million bone. The law was their enemy, he'd been saying. Only the day before, they'd attacked the McCormick Reaper Works, and the law had shot them down, but when, he'd asked, when would it shoot McCormick down (Cries of *Never!*)? Have nothing to do with the law, he'd told them: the law had no mercy, it degraded them, it turned them out in the road. Throttle it, therefore, he'd said, stab it, kill it: if they didn't, it would kill them. And then Capt. Ward, the law in blue, had cried *In the name of the people of Illinois, I command you to peaceably disperse,* and down he'd climbed to say *We are peaceable.*

If peace had ruled in and near the Square that night, it ended then and there. Off in the darkness, a sibilance was heard, a sputtering, and then a spark was seen in an arc through the air, a pounce of fire at the policemen's feet. At once, a great glare grew up from the ground, and a great stroke of sound stunned the minds of all, stilled them for a moment, and then there were moans, curses, pistol-shots, and finally centrifugal flight, the living from dead that lay in blood and disarray

Patrolman Mathias Degan, shockingly mutilated,
died,
and John Barrett, his leg blown away,
died,
and Michael Sheehan, and Thomas Redden

and George Miller, and Tim Flavin
died,
and Nels Hansen in agony died,
and John Reid was shot in both legs,
and Lawrence Murphy lost half of one foot,
the left,
and he took shell wounds in the other,
and in the right hip,
also two bullets in the calf
and one in the side of the neck,
and John Doyle had five wounds,
all in the legs,
                and so it went,
shell wounds right leg
bullet wound right arm
bullet in the back
seventeen shell wounds both legs
three toes shot off left foot
shell wounds fleshy part thigh
shell wound left hip
bullet wound right side
shell wounds both legs
shell wound right jaw
collar-bone shattered,
and Lt. James Stanton
had two shell wounds in the calf,
one in the thigh,
one in the hip,
one in the side,
and one in the forearm,
and Alexander Jameson was shot
through the wrist and in the groin,
                        and so it went
grievous pistol wound
trampled on
right leg crushed
both legs right arm left hand right heel
pistol ball
pieces of shell
bruised shoulder
smashed breast
both arms
three ribs broken
shell wound abdomen,

and Officer Charles Dombrowski deserted,
ran away from all those fallen helmets,
splintered billies,
burst uniforms,
fled bodies full and bodies bled,
found a hole,
and hid

                                   and so it went,
with seven dead, sixty-odd hit,
and one,
that Dombrowski,
who sped from history

All through the night, there were fears of revolution, there were sudden alarms and swift excursions, there were gatherings furtive and murmurous—the city itself seemed to whisper—and there were faces and firearms in countless windows, doorways, piles of stone, and here and there a shot was fired at nothing, and over streetcar rails and curbing, patrol-wagons going nowhere dashed by and disappeared, and looters were abroad, footpads, vags, fingersmiths, ganefs, and the curious too came forth to see and sniff the shambles, the wagon (though the horse was gone), the bloodied pavement, the pieces of—what? what had the pieces been part of?

The sun came up on raids and arrests. Eight particular outlanders were taken—tallow-faced sheenies, mostly, all but one with sebaceous names—Parsons, Spies, Schwab, Fielden, Fischer, Engel, Neebe, and double-g Lingg—greasy names, anarchistic, conspiritorial. As to Lingg, when his rooms were searched, spherical bombs were found, own brothers to the one that was thrown the night before; and as to the rest, all were members of a socialistic organization which published two papers, one of them called *Die Arbeiter Zeitung* and the other, for readers of English only, called *The Alarm*. In various capacities, each of them was closely concerned with these journals, as editor, printer, manager, and the like, and from time to time they published therein excerpts from the work of their master Most, a Bavarian pamphleteer. At the trial of the eight, the prosecutor read many such selections into the record, and as he spoke the printed words, a sweetness came on the air, the privet smell of rope. With book in hand, he paced slowly before the jury, and the boards beneath him rang, as if they spanned a fall, and nooses seemed to dangle for more than eight, for all

(Mr. Grinnell, reading)

Manual for Instruction
on the use and preparation
of Nitro-Glycerin, Dynamite, Gun-Cotton,
Fulminating Mercury,
Bombs,
Fuses,
Poisons,
etc.

(reading *passim*)

Explosives will form a decisive element
in the next epoch:
it is therefore natural for revolutionaries
to learn how to apply them.
The purpose of this treatise
is to publish the simplest methods
for the manufacture of dynamite
and to explain its use and effect —
many mistakes have been made
all of them attributable to ignorance.
Dynamite is exploded by shock,
and it must be handled carefully.
It freezes a few degrees above zero, Réaumur,
and in that state is easily set off.
Moisture has no effect on it,
its principal ingredient being
nitro-glycerin,
which is paraffinic.
The simplest way to explode dynamite
is with a blasting cartridge

(description omitted)

obtainable at all houses
dealing in shooting utensils.
Six to eight inches of fuse will answer
(in important undertakings, best quality only),
for a bomb requires just so much
as will burn in transit through the air.
The cartridge should reach two-thirds
into the explosive material,
so that when the fuse sets it off,
the explosion will explode the dynamite.

The best shape for a bomb is globular.

(emphasis added)

Zinc shells are not to be despised,
nor are tin, or lead, or antimony,
but where an explosion is desired
amongst a number,
the stronger the shell
the more splendid the results,
as, for instance, a gluttonous dinner-party,
where, if the bomb is flung upon the table,
a beautiful effect will be had.

To manufacture dynamite, mix
two parts sulphuric acid
and one part nitric acid,
to which add one-eighth of the quantity
of glycerin.
Gun-cotton is also an explosive
and not much inferior to dynamite.
To prepare,
take unglued cotton wadding,
boil in soda lye,
and dry carefully.
Then dip in a 2-1 mixture
of nitric and sulphuric acids
(see above)
and squeeze dry,
but not with the hands,
and place in a vessel with soda lye.
After fifteen minutes,
squeeze dry again,
and use immediately.
Another powerful explosive
is fulminate of mercury,
which consists of mercury,
sulphuric acid,
and alcohol,
in equal weights. . . .

The best shape for a bomb is globular.

The defendants did not deny that they were members of a revolutionary society advocating the overthrow of the social order by violent means. They did not deny that they had published in their papers large sections of the manual written by Most. Nor did they deny that on the night in question, in Desplaines Street just off the

Haymarket, a bomb had been flung among the police, many of whom had been injured or killed in the ensuing explosion. But they did deny that the bomb had been thrown by any of them, some of whom had not even been present when the blast occurred. In the absence of testimony to prove them the perpetrators, therefore, they contended that they were innocent of crime and ought to be acquitted.

They were in error.

The Court found them to be members of an unlawful conspiracy to destroy the social order and redistribute wealth, and it held that any act committed by one of them, or anyone else, in furtherance of those aims was the act of all. It did not matter that the actual perpetrator could not be identified, nor did it matter in the eyes of the law that the act had not been specifically authorized as to time, place, or manner, nor even that some of the conspirators were physically present elsewhere. What did matter was advocacy and instigation, and where advice to murder had inspired murder, those who had given the advice were no less guilty than the murderer, known or unknown: in law, they were all principals, all murderers. In publishing a call for violence, in pronouncing dynamite to be good stuff, sublime stuff, just the stuff for a party of rich loafers, they became one in effect with him they had stirred to throwing it: theirs was the body, his the arm. *The best shape for a bomb is globular*, Johann Most had written, and when they printed the words, they killed themselves. At any rate, five of them did—three of the eight got off.

Herman Melville, 1819–91

THE CUSTOMHOUSE YEARS

All Fame is patronage. Let me be infamous.
— Melville to Hawthorne

Each morning at eight, he'd set out from Madison Square, walking on a fair day and riding the stage in the rain, and two miles down Broadway he'd go—to Duane, say, or Jay—and there he'd cross to the Hudson, stopping on occasion to stare above the slips, where a palisade of rigging seemed to fence the Palisades. None can say what he dwelt on in such intermissions, nor may even he have been aware of what concerned his mind. There were matters of the moment, the names and berths of ships, the cargoes he was due to inspect; and there were matters of the past, sights once seen, words spoken (to whom?) and heard, the tones of certain winds. Nowhere could he have been free of remembrance, but here, so near to many reminders, the masts, the festooned canvas, the mewing gulls and chloride air, here he must've found himself living in more than one place and more than one time. He was an old man now on one of the days of his six-day round, he was weighing sulphur, counting pelts, stamping chests of tea; and he was also young, unknown as yet and not as yet forgotten, he was watching the *vahine* girls swimming naked out to the *Acushnet,* he was seeing their wet brown bodies, their wet and jet-black hair. So, though no one knows what he thought of on those days beside the dull green river, he may have seen its gulls mingle with other gulls, the ones that cried round the Rock Rodondo, may have seen the hulls across the street meet and gam with hulls across the world, may have seen drays transform to pods of whales, and so faintly as to seem imagined, from no place or from Paradise, he may have caught his hero's name and designation: *Jack Chase, captain of the maintop.* In that same moment or the next, a sobriquet may have surfaced in his mind—*the Handsome Sailor*—and, clearly but a fancy, it may have stirred and then submerged.

[203]

Let me be infamous, he'd said, and Fame let him be, left him at his sere and feckless four-dollar days on the wharves, sought him not among his invoices and manifests, his table of tariffs, his stamping-pad and its purple ink: there were twenty years of such days, and Fame let him be. It was the only work he ever did for pay, and he did it well and with honor, as if it were a charge that lay upon him, for nearly a third of his life. And yet what could he have deeply cared for in those daily dealings with the tricksters of trade, how could his thoughts have stayed with ad valorems and specifics, with false weights and misappraisals, with documents drawn by the light-of-hand—how could he have lived on land those twenty years of days? He was out of his element there, a drydocked ship or one on the ways, a stranded creation, ungainly, exposed, of no avail. If he had a place among the living, or even among the dead, it was where Jack Chase surely was, on the seas or under: the things he did at desks (did he really do them?) were contrary to his nature, were all against his will.

Let me be infamous, he'd said, and so he was for twenty years. Always, though, he was only there in part and only partly of that time, and more and more did he dwell on Jack his hero and the Handsome Sailor, and in the end he may well have joined them, the three becoming one. If so, he may one day have heard himself say *Sentry, are you there?*, and for Ishmael, Jack, and Billy, the long last voyage would have begun.

THE FEUDAL SYSTEM IN ILLINOIS

We are born in a Pullman house, fed from a Pull-
man store, and taught in a Pullman school, and
we'll be buried in a Pullman cemetery and go to a
Pullman hell.
                              —Mary Ellen Lease, a Pullman worker

The fief embraced four thousand acres a dozen miles south of the
Loop, and within it there was raised a small and perfect city where
its vassals might dwell in peace and profusion, as if it were all there
was of a small and perfect world. It was meant to be the seat of all
pleasure, and though it would have been meet therefore to call it
Eden—aye, even Paradise!—it came to be known as Pullman, after
him that had caused it to rise.

It took him longer than God to build his garden, years indeed instead of days, but when done it was no less a place of plenty for
its Adams and Eves, and good gold was there, and bdellium and onyx.
How free from fault his dreamland seemed, how unimpaired! Pristine
he thought the tree-spanned roads, the parks and pleasances, the
shrubberies, and these as well, the church of glaucous stone (Rev.
E. Christian Oggel), the slate spire, the wheel window, and then he
moved in his mind to the Theatre and its Morisco boxes, its morocco
seats, its cloudlike vault of seraphim, and from there he strayed to
the Library and its shelves of many hues, the motley worn by the
bards of the ages, by the travellers and wizards of the physical world.
And on he went, now to his sewage farm where, thanks to some
engineer, shit was made to sink and, presto!, disappear, and then
he found himself before the Hotel on the shore of the lake (veran-
dah 275 feet, first floor finished in cherry). . . .

But most did he delight in those yellow-brick rows where they
who formed his seigniory dwelt. Always on his tours of fancy, he
ended there, in one or another of his residence blocks lettered A
through J, any of the ten thronged tenements that reared from the
eastern part of his dream. He was hardly aware of the crowding,

hardly knew that in each of his mansions, forty-eight families were crammed into pint-size flats, with a crapper for every two such and a tap for every five, and therefore it troubled him little or not at all that his tenants slept in tiers, pissed in pairs, passed sideways down the halls. From the street, the town looked all to the good: there were sodded and terraced lawns, there were elms and lindens and maples shading the flagged and gravel walks. He never entered his ideal buildings, never looked in on any of those bohunks of his, those squareheads and meinherrs, he never smelled or tasted their cuisines, never sat for a while, spoke or listened, never saw the inner side, the lining of their lives.

All he knew about them was that they drew his pay, and for that he may have thought they held him dear, but the truth was that when they uttered his name, it came out like a curse. They hated the beavered son-of-a-bitch, hated his paradigmatic burg, hated above all the wheeled palaces they built there for the rich. They hated the disdainful beauties—the dark green *Despoina*, the scarlet *Artemisia*, the navy *Victorine*—cars that seemed to sneer at those that wore a number, never bore a name—and their hatred grew when wages were cut but rents remained the same.

Times were bad in '93. Ten-cent corn was ruinous, and so was cotton that went for six. Drought blasted the wheat that year, and chinch-bugs ate the straw, and when cold came after the heat, the sheriff came after all. Their land gone, the people took to the roads, in wagons if they had them while those that lacked them walked. They were nomads now, *il popolo*, they were soldiers mustered out and on the roam. Times were bad in '93 and worse in '94. Even the plutes were said to be pinched, and when orders fell off for the *Shenandoahs* and the *Mendocinos*, Pullman bated his rates by a quarter, but his rents, by some law of nature, nary a pistareen. On what they earned now, his workmen couldn't fill the family shirts, couldn't warm their flats (A through J), couldn't cough up for a doctor's bill or even for a hearse—they couldn't get by on six bits a day, and they couldn't afford to die. So they sent him a deputation, and having said their say, they were fired on the spot, and then he got rid of the spot as well by shutting his shops to all—after which the Seigneur betook himself to Elberon for a summer at the shore.

That's when the Railway Union and Gene Debs horned in. They couldn't stand for a lockout of 4,000 brethen, and they called on Pullman to (what's the word they used?) arbitrate, and when heard on the Jersey beach, it was met by such fury that the very waves stayed put in awe. *There is nothing to arbitrate,* the lord of rolling bagnios roared—the *Phryne,* the *Messalina*—and then he made the merest gesture and allowed the waves to break. Mark Hanna didn't approve. *Any man who won't meet his men halfway is a God damn fool,* he said, but Pullman wasn't swayed. *There's a principle involved,* he said, *company control of its own business,* and again, when he flicked a finger, the breakers held their breath.

After that, it was no good thinking that the dust would soon settle on those cozy rows of flats, that any day now the air would clear and show the errant back on jobs that paid them fifty bucks a month less fifty cents for shades—the poor bastards, they even had to rent their shades! No more of that, said the Union, and it took the step for which there was no stair: it called on all cardholders to have no truck with trains that carried Pullmans—an *Autumn Days* in brown and gold, a raven *Desdemona.* Forthwith, engines were abandoned, sighing steam until their fires died. Neither freight nor varnish stirred, and rust grew on rails and track-pans, and on wyes and spurs dust, and food went bad in reefers, and from the yards and rights-of-way, a malodor arose, an almost visible emanation of decay. Nothing moved into, out of, or toward Chicago, no wheel, no piston-rod, no postcard, no rider of the rods. All was still at Englewood, at Blue Island Junction, on the Michigan shore, and out along the Des Plaines. When scabs were imported to break the strike, the strikers broke the scabs, thrashed the scissorbills where found and left them drowned in piss. There was no ado in Illinois except for smoke from burning boxcars and whiffs of roasted meat. They were about to win, the Union thought, but in the end it was the penny postal that did them in. There were soldiers, of course, but it was really the mails that beat them. Those pictures of the Falls that Cleveland swore to deliver cost the strikers seven lives, and the rest were as good as dead well into the next century.

and go to a Pullman hell.

LOGOS IN THE OVAL ROOM

I walked the floor of the White House night after night, and I am not ashamed to tell you, gentlemen, that I went down on my knees and prayed for light and guidance. And one night late it came to me. . . .
—William McKinley

He owed his vesperine vigils to the Philippines: it wrung him and rent him to put the heel on the Isles of Magellan. What, he wondered, was the will of the Lord?—but before he knew, he had to kneel. Kneel in the dark, gentlemen, and into those lightless hours, a luminous Presence came, a golden raying, and to the praying mortal man, it told an Episcopal earful. Take the outlandish Isles, It said, and bring the Word to the Flips. And, gentlemen, therewith Mr. McKinley *Antietam, Opequan, Cedar Creek (brevetted major for gallant and meritorious) high tariff, sound money* rose from the floor quite marvelously disencumbered and took himself to bed. *I slept soundly,* he's said to have said.

Emilio Aguinaldo, 1869–1964

THE REVOLUTIONARY

I doubt if any war has been conducted with as much humanity, with as much careful considera-tion, with as much self-restraint as the American operations in the Philippine Archipelago. . . .
—Gen. Arthur MacArthur

Three-fourths of his blood was Tagalog and the rest, through his mother, Chinese. He was small, like all such paltry people, but in the way of hatred, he seemed to contain more than he was made for, teemed with it, and raging against the Jesuits, he'd scream death to the friars, *Muerte a los frailes!*, but what he meant was death to Spain. To a Spaniard, a Filipino was among the least of creatures, no more than a beast and maybe less, a device of organic matter, really, an engine that ran on rice. Many a one ended its days in the morning: to amuse their betters at breakfast in the park, little brown men were shot against the walls while rolls were being broken and coffee steamed under parasols. It was Spain's old sin, cold blood in pain's presence, the sin of Peru and the Indies, and it was common here as well, in the isles of Magellan.

They were rebels, the dead that so died to provide diversion, and rebellious too was the five-foot Tagal with the Chinese mix. He never deemed himself small or brown or bestial, though, nor did he pro-pose to be droll for alfrescos in the grass: he was only sixty inches tall, but he could see quite far, and he saw, he thought, the last of Spain. At the Seminario San Juan, the Frays had noted his soft speech, his gravity, his masonic ways, but what they'd failed to remark was his crack-shot skill: he could dot the letter *i* and then dot the dot, and in fights in the street, he fought to kill. He, all five feet, became The Revolution.

In the Luneta, executions were still on the *lista de platos*, and the mist of laughter still haunted the trees, but now, in many places, the gentry began to die, in beds and baths, at games and Mass and on their rounds, and posting along the roads, and soldiers were sniped while they picked their teeth and friars while they pissed. And when the fleet met defeat in the Bay, the *gente ilustrada* stayed away from the gardens and refreshed themselves at home. Manila fell, finally, but alas!, it didn't fall to Aguinaldo. It fell (how? by what deceit, what sham with a shell?) to the 20th Kansas regiment, the 1st Idaho, the Pennsylvania 10th, the 4th Cavalry—and the islands were in thrall to another Spain.

For three hundred years, the Filipinos had longed to own their own, to stand upon it seeing and savoring, to laze or lie there as they chose, staring at the sky, at flowers of cloud, at clouds of bats if that's what pleased them, to gaze across the seas at Siam. To have their own was what they'd most desired, to be let alone and lost—*Muerte a los frailes!*—and now, worse than that plague of peccant priests, this host of righteous christers, one of whom,

El Presidente McKinley said

> *one night late it came to me—*
> *to educate the Filipinos*
> *and civilize and Christianize them*
> *and by God's grace*
> *do the very best we could by them*
> *as our fellow men*
> *for whom Christ also died*
> *and then I went to bed*
> *and went to sleep*
> *and slept*
> *soundly*

and during the next three years (with much humanity, with careful consideration and self-restraint), sixteen thousand *insurrectos* were civilized, and two hundred thousand civilians were Christianized to death

Corp. Daniel J. Evans said

> they brought in a couple of insurgents
> and tried to get them to peach on the rest,
> name the villages they were in, the houses,
> and when it would not work, just asking,
> they grabbed a hold of one of the men
> and jerked his head back by the hair,
> and then they took a big tomato can
> and filled it up with water
> and poured all of it down his throat,
> doing the same thing over and over

till the man could hold no more,
and all the while they kept beating him
with a rattan whip,
beating him on the face and the bare back
and raising welts with every stroke
and sometimes even drawing blood,
and then with him all full of water,
they tied him, hands behind, to a post,
tight, so he could not budge,
and then one of our soldiers, a big man
must have been over six feet tall,
he struck the insurgent in the stomach
as hard as ever he could,
struck this little man again and again,
hard blows, never letting up,
as if he could not get enough of the work,
and the insurgent could not avoid him,
being tied, and he got very sick,
but he could not throw up the water
because there was a gag in his mouth

> *with much humanity*
> *much careful consideration*
> *much self-restraint*

> Sgt. Leroy E. Hallock said

the effect of the water cure,
that's what it was called,
the water cure,
the effect on the insurgents was this,
they would swell up,
their bellies would swell up like
I don't know what it was like,
like they were awkward
little men in the family way,
and I saw blood come from their mouth

> *and by God's grace*
> *do the very best we could by them*
> *as our fellow men*
> *for whom Christ also died*

> Pvt. Charles S. Riley said

I was in the Philippine Islands
with the 1st Connecticut

and later with the 26th Infantry
in all for about twenty-four months,
and while garrisoned in the village of Igbaras,
which is in Iloilo Province on Panay
I witnessed what was known as
the water cure,
what the men called
the water cure,
we were quartered in a convent,
and for drinking-water
we caught the rain in a tank
on the upper floor,
a galvanized-iron tank
that held maybe a hundred gallons,
and it stood on a platform under the roof,
and one day when I came in
there was a goodly number of soldiers,
as many as eighty, I should guess,
and they were standing around the tank,
and they had a certain native,
the head official of the village,
and he was being held on his back
directly under the faucet,
and his mouth was being kept open,
I don't know how on that occasion,
sometimes a rifle cartridge would be used
to keep a mouth open,
and a stream of water was coming down
and running right into his stomach,
there being nothing to stop it,
and pretty soon he got filled up,
and then the soldiers began to kick him
and stand on him,
making all that water come up again,
and no sooner was he empty
than they did the business over,
and finally the native told them
what they wanted to know

and then I went to bed
and went to sleep
and slept
soundly

Pvt. Riley (cont'd.)

[212]

and then they let him get dressed,
after which they took him outside the convent,
and there they asked him for more information,
and when he would not give them any more
they gave him a second treatment,
a second water cure
right there in the street,
this time with a syringe,
but it did not do the job they wanted,
so the doctor, Dr. Lyons, his name was,
the doctor got another syringe,
I think they were horse-syringes,
and he threw some salt into the water can,
and then the two syringes
were stuck into the native's nose,
and he was pumped full of that salt water,
and in the end he spoke up,
but it took some doing
on account of the way he struggled,
and before he said anything
the soldiers had to tromp on his belly,
and the water squirted up out of his nose
two or three feet in the air. . . .
excuse me,
did you say did anybody kill the doctor?
no sir nobody killed the doctor

Gen. Arthur MacArthur: Our presence is going to be an un-
mitigated benefaction to the Filipino people. . . .
Sen. Thomas Patterson: Do you mean the Filipino people that
are left alive?
Gen. MacArthur: I do not admit that there has been any unusual
destruction of life in the Philippine Islands.
Sen. Patterson: Thirty-three and one-half percent of one province . . . ?

Aguinaldo lived for a long time. Many more of his people died
before he did.

By God's grace

LABOR WAR AT A HIGH ALTITUDE

I came to do up this damned anarchistic federation.
—Adjt. Gen. Sherman Bell

He didn't come by himself, of course: the miners were armed, and they'd've shot him to hell out of Teller County, tincanned him down to the Springs. To stay up there on that reef of gold, he needed a little help, and he brought a little along—foot soldiers, cavalry, and field artillery. They did their work, the men, the mounts, the wheeled battery, and then they went away, but in the pallid pictures of the day, they seem to be there yet, perpetual, in the streets of Cripple Creek. At a crossing, a Gatling gun is still trained on something not in view, a saloon, a dining room, a sagging staff of telegraph wire; the cannoneers still stand at attention, as if awaiting the next command; and in the timberline sunlight, limber and gun still gleam, still single out a depot, a union hall, a whorehouse on a hill.

They were lifelike once, those rigid images, and now they're nonexistent, gone from first to last. The guardsmen are dead and doubtless at attention in the grave, the chargers have been gathered to the Father of all steeds, and the guns are done with their deeds of gunnery. But even so, the rarefied figures haunt the diggings, supervene, like a double exposure, between the distance and the eye, and it's then that things at rest are set in motion, and the scene becomes alive. Brick walls are blazed by bullets, glass falls with small music, blood flows from duckboard sidewalks into the muck of roads. Six hundred feet down the Vindicator shaft, the car blows up (how far?), and at Independence, fourteen die when a railway station explodes. Those who spurned three dollars a day mill around in pens, and between their derbies and their upright collars, they stare at the enemy, the world beyond the lens. And the marches begin now, not to the edge of town but to the Kansas line a solid week away, and as the miners plod the Santa Fe tracks, troopers prod them with Krags, sabers, ax-handles, whatever will drive the herd, and far behind them smoke rises from a burning union, from dues-books, worn files and furniture, pamphlets, letterheads, a pole and a torn-down flag. *I came to do up this damned anarchistic federation,* the general said, and he kept his word.

The guardsmen are gone from Cripple Creek, and with them the horses and the horse-drawn guns, and the fire is out now and the mire paved, but though the sun is two miles closer, there's still a chill in the air, and when the Independence bombing comes to mind, some seem to feel it in their bones.

DISCHARGE WITHOUT HONOR

The secretive nature of the race is well known.
— report of Insp. Gen. E. Garlington

He meant the black race in general, and in particular he meant 167 soldiers of Companies B, C, and D of the 1st Battalion of the 25th U. S. Infantry. Six of these wore the pale blue ribbon of the Medal of Honor, and thirteen more held Certificates of Merit for campaigns in Cuba and the Philippines and for war along the frontier, but for all their blue ribbons and white citations, they were still members of the black race, and their secretive nature was known: they were four-faced with anyone else and two-faced with their own.

For some years, the 25th had been stationed at Fort Niobrara in the Yankton country of Nebraska, where, a well-behaved outfit, they'd been just as well-received, even by the Sioux. For reasons that no mortal knows yet, they were one day shipped off to Brownsville near the mouth of the Rio Grande, which is about the furthest south the Far South goes. Nobody there had asked for a black garrison, no white, no spic, no in-between, and when someone said *The people don't want the damn niggers here, and they won't have them here,* he spoke for all the living and quite as much for the dead. Trouble arrived when the soldiers did: it came along on the very same train.

Before the affray, which was a ten-minute shoot-up of Brownsville, there were three incidents in the streets of the town, two of them picayune. It was a small thing, trifling, really, that a soldier, one Oscar Reid, was shoved off a footwalk and into the river, a pindling matter, nothing at all. And it wasn't much more, only a sore head for an hour, when Private Newton was slugged with a pistol-barrel — chance-medley, call it, if it needs a name. It was the third encounter that stirred the heart, sped the blood, turned necks above the collar red.

A white woman, a Mrs. Lon Evans, on her way home one evening, was set upon from behind, seized by the hair, and violently thrown to the ground. She screamed, she said, whereupon her attacker fled. On the run, though, he passed through a cast of light from a window, and the woman saw the slouch hat, the blue shirt, and the black face of a soldier. *Infamous outrage,* a headline cried on the following day, and all through Brownsville the cylinders of Colts were spun and rifle-bolts were tried. The hat, the blue shirt, the black face in the night—if seen at all, seen by a woman, and the woman white. It was her word alone, and the word was taken, though no soldier would own to the base assault—but, then, was it not well known, the nature of the race?

At retreat, the soldiers of B, C, and D Companies were told that all passes would expire at eight p.m., after which hour no man could leave the post. Patrols were sent into the town to round up stragglers, and by nine-thirty, every man was accounted for, barring George Thomas, a sergeant, and Private Edward Lee, who, it was later learned, were holed up somewhere with whores. Long before midnight, lights were out in the barracks and even in the officers' quarters, and on the grounds of the garrison, there was nothing to be heard but the sounds of sentries walking and a scavenger's cart on its rounds. At the witching time, no moon could be seen—it was either not yet due or down—but soon the night grew bright enough.

In Brownsville during the next ten minutes, three hundred shots were fired (some say more), and hot steel flew through the air at a muzzle velocity of 2,000 feet per second. The blueblack night was slashed by crisscross flash, and bullets bee-lined into doorjambs and plate glass and ash cans or fell to the earth a mile away. In its flight, one such found the Ruby Saloon, where the bartender stopped it dead inside his body—*Ay Dios!* he said, and he died too.

And then, when the shooting was over, the shooting began. There were civil inquiries and courts martial, there were searches, seizures, and gravimetric analyses, and sleuths were hired to trap the truth and ruses used to catch it napping, distances were gauged, times graphed, stories weighed, and after all it made no difference: no one could prove the soldiers guilty. Townsfolk swore to blacks aswarm in the streets and shooting at random, to the blue shirts they wore, the slouch hats, the sand pants, they vouched for nigger voices and sniggered at the telltale smell, but it was all to no avail: no white could name a black face, and no black would name himself. But, of course, the secretive nature of the race. . . .

In time, the ripples reached Washington, where, instead of licking feet, they rared up and made a splash, broke on the steps of the Capitol and sloshed the Senate floor—they even got as far as the White House to moisten Teddy R. Being Commander in Chief of the Army, he caused an order to be issued directing the men of B, C, and D Companies to come forward and peach, on themselves if they'd done the shooting or on those their knowledge would reach. There was no such knowledge in the minds of the blacks: they'd been asleep and seen nothing; their guns were clean and chained to the racks. No one tested the civilians' rifles, no one made a study of lands and grooves, dug for slugs, weighed the powder grains—no one queried the rednecks, no one accounted for the spics. Might they not have fired those three hundred rounds, shot up the Ruby, and gone off laughing in the dark to bed? If so, it was a good night's work—that is, if you forget the bartender.

On the soldiers' refusal to prove their innocence (secretive race!), they were dismissed without honor from the Army. One hundred and sixty-seven blacks, six with Congressional Medals and thirteen with Certificates of Merit, sergeants, corporals, and privates with centuries of service among them—all were turned off the post with their back pay and a uniform lacking buttons. They went away, some by road and some by train, and for all that's known, they're riding yet or lying in a ditch. In Brownsville, no one cared—the people didn't want the damn niggers there in the first place—and no one cared anywhere else, either.

THE BOMBING OF THE *LOS ANGELES TIMES*

I want those sons-of-bitches to hang!
—Gen. Harrison Gray Otis

Soon after one o'clock on an autumn morning in 1910, a suitcase bomb had gone off in an alley alongside his newspaper plant, and in the blast and the fire that followed, more than a score had died. When, therefore, the General said *I want those sons-of-bitches to hang!*, it was supposed by many that he meant the McNamaras, John J. and brother James, a pair of micks known to be handy with the stuff, the soup, the sticks, or any other name for the selfsame thing: dynamite. In truth, though, the General cared little about his blackened ashlars or windowframes now glazed with sky, still less did he care about twenty-one sets of fractured bone, and least of all was he concerned with brothers John and James. His passion was far more than general, a vast and venatic craze that embraced all who flew in the face of the rich. The brutes of labor, he called them, sluggers, gas-pipe ruffians, anarchic scum, and given his way, he'd've killed them for sport.

The union card! There was nothing under heaven that he hated with more heat. To him, it was the commanding proof of evil, the extra tit of the witch, and he would not suffer them to live (Ex.22.18). So virulent was his aversion that it poisoned even him: from the roorback he printed in his pages, he seemed to be a serpent susceptible to its own venom, a self-bitten old sidewinder dying from within. *I want those sons-of-bitches to hang!*, he said, and he was ready to swing the working class, not one by one but in the pissing mass. They were bitches' sons, the whole twist of them, and when in dreams he saw a coast-to-coast gallows and a horde of hooded stiffs, at the trip of the trap stood hangman he!

For the present, however, there were only the McNamaras, John J. and James, a twain of whom he knew but little. Barely familiar to their own parish, wherever that might've been, they were almost unheard of outside. They were of the undistinguished many, from nowhere come and for nowhere headed, unsung among the living and due for oblivion dead. In some atheneum, doubtless, or in the stacks of someone's mind, the facts about the brothers lie: somewhere their place of birth must be given, the schools they attended, and their grades; some memory must hold their knack with tools, if any, their way with girls, the worth of their word or its lack. But for the General (only a captain, really), it would not have mattered if old registers opened, if lost files were found; it would not have weighed with him that John and James were kind to their own, that they prayed with deep devotion, that they were reckoned good at their trade. For him, whoever their sire, their dam was Molly Maguire: they were dynamiters, and he longed for the day they were dead. *I want those sons-of-bitches to hang!*, he said.

Six months after the crime, the hunt for the brothers ended in their arrest in the company of one Ortie McManigal, who soon broke down and confessed to having been an accomplice of the micks: they'd prepared the stuff, he swore, they were the wizards with the sticks. At once, from their own and other unions, cries of Frame! arose. They were innocent, their multitudes contended, they were faithful sons and wafered Romans, John and brother James, they'd been nowhere near the *Times* that night, they'd played no games with thunder tubes of dynamite—indeed, it was an open wonder if there'd been a bomb at all. Tales were told of gas mains leaking in the basement, of fumes that filled the telegraph rooms, and since no repairs had been made by the General, his was the blame for twenty-one deaths, not the boyos John and James. A fund was raised to defend them, most of it ponied up in small change, in five-cent pieces and Indian heads that came out of wages, fares, lunch money, pin money, pennies saved for penny plain, came from nighabout and far away, from Gary, Cincy, Scranton, and from Tipperary too. *We are innocent of the crime with which we are charged*, the brothers said, and when the purse hit a quarter of a million, a great slouch of a lawyer was hired to pluck them from the rope.

It's a fair enough suppose that at least once before the trial began, he took himself over to First and Broadway to gaze at all that was left of the *Times*, a facade, a roofless ruin three stories high. And being there in its presence, he may have imagined his way back to when the pile was still ablaze: he may have seen pumpers throb and hoses crawl, and while he stood there, a wall may have crumbled or a floor fallen in, and he may have stared through vacant casements at squares of vacant space. And as he turned to go, who can say?, he may have thought *Ah, well, the old General's got his open shop at last.*

But behind what he may have done or said or given the run of his mind, there was a dark and dreadful void. For all the backing the brothers had received, for all the street-meetings held in their cause, the parades, the pamphleteering, for all the fees the faithful had paid for with meatless meals and heatless hours, for all the class-love of their kind, the lawyer was never sure that the brothers were as pure as claimed, that John and James were in the clear. Ortie McManigal had owned up to much more than even a flighted liar could've fancied: in his avowal, there were names, dates, and times of day, and he'd cited the disguises worn when the sticks were bought and the places where they were stashed, and, worse than mentions merely, when put to proof, they were always found to be true. The great lawyer grieved, therefore, when he thought of the trial ahead, and to keep it there, still to come, he took weeks to pick six jurors for the case against the micks. He never did fill the box. The end was known now, before the beginning, the noose was where the brothers were bound for, and no eloquence would keep them alive, no close questioning, no rube or urban shrewdness, no surprise — John and James were due to die. The great lawyer faltered; he couldn't lead the way.

On a certain day, and many say so, something was sensed in the courtroom air, and though no one knew what the addition was, a flavor, a wave, or even a hue, it was there, and it seemed to grow. It did grow, from the merely apprehended to the real, and when afternoon came, John and James were brought from their cells and placed before the Bench. No longer did they claim to be unspotted, nor did they cast again the charge of Frame! They wished now, said the great lawyer or someone in his stead, to withdraw their plea of innocence: they were not innocent, as so long they had insisted and the working world had believed; they were guilty, the great lawyer said, or whoever had risen to speak the stunning word. There was a silent moment in the courtroom while thought and breathing stopped, and then in the minds of all, the word went off like those other sticks of John and brother James. So actual was the explosion that some could've sworn to a flash of fire, a smell of smoke, a ringing in the ears—and then all, the numb, the deafened, the disenchanted, flowed toward the doors as though trying to escape.

Among the betrayed as they went from the room, no few wept, and all across the country, there was gloom. In the streets of many cities, union cards were strewn, and it would be long before the dismals died. John got life for the crime, and James served ten of his fifteen years. Labor got a blue-black eye and the hardest time of all—the open shop.

THE SCHOOL AT CARLISLE

The Indians were like other people.
— Capt. Richard Pratt, supt.

The white people are all thieves and liars.
— Spotted Tail, Brulé Sioux

His father was half Irish and half Indian, and his mother was No-ten-o-quah, a Sac and Fox of Black Hawk's Thunder clan. That might've made him a white of the quarter blood, but if so, he was white nowhere else, not in his skin or hair or eyes and never in his mind. *Son, you are an Indian,* he'd been told, but there was no need for the telling: Sac and Fox from the start, he was Indian still when he died.

He was sixteen when sent away to Pennsylvania, and getting there in a shirt and buckskins and a hat worn straight, as if it would spill, he soon was wearing brass and blue at drill and while attending class. They taught him much they thought would be useful when he returned to the plains, such things as Grammar and Composition, so that he might hold literate communion with Maggie Stands Looking and Joseph Loudbear and Runs After the Moon; and he was instructed as well in the science of order, which is Mathematics, to the end that he might know the relation between magnitudes, especially the savage and the civilized; and to these insults was added this injury, a course in the history of the whites.

They did not teach him his mother's language. It counted for nothing that *Noten* meant the Wind, and that a Wind on the Way was *Notenkao,* and they were unaware that *Mamaka* stood for Butterfly, or else they didn't care. Nor of importance were the things of her belief. What did it matter that the Great Spirit was a white-headed old man seated forever in the Empyrean and forever making smoke?, that the Spirits of the Waters were panthers that dwelt in swamps and falls?, that four serpents supported this island, the earth?, that each person was possessed of one soul only, and when death came, it left the body for the Afterworld, following the White

River, as they called the Milky Way—what did it matter? They did not nourish the customs of the unenlightened race—how primitive the practice that during connection the newly wedded must touch nowhere else, lest their children be born deformed or strange! And of what value were the rules for the training of the young, as those that dealt with the First Kill Feast, with Dream and Winter Fasting? And who in these latter days observed the Ceremony of Initiation, listened to the gourd rattle and the sacred drum, sang the Entering Song—*My arrow is flying around*—who sweated in the sweat lodge now, what naked boys and naked girls sat fainting in the steam? . . . Forget your ways, they seemed to say. Forget that your mother was Sac and Fox, that your father said *Son, you are an Indian*.

In those old Hessian barracks at Carlisle, a forge was installed, and a shop for carpentry, and sewing machines, and tools were found for smithing, tinner's tools, tools for making harness, shoes, and clothes, and Pawnees, Kiowas, and Arapahoes bent russet faces over shuttles and bobbins, over anvils, lasts, and pairs of traces. And in other rooms, they learned the proprieties of business correspondence, they learned how to sum in numbers instead of in the dirt, how plants and animals evolved, and even how to dance the polka—all such being handy for their future on the plains—and among them was the son of No-ten-o-quah, the Woman of the Wind.

He was drawn, who can say why?, to the field of force called electricity. He may have been reminded of his mother's clan, or he may have heard the word for Light in Front of Thunder, who now knows?, but it was just that fundamental quantity in nature that he wished to understand—the Fire that Came before the Sound. Woeful it was, but no such course was given at the school, yet how his spirits must've risen when they put him to work at threading a needle and rocking a treadle!, how savory the textiles, how vivid their hues! Or did he jump from a window and simply run, run, as if to outspeed *Noten*, the Wind . . .?

The West Virginia Coal-field Wars, from 1912

THE BALDWIN-FELTS DETECTIVE AGENCY

*I warn this little Governor Glasscock that unless
he rids Paint Creek and Cabin Creek of these god-
damned mine-guard thugs, there is going to be one
hell of a lot of bloodletting. . . .*
—Mother Mary Jones, 1831-1930

Glasscock!

They say I'm a foul-minded old woman, and I don't deny it, but
Glasscock—why, Herself, Mary Mother of Jesus, would've sniggered
at the name! I've heard of a glass eye and a glass jaw, but a glass
dinglebob is a new one on me, and I've trod this sinful earth for eighty
sinful years. Glasscock! His wife must've had fears for her life: he
might've shattered in her belly, hell, he might've cut her in twain.

He was a Republican, which is a man with a squint in one eye
and a mote in the other, but this Glasscock, he was blind in both,
the kind that misses the hole and pisses on his shoes. Trouble was
coming to the coal-country, but for all he knew about it, the tipples
could've been up the Nile a thousand miles instead of an hour away.
There were portals at every turn, galleries under every hill, but he
never left the surface to learn what lay below. Maybe he couldn't've
stood the darkness, the swamp-smell of rot, the dripping of water
from the overhead world, the daily dread of a caved-in roof. He never
tried himself, though, little Glasscock: he never went inside a mine,
where the mules and the men, the asinine, were.

He was surprised, therefore, when a strike-call came, and even
more so by the wherefore and the why. He didn't know that the
miners were paid by the carload, and that when a car was built up
bigger, the digger was getting a shave: cribbing, they called that little
trick, but the word I use is theft. And it was thievery too to fine
the men for slate in the coal: a few streaks of bone, and the weighmen
docked their pay. May the devil shit that flying!, they said, and out
of the adits they boiled, 7,500 of them, to kick about their loss of
wages, about weighmen that weighed for the boss. What they got
for their pains was more of the same: at the fifty-five mines on Cabin

Creek and the forty-one on Paint, they got three hundred gunmen from Baldwin-Felts. Trouble wasn't coming no more; it was there.

They weren't detectives at all—they couldn't've detected the sun; they wouldn't've known where to look. They were simply shooters that hired out for ten a day and found, and as such they shot at what they were shown. They leaned toward black suits and black hats, and their rifles too seemed black apparel, less to be carried than worn. Their favorite game was union labor, but if none was around, non- would fill the bill. Christ, for ten a day, they'd've killed their children.

Those gullies where the Paint and Cabin ran, they were company land for twenty miles along both banks and all the way up to the ridges. The miners lived on the sidehills in shacks that simply hung there, like cuckoo clocks on a wall, and the strikers no sooner struck than they were stricken back: they were kicked off the company earth. Their spindled kids, their sick and washed-out wives, their goods and bads, their lives' sad rags—all were loaded into freight-cars, hauled across the boundaries, and dumped beside the tracks. There, in whatever they could build to keep the heat in and the freeze out, they stayed and starved through a year's four seasons. Bad cess, but worse was on the way: the scissorbills, the scabs. *Steady Employment at Good Wages in the Mines of West Virginia*, the ads read, *No Strikes, Free Transportation.*

That's when I showed up, eighty and then some, profane as charged, and full of flame, and at a rally of the boyos on the State House steps, I tried to warn the Governor about the bloodshed on the way, but the crystal prick had fled Charleston, cut a stick and hidden in the hills. What was I to do, God damn it! I couldn't tell the men to go die, to lie down and stay still, so I said some more that day. *Arm yourselves and kill!*, and kill the devils did.

Some of the killing I was there to see, as when they caught those two mine-guards in an ambush: Bob Stringer they shot dead, and the other they winged. W. W. Phaup, that one was, and I remember his coat being dyed with blood, and I tore it up and passed the pieces around, and the strikers, I can see them yet, they wore those red swatches like ribbons of honor

and I remember Matewan in Mingo County
when the miners called a strike,
and the company brought in a dozen guards
from Baldwin-Felts over in Bluefield
to serve the writs of eviction,

and led by Lee and Albert Felts,
they served the papers as ordered,
and they were waiting for the train back
when Sid Hatfield and Ed Chambers
walked up to them on the streeet
and shot Lee and Albert in the head,
after which shots poured in from everywhere,
the doorways the roofs the windows,
and by the time the town was quiet again,
seven more guards lay dead,
and two miners,
and the Mayor,
feller name of Testerton,
I remember,
and I remember how the guards got even
for that massacre,
Buster Pence
and Bill Salter
and Everett Lively,
the three of them
getting themselves assigned
to protect Hatfield and Chambers
a couple of months later
when they came to testify,
and right in front of the Courthouse,
they shot them down and killed them,
I remember all that and more,
I'm dead now but I remember those things,
and best of all,
I remember that name
Glasscock. . . .

   God! To be called Glasscock from your bed of birth to your earthly grave!

BIRDS OF PASSAGE

You can't educate a procession.
— Arthur Gleason, *International Magazine*

In the late summer, the hops were ripening on the ranches at the topmost end of the central valley, and from God knows where, the fruit-stiffs were coming to pick the pale green cones from the sagging vines. To the fields of the Durst brothers, twenty-eight hundred were on their way from other harvests, from orchards stripped and shaken groves, and, boes of the bindle all, ragheads, flips, skibbies, spics, and blue-eyed whites, they were coming in their wobbledy wagons and on their bare and fingered feet, they were riding the rods of local freights, they seemed, being birds, to be gliding in on air.

Long before the hiring began, the bald brown hills had become a slum looking down on the neat and straight-street city of hops. On the slopes, the twenty-eight hundred, with only a dozen privies to hold their soil, had already filled them full and flowing, and now, squatting wherever seized, they made all outdoors their toilet. In the heat—at sunup, it was 95 and warming—the whiff was almost a solid, a new component of the atmosphere, something so nearly visible that there were some who tried to brush it aside. Over the stool-tufted ground, blue flies wove and wound in oval orbits, and the sound they made was that of swarming.

What wells there were—for all those picker-people, five—went dry with an hour's use, and since they washed and bathed on the pumping platforms, soap, silt, and excremental rinsings ran back down the shafts. Still, it was water that came from the spigots, and while it lasted, they filled their demijohns and drank it in the fields. Out there, at 110 between the rows, it was soon gone

It would only do for about three hours,
              someone said,
and to get more, I had to go a hot mile
and a hotter one coming back,

                    and someone else said
Water was brung out on the lunch wagon,
but it was only free
if you bought your lunch,
                    and another one said
Jim Durst come out with a barrel of water
which he was suppose to give it away
free,
but he claimed if he done that,
he wouldn't be able to sell
his ice cream cones
and limonade,
                    and another one said
His limonade was no damn good,
wasn't limonade at all,
only water spiked with citric acid,
feller at the druck-store told me
it'd cut your inside out of you,
                    and another one said
I could've stood the walk for water,
but I couldn't afford the time.

The going wage was a dollar for a pick of a hundred pounds, a
dime of the dollar being held back to ensure that the people stayed
for the three-week season: if they quit, for whatever reason, the dime
was forfeit to the brothers Durst. A beggarly game, the pickers called
it

I never got but ninety cents a day,
                    one of them said,
and I stayed the season.
He made you pick too clean,
wouldn't stand for stems
or leaves no bigger than your fingernail,
had you picking twice
for the same price
was what it come to,
                    and another one said
they gave a mighty close inspection,
only two hops to a stem,
or you done it over again,
but it never said that in the ads,
and instead of you making four dollars a day,
the way it said in the circular,

it was more like two
and sometimes less—
they was one pore sonabitch
he got seventy cents for a day in the sun.

And there was sickness among the people in the camp on the hills. Some rented tents from Durst, and some lay under rags affixed to poles, but many slept in the open on piled weeds and skiffs of straw, and what with their scattered garbage and omnipresent shit, it was small wonder

I had malarial fever,
                    as one mother said,
and so did many women I knew,
                    and another said
They was a family that they all had typhoid,
                    and another said
I didn't rid me of the fever
till I got back to San Fran,
                    and another said
Every year we picked for Durst
he had fever on the ranch.

Small wonder too that the Wobblies, so few in number, could stir the pickers into making a kick. Only a hundred or so were card-men, and of those many were fresh from other fights, still blue from other beatings, still pissing blood, still, as in cartoons, with blanks instead of eyes. But thirty-some smoldered yet, and one in particular blazed—Dick (or Blackie) Ford. At a meeting called to protest against conditions in the camp, he had a crowd of fifteen hundred cheering every second word and whistling in between. Most of them didn't really savvy him, because he spoke in American and they in outland ways, but all the same they seemed to gather that his voice was theirs, that he was saying for them what they couldn't say themselves—who knows how they knew?—and therefore when he damned the Dursts and their deputies, the pickers in their lingos cursed the bastards too. *Knock their blocks off!* he cried, and when one of the badges tried to arrest him, the Hindus, the Swedes, the Greeks, the whole kit and cargo fell on the sorry scissorbill and beat his bravery into his pants. After that, there was a three-acre free-for-all that ended with four dead among the hop-vines—the District Attorney of Yuba County, a Wheatland sheriff named Riordan, a black

Porto Rican, and someone merely called *the English boy*. The rest of the posse fled, or they'd've gotten their comings too.

At dawn the next day, the militia came, and the pickers went back to work. Nothing had changed, not even the weather. It was still 110 in the sun, and by noon or sooner, canteens ran dry, and Jim Durst was out there with his ice cream cones and his limonade and his barrel of water at a nickel a glass, and inspectors were still faulting the pick for twigs and leaves, and the pay was still a buck or less per hundred pounds, and up on the hills, the children were still playing in their own and alien squit. All was the same in the hop-fields—except, of course, for Prosecutor Manwell, and the mick deputy, and the dark-skin spic, and that English boy.

As for Blackie Ford, he was arrested and put on trial for the part he'd played in the riot, and while it was conceded that he'd committed no battery himself, that he'd neither fired a shot nor struck a blow, he had incited others—*Knock the blocks off the scissorbills!*—and therefore, when death ensued, he was guilty of murder. He drew a life sentence for that.

For the rest, though, nothing had changed: they'd come to Wheatland to pick, and having picked, they'd gone. Like the birds. . . .

THE NIGHT WITCH DID IT

*When children cry out in their sleep, it means the
night witches are riding them, and you must wake
them up, or next morning you will find them
strangled to death.*

—Negro folklore

Mary Phagan was a white girl of fourteen, and the chances are
she never heard of cacodemons that rode the young at night, never
knew what the blacks all did, that no one was immortal in the dark.
Just before she died, therefore, she could hardly have cried out that
fiends were upon her, and yet to all seeming they were, even as in
the legend. When found, she had a rope of jute around her throat,
so tightly drawn that her tongue protruded for half its length. She
lay on a slag pile in the basement of a pencil factory, her face tumid
and discolored, and from a gash in her scalp, she'd bled until her
hair was a nameless shade between blood and brown. Her body,
wherever visible through a breading of cinders, was skinned down
to the derma, as if she'd been dragged for some way along the
splintery floor. Her drawers were stained with urine, her mouth was
filled with graphite and cedar sawdust, and some of her fingers were
bent back and out of joint. There were two notes lying beside the
misused body, and one of them said *The night witch did it.*

Witch it may have been, incubus, rider of the nighttime hours,
but even so, no hue and cry of witch was raised: who could bring
that kind to book, what law would make it swing? Better, it was
thought, to look for guilt where all guilt flourished, in the natural
world of men. Better to leave ghosts to the ghastly, the casters of
spells—hell's hosts belonged to hell. There was deuce enough in
earthly beings, and two such readily sprang to mind.

One of them was foreign to Georgia—Leo Max Frank, a Jew from
the state of New York. An engineering graduate of Cornell in the
class of 1906, he'd gone to Atlanta to act as superintendent of the
National Pencil Factory, owned by an uncle. There, not long after-

ward, he married a Lucile Selig, and until the year 1913, the couple resided with her parents, who were said to be cultured and who were certainly rich. Outside the tacit ghetto of Atlanta, Leo Frank had no standing whatever; within it, as a Jew of German descent, he was of superior rank and merit, a leader undisputed by the led. In his physical being, he was unimposing, a man of slight build and medium height, with no characteristic more striking than the pince-nez he wore before his prominent eyes. He was in his twenty-ninth year when Mary Phagan went to the factory for the day's pay that was owing to her—$1.20 for ten hours' work.

The other mortal who might've filled the bill was a Negro named Jim Conley, described as short, stocky, and, for what it may have meant, ginger-colored. He was not a Mechanical Engineer, nor had he descended from a family of German Jews in Brooklyn. In and around Atlanta, he was known as a liar and a petty thief, often seen on a chain gang and fined times without number for breaches of the peace. Nervous in manner and never at ease, he seemed to have a liquid essence, and if so, it was whiskey-fed, for he was nearly always drunk. During the two years prior to the death of Mary Phagan, he'd been employed at the pencil factory as a furnaceman and sweeper.

Little Mary Phagan/ She went to town one day The day was a Saturday late in April, the Confederate Memorial Day, and early in the afternoon, there'd be a parade through the streets of Atlanta, and many would march behind the Stars and Bars in their old regiment-als, behind flags ragged, faded, torn by shot, and all along the way, heads would be bared for the Gray who'd fought the Blue from First Manassas to Appomattox. *She left her home at eleven/She kissed her mother goodbye* For the occasion, Mary dressed herself in her best, a poor enough showing, true, but she did have a mesh bag that she prized and was proud of, a vivid parasol, and a pretty pair of shoes. *Not one time did the poor child think/That she was a-going to die* No one knows whether she saw the parade or any part of it, a color guard, a military band, a slowly passing line of old soldiers, nor does anyone know whether she caught a glimpse of her doer-in. When her body was discovered by a night watchman, her lavender pongee was a silken ruin, ripped and spattered, and one of her gunmetal shoes was gone. The parasol turned up later at the bottom of an elevator shaft, but the reticule ($1.20 plus carfare home) was never found. *Now little Mary's mother/She weeps and mourns all day.*

Because of the holiday celebration, only a handful of employees were at the pencil factory that morning, and those few had come voluntarily to perform some minor maintenance work on the machinery and would leave at noon or soon thereafter. Leo Frank, however, was writing a series of reports for the company, and save for a lunch-hour recess, he'd remain in his office until the day was well along. On being questioned by the police after the discovery of Mary Phagan's body, he was said to have been in a state of agitation *apparently high-strung, a fluent talker, polite and suave, smokes incessantly.* He was arrested on suspicion of murder, and Conley was jailed two days later when it was reported that he'd been seen trying to wash bloodstains from a shirt.

At Frank's trial, the black man became the chief witness against him. Liar, thief, convict, souse, he swore the Jew's life away with the story he told on the stand. On the day stated, he said, he'd been at the factory at Frank's request, and for one purpose only — to stand lookout while Frank seduced Mary Phagan. He'd been instructed to remain downstairs, he said, and on the girl's arrival, he was to send her up to the second story, where Frank's office was, after which, when Frank stomped on the floor, he was to lock the outer door and await a second signal, a whistle, which would indicate that Frank's purpose had been accomplished. Conley had done as told, he said, but when the whistle came, the girl had not appeared. Instead, Frank was standing at the top of the steps

> shivering, trembling, rubbing his hands.
> His eyes were large,
> and they looked right funny.
> He looked funny out of his eyes.
> He said, "Did you see that little girl
> who passed here just a while ago?"
> and I told him I saw one come along,
> and he says,
> "Well, I wanted to be with the little girl,
> and she refused me, and I struck her,
> and I guess I struck her too hard,
> and she fell and hit her head,"
> and he said,
> "You know I ain't built like other men."
>> (the reason he said that was
>> I had seen him in a position
>> I haven't seen any other man.
>> A lady was in his office,

and she was sitting down in a chair,
and she had her clothes up to here,
                    (indicating waist)
and he was down on his knees,
and she had her hands on Mr. Frank)
He asked me if I wouldn't bring her
                    (meaning Mary)
so he could put her somewhere,
and he said there would be money in it.
I found the lady lying flat on her back
with a rope around her neck.
Cloth was also around her neck,
like to catch blood.
She was dead,
and I came back and told Mr. Frank
she was dead.

Nor was that all that Jim Conley testified to before a judge and
a jury and a courtroom crowd; he bore witness to much more to all
these and, through the open windows, to the minatory mob outside.
Five thousand, there were, and they filled the streets so full that
trolleys could not pass, and on sheds across the way, hundreds stood
in the sun all day to cheer the black and mock the blackhearted Jew.
At Frank's direction, Conley said, he'd written the two notes placed
near Mary's body, and for so doing, Frank had paid him $200. And

Mr. Frank looked at me and said,
"You go down there in the basement,
and you take a lot of trash
and burn that package in the furnace."
And I said, "Mr. Frank,
you are a white man, and you done it,
and I am not going down there
and burn that myself."
He said, "Let me see that money,"
and he took the money back
and put it in his pocket and said,
"Why should I hang?
I have wealthy people in Brooklyn,"
and I said, "Mr. Frank, what about me?"
and he said, "Don't you worry about this.
You just come back to work Monday
like you don't know anything,
and keep your mouth shut.
I am going home to get dinner. . . ."

The night witch did it.

It was the law of Georgia that no one charged with a capital crime could testify in his own behalf; a defendant might, however, make a statement to the jury, not under oath, and it would rest with the jury to determine its weight. Frank elected to avail himself of the right, and he prepared the statement himself. It took him four hours to read it, all through an afternoon, to the silent, watchful, sweating talesmen. It was simply written and ably delivered (*Cornell graduate, fluent talker, rich Jew*), it revealed with great particularity each of his doings on the day of the parade, and it ended with

> Gentlemen,
> I know nothing whatever
> of the death of little Mary Phagan.
> I had no part in causing her death
> nor do I know how she came to her death
> after she took her money
> and left my office.
> I never saw Conley in the factory
> or anywhere else on April 13, 1913.
> The statement of Conley
> is a tissue of lies from first to last,
> and as to his helping me dispose of the body,
> or that I had anything to do with her
> or to do with him
> that day
> is a monstrous lie.
> The story as to women coming into the factory
> for immoral purposes
> is a base lie, and claims to have seen me
> in indecent positions with women
> is a lie so vile
> that I have no language
> with which to denounce it.
> I have no rich relatives in Brooklyn.
> My father is an invalid
> of very limited means.
> Nobody has raised a fund
> to pay the fees of my attorneys.
> These have been paid by the sacrifice
> of the small property my parents possess.
> Gentlemen, I have told you the truth.

The night witch did it.

But there was no night witch in it. After a trial that had lasted twenty-nine days, the jury was out for only three hours, including a one-hour intermission for lunch (chitlins and poke sallat? winnies and coke? hot plates with bull-fuck gravy?), and their verdict was Guilty. For the first time in Southern history, a black man's word (liar, thief, jailbird, boozer) had been taken against a white's—that is, if Jews are really white.

In the streets, the crowd acclaimed the verdict, and on Sunday next, it'd serve all cracker preachers as a text. Tom Watson, old Populist editor of the *Jeffersonian* (the *Jeff*, the rednecks called it), wrote

> We Georgians save our kisses
> for our wives and children.
> Mary Phagan was only a factory girl:
> she had no mighty connections.
> Frank belongs to the Jewish aristocracy,
> a rich depraved Sodomite.
> The Jew basks in the warmth;
> the child has fed the worms.

Frank's appeals were denied all the way to the Supreme Court of the United States. Thereafter, his sole hope lay with John Slaton, governor of Georgia, and four days before his term of office ended, he issued an executive order

> The performance of my duty
> under the Constitition
> is a matter of conscience:
> the responsibility rests
> where the power is reposed.
> I cannot endure the constant companionship
> of an accusing conscience,
> which would remind me in every thought
> that I failed to do right.
> This case has been marked by doubt:
> the trial judge doubted;
> two judges of the Court of Georgia doubted;
> two judges of the Supreme Court doubted;
> one of three Prison Commissioners doubted.
> Therefore, in accordance with my duty,
> it is ordered
> that the sentence in the case of Leo M. Frank

be commuted from the death penalty
to imprisonment for life.

Tom Watson raged and wrote

The State of Georgia has been raped!
We have been violated, and we are ashamed!
The breath of some leprous monster
has passed over us,
and we are unclean!

One month after Frank was removed from the death cell to a penitentiary at Milledgeville, while he lay asleep, his throat was cut by a convicted murderer who worked in the prison kitchen; the weapon was a butcher-knife. In the *Jeff*, Tom Watson wrote

Kosher!
The knife used on Leo Frank
was also used for killing hogs.
Let the Jews of Georgia beware.

But Frank survived the assault, and within a few weeks' time, he was released from the hospital and returned to the barracks. He lived for one more day. A band self-styled the Knights of Mary Phagan, broke into the prison compound, seized Frank, and drove with him to a place called Frey's Gin, a hundred and seventy-five miles away. There they hanged him from an oak tree not far from the house where Mary had been born. No one was ever prosecuted for the lynching, although photographs of the party were sold all over Georgia for the next fifteen years.

The night witch did it.

Four people swore that Jim Conley had murdered Mary Phagan. Annie Carter, a black woman, knew that he had committed the crime, because he told her so; and the Baptist minister Ragsdale knew; and William Smith, Conley's lawyer, knew; and, name unknown, a fellow convict knew. But the people of Georgia didn't want Conley. They wanted the Jew, the Jew, and they'd've taken Christ Himself and hanged him twice, once to cover the Resurrection.

Was Leo Frank the Sodomite? Or was it Jim Conley, who, in letters to Annie Carter, wrote

Now baby
you have that right hip for me

cause if you hold your fat ass
on the bottom
and make your papa go like a kitty cat
then you have won a good man—
that's me

and he wrote

if you let papa
put his long ugly dick
up your fat ass
and play on your right and left hip,
just like a monkey playing on a trapeze,
then Honey Papa
will be done played hell with you

and he wrote

Give your heart to God
and your ass to me. . . .

The night witch did it.

CAUSES OF DEATH

riddled with bullets
— newspaper report

assault on a white girl
  shot thirty-two times
suspicion in the murder of a white girl
  beaten and shot to death in jail
speaking disrespectfully of a peace officer
  shot to death
accused of slashing a sheriff
  hanged from a light pole
accused of robbery and murder
  riddled with bullets and burned
suspicion of rape and murder
  tortured to death and hanged
accused of assaulting a white woman
  shot seventeen times and hanged
accused of attacking a white man
  shot to death by a mob
charged with stabbing an officer
  shot to death by four masked men
accused of an unnatural crime against a white boy
  shot by a mob
charged with rape
  riddled with bullets
accidentally running over a white boy
  shot dead by brothers of the victim
accused of raping a white girl
  beaten and riddled with bullets
accused of killing a white man in a gun-fight
  shot to death in a doctor's office
accused of nothing after the death of a white
  shot as an example

assaulting an arresting officer
beaten and shot dead
accused of defending himself against whites
missing
mistaken for someone else
beaten and shot
accused of attacking two white men
hanged by a mob, riddled with bullets
resisting arrest by fleeing
shot five times in the chest
accused of kissing a white woman's hand
bound hand and foot, shot, and drowned
accused of killing two white women
killed, dragged through town behind a car
accused of disorderly conduct
shot, drenched with gasoline, burned alive
suspected of stealing from an employer
clubbed to death
accused of striking a white man
hanged opposite a cemetery
no charge
flogged to death
accused of burglary, murder, and attempted rape
hanged, shot fifty times
accused of rape
riddled with bullets
accused of attempted rape
hanged, throat slashed
accused of being drunk, not under arrest
flogged to death
accused of killing a policeman
*shot in his cell after the U. S. Supreme Court had
granted a new trial*
whipping a white man who had drawn a gun on him
hanged from an oak, riddled with bullets
accused of being too smart
shot and dragged through town
accused of improper conduct toward a white woman
hanged, weighted down, sunk in a creek
accused of writing an indecent letter

        shot
speaking disrespectfully to a young white woman
        whipped to death
accused of murdering a white man
        hanged while jury was deliberating
accused of assaulting a young white girl
        hanged, shot, cut down, hanged again
accused of carrying copies of Huey Long's "Every Man a King"
        found with rope around his neck and shot several times:
        verdict of Coroner's jury—suicide
accused of killing a white storekeeper
        burned to death with blow-torches
accused of robbing an elderly white woman
        lynched in an orderly manner, without shooting or other
        irregular conduct
understood to have had some difficulty with the white foreman
of a lumber mill
        found in a river bound hand and foot
charged with the murder of an employer
        taken from a hospital bed, hanged, cremated
accused of attacking a seventy-year-old white woman
        hanged by a mob of five thousand men, women, and
        children
charged with rape and murder
        chained to the rooftree of a schoolhouse, doused with
        gasoline, burned along with the building
accused of drawing a knife on two white men
        battered body found in a river
no charge
        shot by a band of ten in mask and robe
accused of assaulting a white girl
        hanged after release for lack of evidence
accused of attempting to vote
        bullet-ridden body found in a river
accused of entering a white woman's bedroom
        hanged to a blackjack tree
accused of killing a white woman
        killed resisting arrest, body dragged for two hours,
        dismembered, burned in a bonfire
suspected of attacking a white farmer and his wife

hanged and burned, teeth distributed as souvenirs, head
cut off and placed on exhibition

flogged
hanged
burned
drowned
dragged through the town
riddled with bullets
riddled with bullets. . . .

The passenger-pigeon, ?–1914

A RIVER OF THE AIR

Sometimes we have mighty Flocks flying over us, yᵉ
Welkin in a manner obscured & covered with yᵐ
— A. W. Schorger, from Cotton Mather

Earlier, even, they baffled numbers. As well try, some said, to poll the sky, to call the roll of the stars and rain: how tell untold profusion? Still, they did try, and when numeration failed them, they spoke of *thickened clowdes* and *ayerie regiments*, but no whit better did words reckon the birds in their multitudes. Of one thing only were all men sure: there was no end to the endless creatures; their flights would last till the last of time. Over the prairie, they were *thickened clowdes*, and they were *ayerie regiments* on the plains— they whirled across the land in storms as vast as states (an Illinois was on the wing, and it took all day to pass!), and they left behind them snows of down and drifts of dung, and the sound they made in coming hung when they had gone.

Movable and wandering, they were, and so were they styled by all. *Wuskowhan*, the Narraganset named them, meaning the wanderers, and to the Choctaw they were *putchee nashoba*, which conveyed that they were lost. *Wandertaube*, the Germans had it, and *ringle duif* the Dutch, but whatever called, in all truth they were movable and wandering things, water-wild, an air-borne flow of wings, and so they'd be forever, a river on the fly. Forever, all agreed, but in time forever ended.

How did those *ayerie regiments* die, how did the countless come to none, the running stream of *clowdes* go dry? Where day was, they latened the hour once—a dust of birds, they set the sun, and they were long, long, in going by

Audubon said
a column of one mile in breadth,
which is far below the average size,
passing over us for three hours
at the rate of one mile in the minute

[244]

will give a parallelogram of 180 square miles.
Allowing two pigeons to the square yard,
we have 1,115,136,000 pigeons in one flock.
The astonishing bounty of the Author of Nature,
                              Audubon said

How befell it, then, that the many waned to none?
They were spring-snared in whole jimbangs: a single tripping would
sometimes save (save was the word they used) 1,500 and all too often
more (astonishing bounty, Audubon said), and with a head showing
in each gap of the net, it would look like a coverlet, a great tufted
bedspread heaving. It was a catch of heads, not birds, a bag of steady
staring eyes, it seemed, and they'd gaze at their savior as he slew
them in one of several ways: by crushing their skulls between his
thumb and forefinger (a tiring thing, they being so numerous), by
pinching their necks with a pair of pliers, or by decapitating them
with his guillotine of teeth.
How did the many wane . . .?

                              someone said
     you had a solid mass of birds to fire into
     as far as your shot would carry,
     and you'd kill a dozen or two per shell —
     all you had to do was shoot
     till it became monotonous

                              and someone else said
     Doc and I were completely sick of it
     by 11 a.m.
     Always supposed I could load & fire
     as long as anything showed itself,
     but for once I was beat.
     We shot sixty or seventy an hour —
     our heads ached when we fired,
                              but all the same,
     they were back six days later,
                              he said,
     and had some good shooting
     at single birds, or twos and threes,
     killing fifty by noon,
     after which the birds came on in earnest,
     and they shot away till their guns got fouled,
                              and he said
     they could've killed a hundred apiece

with fishpoles,
so close did the pigeons pass them

The days of the innumerable, how were they numbered . . .?

and between first light and sun-up,
                                    someone wrote
a roar came as from a thousand threshers,
a thousand steamers with open valves,
a thousand trains on a thousand bridges —
it was the pigeons on the rise from the roost,
flight after flight, cloud after cloud,
and we fired till our guns got hot,
too hot to hold or load,
and while they cooled in the damp leaves,
we snapped pistols, threw clubs and stones,
and something fell, sometimes two,
at every try.
We were only at it for an hour,
but we took 2,500. . . .

How did the *ayerie regiments* die?

TWO BLACK CASKETS AND ELEVEN WHITE

> *It was a sickening, disgusting, disgraceful piece of*
> *work. . . . I wish I could forget everything about it.*
> —Lamont Montgomery Bowers, 1915

He was Rockefeller's son-of-a-bitch, and he ran the Colorado Fuel and Iron Company, a beanhill to the richest man in the world, but somewhat more to anyone else, for it came to three hundred thousand acres, give or take a township. Under those forty square miles, lustrous seams of bituminous lay, hardened streams, dense and bottomless, and when prisms of such were brought to light, they made the richest man still richer, and he prayed God a little harder than before. If his son-of-a-bitch ever besought the Lord, it wasn't for a saving grace; it was for coal without end and foreign-borns to delve it, wherefore he may have bent a knee for more hunger in the Balkans, more Greco-Turkish war.

If he did, he got his wish, and to the galleries under the Purgatoire, to the tipples of Stinking Creek, many different peoples came. The Croats came, and the Bulgars, and Serbs and Montenegrins came— the no-spikka peoples came from famine there to famine here, from that war to this war, and for fifty cents an hour, they niggered in the mines. In three years' time, six hundred of them died beneath the ground, a mile or so lower than their graves would've been if their parts were ever found.

As the son-of-a-bitch saw them come and watched some go, he may have wondered what they thought they'd left at home. The greeners! The swallowers of flies!—they'd brought along the squalor they'd fled, they'd worn their gloom and ignorance, borne their every stone. He must've hated them for inflicting the pain of pity, for punishing him with their plight, and when they complained of his crooked weighmen, he fired a batch and drove them from his sight. The rest kept on kicking, though, about picking slate for nothing, about timbering the stalls and clearing falls of rock—dead work, they called it—he fired some more (out of pity) and clubbed a few in the streets. A slew of them remained, and in that broken inglés they spoke, they laid claim to the right to trade where they pleased, to an eight-hour day, and, fie and for shame!, to a union. That last got some Adriatics shot, and to the surprise of John D.'s son-of-a-bitch, lead was fired back. There were corpses then on both sides, and many more to come. *I wish I could forget everything about it.*

The scene he couldn't iris out was the town of tents his men set afire, the dirty skirt of smoke on the sky, the bloodshot snow in the wagon road. *I wish I could forget,* he said, but even as he made the wish, he knew he never would. Such things were there for good, with the frozen clothes that hadn't burned, the mattress springs, the crooked flues amidst the ash. *I wish I could forget,* he said, but he knew they'd be there to the last, they'd be in his mind and right behind his eyes. He'd see stoves, pails, kettles, the blackened bits of scattered lives, he'd see the pits where thirteen wives and children charred, a magma of shard and tin, a hash of broken ware. He'd see, no matter how old he grew, the hung-out wash with its starch of cold, it'd still be there, still flying on his dying day. *I wish I could forget,* he said. The shirts and drawers, the pairs of hose, the mittens and the belly-bands, the snot-rags, scarves, and camisoles, faded, frayed, torn, made over, little when bought and worn to less—on a winter wind in his brain, they'd stiffly ride forever, ghosts of those who'd died in cellars under the tents. In this life, his last sight would be two black caskets and eleven white—and in the next (*I wish I could forget*), his first might be those adamant clothes.

He lived to be ninety-six. He must've been afraid to die.

WARREN K. BILLINGS

the little auburn-haired boy
—Frank Oxman in the Mooney trial

That's all he ever seemed to be, something small among greater things, the witness of some commotion, and remembered mainly for the color of his hair on the rare occasion when he was remembered at all. At the center of the stir was Mooney always. It was Mooney who counted, it was the martyrdom of Tom, it was Tom's twenty-two years at "Q" that were mourned—and yet he too had been imprisoned, he for twenty-three. If he dwelt on such neglect, if it troubled him to have been so far forgotten that even his name was unfamiliar, he failed to complain; indeed, for all that appeared, he preferred the shade of Tom to fame.

His life began in the Catskill foothills, the Shawangunks, and it ended, for nearly every useful purpose, at the corner of Market and Steuart in the city of San Francisco. There, while a parade was forming on a summer afternoon, a bomb exploded amid waiting marchers and watching crowds, and ten were dead and forty maimed by the time the score was told. There, along with a suitcase that someone had left beside the Ferry Exchange (cigars, newspapers, postal cards), a third of his life went up in a blast of blood, gray matter, bone, and rags. The someone, several later said, was a boy with a head of auburn hair.

They were no exemplars, those who placed him there, among them a whore addicted to morphine and a part-time waiter with lues of the spine and brain, hardly the kind whose word was worth the pain of hearing. Still, they did swear that just before the detonation, they'd seen there or thereabouts a boy with reddish hair, and in such of his history as came to light, there was much to bear them out. Born into poverty, one of nine children raised by a widowed mother, he learned early that living would be as hard as the road was long. Few would care, and none would spare his back the load. (*I was always overworked*, he said, *and always underpaid*), and he drifted, therefore, from this grind to that, ever seeking what he'd never find, over-pay for underwork, and in the course of the quest, he drifted as well across the country—and what was he not on the way! Bellhop, errand boy, dishwasher, swamper, a helper here, a holder there, a hand at the end of a board; gambler, burglar, streetcar conductor, apple-picker, ditch-digger, plant for a union in a shopful of scabs—what was he not en route to the Bay! He was nineteen when he got there, a peaked peewee with an outsize dome, but to Tom Mooney, whom soon he met, he looked like the sort to scratch a match on, the kind who'd light him a fire, and Tom turned out to be right: wherever the redheaded runt showed up, so did flash and burning.

Once, though, there was neither. For twenty-five dollars and his railroad fare, he hired out to a stranger who desired that he carry a valise from San Francisco to Sacramento. He neither knew nor asked what the valise contained—maybe he was bemused by the high pay for the day's work, by the prospect of a ride through the Delta, by one shot too many of booze, but whatever had persuaded him to take the job, it came to no good end. He'd hardly climbed down from the cars than he was pinched by a pair of detectives, who seized and inspected the valise: it held sixty sticks of dynamite. Indicted for knowingly transporting explosives on a public conveyance, he based his defense on a plea of confession and avoidance, in that while he'd possessed the valise, he'd never opened it, wherefore he couldn't be charged with the knowledge specified in the statute.

Well, maybe so. Maybe, as he claimed, he'd let himself be a chump for a stranger in the street, maybe he'd ridden without a thought through the sloughs and swamps of the San Joaquin, maybe he'd never wondered about the grip beneath his seat, never opened it, never known that he might've gone up with the train and come down with the trash—maybe, in good truth, he was innocent. But for him, the truth was only what the jury believed, and it believed that he was lying. Of no help to him at all was the fact that at the time of his arrest, a pistol was on his person along with a set of jimmies. He was given two years in Folsom—high pay for the day's work—but they let him go in thirteen months.

Returning to San Francisco, he fell into his old ways, straying from job to job and playing poker in between; he also took up with Mooney again, though well aware of the danger (*We have got a red shirt on the son-of-a-bitch*). Even while in prison, he'd known that the trolley lines and the PG&E were out to break the unions down to units of one and Big Tom to something less, but in the man's presence, he always found himself looking up, not so much at someone taller as at something off the ground, a bird in flight, a cloud. The price of such worship was steeper this time: it came to twenty-three years.

Wherever rumor ruled, Mooney was a dynamiter. It was widely supposed, though never proved, that he'd blown up the power masts of the PG&E at San Bruno, and, earlier, he'd been three times tried in Martinez for the possession of explosives, winning acquittal in the end despite testimony that on a skiff he owned were guns and ammunition, a contraption of dry-cell batteries rigged to an alarm clock, a dozen or more blasting caps, and a sizable spool of wire. As for his little redheaded adorer, had he not done time for having done Tom's work? Small wonder, then, that at his trial full faith was given to a whore and a syphilitic when they swore to having seen the pair just before the bomb went bang at the newsstand wall. It made no difference that Mooney had been a mile away at the time and the redhead even more: they were known dynamiters, and guilty if shown to have been on the planet.

And so back to Folsom the dapper one went, but for more than a score of the following years, all the Donner and Blitzen broke over "Q," where Big Tom had been sent to die adangle from a rope. He didn't, little thanks to the car lines and the PG&E: it was the thunder and lightning of the nobodies, meaning the people, that saved him for a four-foot cell, and a tight fit it got to be by the time they let him out to march past the Steuart Street corner—another day, another parade. Meanwhile, up along the American River, the great wall of Folsom kept all invaders from the half-mile world within. There, for three and twenty years, dwelt the boy with the auburn hair; there he rose in the morning and lay down again at night; there he quarried rock for future cells, for coming generations, for cons as yet unborn; there he ate, bathed, squittered, and pumped himself off; there he stopped passing time and let time pass him, became one of the stones in a stream—all for having been seen, or so they'd sworn, by a syphilitic waiter and a whore who used morphine.

What he thought of during that middle third of his life cannot be known from his written or spoken word. He must've had thoughts beyond the ones expressed, beyond even his own knowledge—there must've been a further universe of the mind that he was unaware of, a place in which he was immured against himself, a mental Folsom. With it, he existed; without it, he must've died. From "Q" came the sound of old and new alarms, freshets of letters, protests, petitions, directives, calls to arms: about its towers, or so it seemed, bolts of fire flashed. All the to-do, all the smoke and dust and whirling wind, were down on the Bay at "Q," far from where the forks of the American joined at Folsom. There, in the quarry, in the shoe factory, over a chessboard, or working at his clock-repair, the boy with auburn hair grew older, living so little that he might've wondered why he aged at all. *A lifer making timepieces run:* How could he have touched such things, the measures of the things he'd missed?

And so past him, past the stones in the stream, flowed the American toward the Bay, where, joining other streams, it may have kissed the feet of "Q"—and thus, though many a mile apart, the two may have come together, Big Tom and the little redhead, one of them silent and the other roaring at four straight Governors deaf to all but the PG&E and the railways of the street. It took twenty-two years before his claim of Frame! was heard; it took a fifth Governor to set him free to step up along Market and, with two hundred thousand waving, turn his head toward the Ferry Exchange.

No one knows why, but it took still another year to spring the little redhead. Maybe he was so quiet up there with all those clocks and watches that they overlooked him, maybe his shirt was redder than Tom's, maybe they simply forgot him. Whatever the reason, when he came back to Frisco, no parade was held in his honor, and there were no cries, no cheers, no fluttering hands from the Embarcadero to Van Ness. Many times, in the years to come, he'd stop before the Ferry Exchange, but always he'd seem to be alone in a crowd, a stone in a passing stream.

AN ALBUM OF PHOTOS AND POSTCARDS

The Photos

barricks at Ft Logan Colo where we are quartered

The silver salts have broken down, and blacks and whites are shades of brown now, autumnal. The snap takes in the length of the barrack aisle—a still of motion, nearly, for between two rows of cots, the flooring all but flows. So with the piecemeal uniforms that hang from hooks in the bald pine walls—cuts of meat, they look like, shanks, loins, rounds, only lately wholes in herds and streaming on the plains. On the mullion of a door, a razor-strop is a dark streak in the stark wood.

our companys squad of litter bearers

They stand in a long single slant across the print, every second man shouldering a stretcher furled on a pair of poles. Beyond the drillground, a world with no horizon seems boundless: earth and sky merge in a beige blank where, who knows?, the dead and wounded lie strewn among the stars.

this is the send off the boys got at Littleton Colo. 10000 people were at the depot when this was taken

All ten thousand, except for two, have turned away to fix on what the hard edges of the shot exclude—the tracks, the train, the troops. It's a picture of backs—collars, shawls, ten thousand heads of hair and hats, less the nearby pair agaze at what? astare at whom? Behind them, all those hats and all that hair, a foxed and faded sky, and a sign on a cross that says LOOK OUT FOR THE CARS to all the world but two.

The Postcards

1. A view of Immaculate Conception Church, Albuquerque, N. Mex.

we are now at San Marcial N M it is 6.30 p m

2. A view of the Library, El Paso, Tex.

Somewhere in Texas, this is Thur 1 p m we are stoped for water so will write a little. We are going South east and things here are awful nice crops look fine wheat being thrashed. it is awful hot here but no sand. I will hand this to some one to mail as we do not leave the train except for a little brether three times a day

3. A view of Lake Purdy, near Birmingham, Ala.

We are just coming to Meridian Miss it is 3 a m. we are traveling right along lots of woods here and corn fields. crossed the old Father of the waters yesterday on a ferry, just a wide Platte thats all

4. A view of Stone Mountain, Georgia

going thru old Civil War zone of georgia. Country here is very pretty. Red-cross furnish these cards and mail them. Some writing, 60 miles an hour

5. A view of Crescent Ave. Greenville, S. Car.

in Caralina noon 6-15-18. the South certainly is a fine place. The picture on the other side is a picture of a Cedar of Lebanon tree that somebody brought from Palastine a hundred yrs ago

And then pages, pages, that remain unused. No more tinted schools appear, no more falls, forts, courthouse squares, vain the search for raw wood halls, nor are faces turned away here, nor vacancies of sky. And yet *just arrived*, the spaces all say, *am feeling fine.*

THE TROOP TRAINS

*in honored glory an American soldier
known but to God*
— Arlington

With their stained-glass transoms and their garnet plush, the wooden cars were the going thing of a bygone age. But they were old-style now and, worse still, old, and on their rusted trucks, they rolled ungainly, relics drawn by relic engines, and they were a blue moon on the way to piers along the Hudson, to wharves on Delaware Bay. Gazing from the windows, many must've thought they'd never arrive: the tracks were interminable, laid, it seemed, by the trains themselves, and as in some dreamed-of pursuit, the end was never the end just reached.

Slowly went those crossings of the country — or was the country passing while the trains stood still? After days at the dusty glass, few were sure they knew: there were spires and streams and staves of wire, there were hills and stubblefields, and smoldering cities were seen, hills and rain in the distance, wind-marred grain, and where snow was in season, it capped the trees and coped the walls, and children waved from every station, every stack of ties, and flags flew night and noon, bands played in braid and brass, and whistles blew off martial steam: for days on end, endless things went gliding by. But which, some wondered, were on the move?

Two to a seat, the soldiers rode to the trains' commotion, and acting out the asperities of the roadbed, they trembled over trestles, shook when shaken, banked for the curves, some in the stupor of boredom and some while dead to the world. In the tinted light, smoke seemed to sigh in several hues, heaving for horseplay, laughter, and paper gliders, and in the aisles the litter grew, the done-with bits of wholes, the seeds, the rinds, the stubs, the wrappers, and still the trains drifted or the drifting miles went by.

Somewhere in one of the cars, a soldier breathed through the reeds of a mouth organ, and into the roundabout din, he made soft sounds that no one heard: it was a tune new and nameless, as though then and there composed. He was one of many in a certain battalion, no marvel of the time or place or the race he came from, no bright star of morning, and when lost to view, he was simply lost to mind, the so-so kind that made no mark, left no afterimage on the eye. Few could tell how tall he was, recall his features, his words and ways, and rare the invitation to join a game or group, to fill an empty chair—nor, rarer still, did he try. He was unaware of being omitted— he never saw the idle chair, and he'd pass the going game as if he didn't care to play. He'd go his way, that solo soldier, and soon, at the next gantry, say, he'd cause air to stir in a mouth organ's reeds.

He had no thoughts, or none he knew of, as he leaned against the sill, taking in the sun and shade, the day and night outside: no word was spoken, no scenes took place in his mind. He was merely, at that moment, spending a moment's time. All the same, there were things he knew in unknown ways, places, names, sounds, meanings, and within his head they turned and tumbled, a blizzard of singletons somehow sequent, and from it he drew a sense of times that were coming and when the times would end.

He sat there, the soldier, and made his minor music of the smoke, the jokes, the odors on the air, played it softly so that none but he could hear, and all the while those unknown things were snowing in his mind, whorls of words he'd never learned and sights he'd never seen. There was a dark wood (where?) with a strange name, and it was filled with fireflies in crisscross transit, death in orange arcs, and above the wood there were stars in a great sped-up night, and one of these (he saw it!) fell—he saw it fall at his feet. And he saw this too, four caskets being levied from where they'd lain in the ground, encrusted, stained, mephitic, and he saw someone walk three times round them and stop at one not knowing why (had he heard thin music?), and on that casket he placed a rose.

All these things were known to the soldier before they occurred. He saw them in that railway car. He knew even then where the car was going. . . .

A SWIM IN LAKE MICHIGAN

*The colored people suffered more at the hands of
white hoodlums than the white people suffered at
the hands of black hoodlums.*
  — Cook County Grand Jury

Off and on, it lasted through four days at the summer's height,
and when the numbers stopped coming in, dozens had died, and hundreds still bled somewhere inside their skin. The finding for once
was right: there were more blacks dead than whites, more black
bones cracked, more black lights and livers bubbling. It'd been hot
that Sunday, blistering, the papers say—the air seemed to dance in
the distance, and underfoot the pavement gave. It'd been hot in the
parks, the streets, the darksome portals, even in the shade—it'd been
hot, but not off Cottage Grove, not for black Gene Williams as he
swam away from the beach. He was headed for a raft that bobbed
before him, and when he reached it, he climbed aboard, dwelling
perhaps on ancient charts, on the rumored isles of little-known seas,
and then, supine, he lay looking up at the sky and listening to the
slap and suck of planks beneath his back. He trailed his hands in
the water—why would he not?—and now and again he bailed some
up and let it drip on his mouth and eyes, and the raft drifted, drifted,
and the cries of friends, their talk, their laughter, grew fainter all
the while.

No sign was posted on the shore, no line drawn to show where
its pair of zones began and ended, but all the same, they were there,
and plainly, though only in the mind, and from one's own to the
other, neither black nor white had a right to pass. On a different
day, Gene Williams might've been aware of the bearing of the raft,
might've seen and changed its course for trespass—and to him,
trespass it was. There were lake and land enough, he thought, and
he did not mind the place assigned to his race. But on this day of
the Lord in late July, he knew nothing of this whereabouts. He lay
on no lashup of flotsam in forbidden waters; he strode, it seemed

to him, some dreamed-of deck, he commanded the currents, summoned the wind. And gazing at a gull in the air, at cloud-explosions over Illinois, he was still unaware when a rock struck his skull, rolled him off the raft, and drowned him a short way—a stone's throw, one might say—from the Twenty-ninth Street beach.

One George Stauber had stooped for a bolt, hurled it, and killed Gene Williams. George Stauber, white and sinless, had made the cast, but why has his name lasted and his life been lost? Staub meant dust, and dust he'd made of a black on a raft, dust he'd made of himself. But the name, the name has been remembered.

They say Patrolman Daniel Callahan refused to arrest him, and they say he even kept them from saving Gene, and they say they whaled the shit out of him before he could call for help—and then it was all a far way past the last place to stop more murder. A battle-royal on the beach began and chases through the streets, guns and knives and knucks appeared, and there were raids and barricades, captures and deliveries, and ever it was cut and come again.

That night, white gangs beat, stabbed, or shot thirty-eight blacks, and blacks stormed cars, trains, and trolleys, and brained anyone who was white. They left two dead and fifty hurt.

Shops were shut and theatres closed, and children stayed indoors and played games like those they'd seen outside. The stockyards, the Loop, the depots and tracks of the Central of Illinois, everywhere blacks met whites and clashed, and by the second night, twenty more were dead and other hundreds slashed and clubbed. Doors, railings, windows went, and poles and lights and wire, and Policeman John O'Brien was shot in the arm, and in a rampage on State at Thirty-fifth, a Martin Webb, white, shoved off with a crack on the pate, and plugged by a black, Officer John Simpson quit this world at Mercy Hospital.

On the West Side, a mob of Italians, stirred by a story that a nigger had gotten a ginny girl, shot an innocent black named Lovings.

Forays, sniping, random firing into crowds, and in a car containing five whites, three were found dead and the others bloodied. The Death Car, it was called, and in one much like it, a second Death, four more rode to where their lifelines ended.

Someone shot Detective Sergeant Middleton.

And then, on Wednesday, rain came, and the heat died down and the beatings and killings too. By that time, though, there'd been enough of both to last till the next raft was built. Twenty-three blacks and fifteen whites had no more need for zones and beaches, nor, indeed, for stones and rafts. And three hundred and forty-some blacks had been injured and so too some two hundred whites. Of Gene Williams, black swimmer in a near-white lake, black voyager, black dreamer, one must suppose he's adrift as before, adrift on those little-known seas.

IN WOODED WASHINGTON

Tell the boys I died for my class.
— Wesley Everest

Everset, he was called by some, and there were some who called him Everett, but they were wrong, the lot of them: he was Everest. But beyond that, little enough was known of him—to many, he was a nobody with a name; to most, he was nobody at all. He'd been a lumberjack once, or so it was said, and a soldier-boy in France, but there even the town-talk ended. He seems to have lived his life hardly seen and hardly ever heard, lived it in the shade, you might say, while awaiting the coming of one particular day. He'd been born to perform a single act—defending his Wobbly union hall when the Legion made its raid. He had a pocketful of clips for his .45, and when he'd spent them, as if meant for that and nothing more, he had about twelve hours to go in and around Centralia. Wesley Everest, the name was—the name *is*, because it's still adrift on the hills up there along the Chehalis, it still festoons the pines, the mills, the air, but unlike smoke from a sawdust kiln, it will not blow away.

Back in '17, when the war came, there was money to be made in almost anything, and it stood to reason that the more you had of it, the richer you got—wood, for instance, wood in the shape of trees. Time was when it could've been stacked in a yard, straight-grained and sun-dried, and it could hardly be given away—sixteen dollars a thousand, it was, and they'd even deliver it. But once war was declared, things changed, and they did so fast. Fir and cedar jumped to a hundred dollars a thousand, and Sitka spruce clear fetched a thousand a thousand. There was great joy in the Northwest, especially among the owners of the trees.

Twelve hundred billion board feet of standing timber, some of it full of years at the time of Plymouth Rock, belonged to a dozen companies. That was a main and mortal sight of wood, and having nothing better to do, they could've built a bridge with it five miles wide and clear across the country, or they could've roofed over Montana and both Dakotas and had enough to spare to fence off Canada—but bridges, roofs, and fences never entered their minds. They intended to fell those conifers, to saw them and sell them, every tree, branch, leaf, and cone—but first, though, they needed woodsmen, and that's where the long-log Wobbly came in, Wesley Everest. They offered him and his brother Bunyans the rate they'd paid before the war—two-fifty a day, with three rounds of company slop thrown in and a flop in a company bunkhouse, a muzzle-loader, like as not, the kind you crawled into from the end. The Wobblies thumbed their noses and began to organize.

Centralia organized too. It got up a parade led by the Mayor and the Governor and followed by Company G of the National Guard and a brigade of broadcloth bulls disguised as Elks, and when it passed the union hall, it broke ranks and did the work the march had been called for. All those sellers of wares, all those Elks and shrieves and Legionnaires, they stormed the building, they broke every window and every door and even tore down the walls, and, once inside, they simply vandalized. Chairs, tables, pictures, partitions, all were turned to trash, records and files were burned, and for some queer reason, the flag was tossed on the pyre. A merchant stole a desk, though, and a phonograph was carried off by thieves unknown. Wobblies found on the premises were clubbed to the floor, kicked while down, and picked up again by the ears, after which they were stripped naked and whipped out of town. The poor bare-assed bastards didn't come back for a solid year.

They did come back, though, and they were wearing clothes, and it wasn't long before they held a meeting of logging stiffs at which a young man in an old army jacket and stagged overalls went up and down the aisle handing out union throwaways. The town's response was a second parade, and no one made a secret of the impending second raid. The merchants, the Legion, the owners of the mills, all of them spoke of it to all who'd listen

since the Armistice, the radicals have started in again
the businessmen don't want any Wobblies in this town
if I were the Chief of Police, they wouldn't stay here twenty-four hours
if the agitators were taken care of, we would have very little trouble
sooner or later, they're all going to be hanged

spoke of it in the streets and stores, the whorehouses, the corner saloons, spoke of it in twos and threes and crowds, spoke in heat and loudly, so that those of a mind to drag their feet were made to tag along, and what they said in cold blood, the papers said in Bold

> *a committee of citizens has been formed, and its object*
> *is to combat I.W.W. activities*
> *it is high time for people who believe in the lawful and*
> *orderly conduct of affairs to take the upper hand*
> *if the city is left open to this menace, we will find ourselves*
> *at the mercy of a band of outlaws*
> *what are we going to do about it*

The *Centralia Hub* announced the event for the first anniversary of the ending of the war, and it published the line of march, so laid out as to pass the union hall twice, once going and once coming back. The Legion met and voted to appear in uniform.

Armistice Day 1919 ws like many another day in the Northwest, damp, gray with mist, and what sun got through no longer warmed Centralia vale. At City Park, where the columns formed, breath hung on the air, trailed from sailors and marines, a contingent of Elks, a scout troop, and a group of girls decked out in Red Cross rig. The postmaster carried a coil of rope, and so did a clergyman. The trouble started on the second pass, after the parade had about-faced and headed back toward the park. Someone put two fingers in his mouth and whistled through the split, and someone else cried

> *let's go! at 'em, boys!*

and formations went to pieces in a rush on the hall. The Legionnaires got there first.

The charge, over flindered glass and riven wood, carried them through the doorway and into the hall, but this time their whipping boys had guns, and lead caught them front and rear, some from within the hall and some from across the street, and six of them fell, three wounded and the other three dead. In the aisle, as before, was Everest—not Everset or Everett, but Everest—but he had no throwaways in his hand that day. He had an army automatic, and when the hall was crashed by the Legionnaries, he began to fire at what he could hardly miss from ten feet off. Among those he hit was the leadaer of the dragonnade

> *my God, I'm shot!*

he screamed, and before he died, he said

it served me right. I had no business there

Everest kept on shooting until he was driven from the building. He still had a clip or two for his Colt, and as he fled he fired back to delay pursuit, but it was a river—not the black Acheron, but the Skookumchuck—that finally stopped his flight. Before he ran out of bullets, though, he killed another man, and then, throwing his gun away, he said

if there are any bulls in the crowd, I'll submit to arrest. Otherwise lay off me

No one in the crowd saw fit to show a star before laying hold of his person, and when they did, they caved in on him, and he was hit with whatever they'd brought along, fists, feet, ax-helves, bike-chain, and pipe. One of them butted him with a rifle, crushing his lips and stumping off his teeth, and he was cursed, spat on, clawed at, and slapped (by a woman), and his arms being held, he was slugged in the belly and kicked in the groin, and then a rope was produced (the clergyman's? the postmaster's?) and placed around his neck. He said

you haven't got enough guts to lynch a man in the daytime

and he was right.

They needed darkness, and they even shut the power off to douse the glim of night. It must've been twelve or so before they got their gism up and sneaked around to the jail, and finding the cell-door open, they took Everest out for a spin. Wherever they were going, they beat him all the way, tromped him with their boots, stomped his broken face, whaled his shins and head. He failed to beg, though. Instead, he struck back, God damn it!, drew blood from someone, actually—and then the someone flashed a razor and slashed him loose from his balls, saying

that's about the nastiest job I ever had to do

Did he throw them from the car?, you wonder, and did they land in the road, a ditch, a puddle of mud? Or did he stow them away, take them home, show them off in alcohol? And in times to come, did he dream of what he'd done, *nastiest job*, and wake up wildly, wildly looking down?

What was left of Everest they hanged from the bridge across the Chehalis, but when the knot showed signs of coming loose, they hauled him up again, retied the noose, and pushed him off a second time. When the knot held—they could hear it break his spine—they got their rifles and poured a pound or two of metal into him and then rode off to spread the tale. An unknown knife cut him down before first light, and floating on the current, he wound up beached on a bar. Not wanting him found there and in that condition, they came back for him, slung him into a packing-crate, and buried him somewhere out along the railroad track—and that was the end of Wesley Everest.

The Coroner made his report to the Elks Club. He declared that Everett or Everset had broken out of jail, gone to the Chehalis River bridge, and jumped off with a rope around his neck. Deciding that the rope was too short, he'd climbed back up for a longer one, and then jumped all over again, this time breaking his neck, after which he'd shot himself forty-seven times. There was much laughter.

But the name was Everest—Wesley Everest.

DICK THE BOOTBLACK

In the world's six thousand years of history the
Negro remained a beast in the woods
                    —editorial in a Texas newspaper

It started when Dick Rowland, nineteen years of age, entered an elevator operated by Sarah Page, a white girl, and accidentally stepped on her foot. A chance event is all it was, a happenstance, a stumble, and it would've come to nothing bigger but for this: clumsy Dick was a Niggertown nigger.

and didn't even learn to cook his meat

He'd stepped on her foot, this shoeshine shine, dust in the daily grind, hardly worth a tinker's curse, but what made a picayune worse than mere was this: Dick Rowland was a coon.

he worshipped fire, thinking it was a god that feasted on
dry sticks

That made no great matter grow, turned a mindless touch to something meant, swelled little then and there to much.

the Negro, through sixty centuries, never wrote a book

He'd defiled her, the dinge, tinged her purity—there was the blight, on her white cotton stocking. And now suddenly a pistareen seemed to become a passenger in Sarah's cage, asweat and outrageous, impingent, a deep-dyed prick indicative—and Miss Page slapped the colored face.

never composed an opera
never painted a picture
never carved a statue

Dick fled, and Sarah raised a hue and cry, and before three more days were out, fifty whites were dead, and each took with him four of the rude and impudent race.

never sang a song that would grace music's kingly realm

It was a fluke. All he'd done was step on her foot.

and he has the gall to want a place at the council board
of the white man's civilization
it will never happen, gentlemen!

Frank Winfield Woolworth, 1852–1919

A BLIZZARD OF PICAYUNES

Some of you have got the habit of placing goods on the
5¢ counter without looking at the article to see if you
can get 10¢ for it.
                              —F. W. W., to store managers

He was puny born and scrawny growing, a pindling boy too short
on vim, tall, thin, the drawn-out sort that flagged at work and puned
around at play. He couldn't last, said the small-town dawdlers: he'd
never conquer the soil or the seasons, he'd succumb to some
machine. What they forgot, the wiselings, was the benign, the wine
effect of trade; they reckoned not the tonic Gain. It was they therefore
that fell away early and he that lived to see them fall — he may even
have brought them farewell gifts, useful little articles from the ever-
teeming bins on the counters of his stores

> papers of pins, they may have been, and things of tin, and things
> of wood, and button-cards, and carded hooks and eyes, and there
> were thimbles, celluloid barrettes, flour dredges, and whistles
> to summon the police, and for those that time had ticked and
> taken off, there were keys for winding watches and dustpans
> for their dust, and to their low green homes, he came with dolls
> and games and fine-tooth combs, with eye-glass frames and
> sewing-kits, with tinsel for their Christmas trees should these
> be found beyond the grave, and he may have come with corset-
> steels, pacifiers, candy, with twine, picture postals, signet rings,
> and soap — he saw them off, those old deniers, those doubting
> Toms and Dicks and Harrys, he buried them all in knicks and
> knacks and tinker's damns, in barber's thread (whatever that
> was), in boxes of tacks, lamp wicks, cuff links, he sped them
> to hell with suspenders, egg whips, sheet music

They scoff no more, he must've thought as he opened his thousandth
store — or were there eleven hundred now? twelve? He'd lost track
of numbers of late, he no longer remembered the riches he'd wrung
from trumpery and sallow sales-girls, he no longer cared about much

except those overripe bananas he devoured by the bunch. He didn't know that he'd die soon and that no one would bring him a bow-tie for a nickel, a stickpin for a dime.

The Bridgewater Trial, 1920

BARTOLOMEO VANZETTI

*I think he looks enough like the man
to be the man*
— Alfred Cox, prosecution witness

In the town of Bridgewater, Massachusetts, at about half past seven
o'clock on the morning of December 24th, 1919, an attempt was
made to hold up a truck transporting a payroll from a bank to a shoe
factory. Despite the early hour and winter weather, several
pedestrians were abroad, and some of them saw two men, one armed
with a revolver and the other with a shotgun, open fire on the truck.
The fire was returned by Cox, the payroll guard, and the two men
were beaten off, escaping from the scene in an automobile. No one
was injured during the shooting, and nothing was stolen.

Statement of Earl Graves
The man with the shotgun was 5′ 6″ tall, 140 lbs., age 35 years,
dark complexion and black moustache and looked like a Greek.

Statement of Alfred Cox
The man with the shotgun was a Russian, Pole, or Austrian,
5′ 8″, 150 lbs., dark complexion, 40 years of age.

Statement of Benjamin Bowles
The man with the shotgun was 5′ 7″, 35 or 36 years, 150 pounds,
and was an Italian or a Portuguese.

Statement of Frank Harding
The man with the shotgun was 5′ 10″. I did not get much of
a look at his face but I think he was a Pole.
—from Pinkerton reports, Dec.1919

On the 15th of April, 1920, in the neighboring town of Braintree,
another payroll robbery was attempted, and this time the bandits
succeeded in making off with more than $15,000 after shooting to
death the paymaster, Frederick Parmenter, and Alessandro Berardelli,
a guard. There too dark men were seen, of middling height and
slightly built—Poles, some swore, and others Greeks, with hard and
bright black eyes like coals.

Twenty days later, while riding on a streetcar headed for Brockton, the defendant Bartolomeo Vanzetti and his companion Nicola Sacco, both of them known for their anarchistic beliefs, were arrested as suspicious characters. They were found to be carrying weapons, Sacco a .32 Colt and Vanzetti a .38 Harrington & Richardson; in addition, the latter had four shotgun shells in his pocket. At the police station, after an interrogation touching on their radical activities, they were held on a charge of unlawful possession of firearms. At the time, there was no inquiry concerning the attempt in Bridgewater and the holdup in Braintree.

The police were behindhand in realizing the correspondence between the prisoners and the descriptions contained in the Pinkerton reports—the dark hues, the black hair, black hats, and black shoes, the coats that came to below the knees, the broken English spoken by the Russians, Greeks, Portuguese—but gradually *sallow complexion, foreign-looking* it grew upon them that what they'd been seeking they already possessed: two extraneans with dingy skin (*severe eyes*, someone had said) and blueblack hair. It was held to be a little thing that there were discrepant heights, that weights and ages disagreed, that what some had been sure were Austrians, others had seen as Poles. It was of no importance that time had worn at memories of a face, a color, a fancied place of birth, and no matter that the day had been dimmed by a recent rain, that mist still grayed the air. What counted was this—in cells nearby, there was a pair to fit a pair of crimes.

Vanzetti, a sometime fish-dealer, maintained that he could not have taken part in the Bridgewater attempt on the 24th of December because, in response to the usual Christmas demand, he had been peddling eels to his customers in Plymouth many miles away. The Grand Jury indicted him nevertheless, and he was tried alone, for Sacco, a factory employee, was able to establish that he had been at work on the day of the crime. There would be other days, though, and other crimes, and both would die for them on a summer morning that was still seven years off. It would be a long hard road all the way, but they'd come to that end from this beginning: *He looks enough like the man to be the man.*

Q.: Describe the man.
A.: He had a long dark overcoat. Slight build. Not a heavy man.
    He had a short croppy moustache. Well trimmed.
Q.: What color?

A.: Dark.
Q.: Any other description?
A.: He was a foreigner.
Q.: Where is this man now?
A.: (indicating Vanzetti) I think it is this man behind the rail.
I think he looks enough like the man to be the man.

Vanzetti was tried before Judge Webster Thayer and a jury in the Superior Court at Plymouth. Assisted by William Kane, District Attorney F. Katzmann appeared for the Commonwealth, and the defendant was represented by John Vahey and James Graham. The proceedings, during the week they required, were orderly and free from hostility; indeed, throughout the trial counsel referred to one another as brother.

In the stenographic minutes, there is no record that Vanzetti was called brother by anyone. Benjamin Bowles called him

a tall man about five foot eight with a dark moustache, long coat, no hat, high forehead, about twenty-eight or thirty years old or somewhere along there, face kind of red, high color,

and Alfred Cox called him

a man of medium complexion, with prominent cheekbones, a short well-trimmed moustache, not awful small but short, dark, struck me immediately as being a foreigner,

and Frank Harding called him

a dark complected man, rather broad face, round head, heavy dark moustache, face red,

and Richard Casey called him

swarthy, dark hair, short moustache, prominent nose,

and Georgina Brooks called him

some kind of a foreigner, he was a foreigner, and he had a dark moustache and a dark hat on,

and Maynard Shaw called him

a foreigner, I could tell by the way he ran, a foreign look, sort of sallow, foreign, that would describe it, not white, not negroish, but either Italy or Russia, might be a Mexican, I would not say he was an Alaskan or an African.

[271]

He was called many things during that trial—a man with a shotgun, a man with a long dark overcoat, a man with short black hair that stood up straight, a man with a croppy moustache well trimmed, a man between 5' 6" and 5' 10" with a severe look, swarthy, dark complected, foreign, not quite negroid, not quite white, not an Eskimo and not a nigger but somewhere in between, a Russian, maybe, a Pole, a Greek—but no one in that courtroom ever called him what the lawyers called each other: brother.

They were seven days in that Plymouth courtroom, and what they said there is spread over three hundred pages of questions and answers dealing with the weather, the time of day, the coign of vantage, with distances and sounds, with colors, kinds, sizes, speeds, with what was seen and what was done, but everywhere, layered in with all the rest, there were references to foreigners firing and foreigners on the run, to dark hair, dark overcoats, dark eyes, always there were pictures drawn of middling men, swart but not negritic, wan and yet not white—and never once in all those pages did someone call them brothers.

The jury was out for five and a half hours, part of which time they spent at lunch. In the end, they returned a verdict of guilty against Vanzetti, guilty of assault with intent to rob and assault with intent to murder, and he was sentenced by Judge Thayer to not less than 12 nor more than 15 years in State Prison. He served only seven years of the term: they got rid of him for the Braintree murders, and while they were about it, they got rid of his brother too—Sacco.

THE MAN WHO LOOKED LIKE A PRESIDENT

I am not fit for this office, and
I should never have been here.
—Warren G. Harding

The Mansion was written all over him. He had the frame for the place, he had the face, the hair, even, a mist-gray, fine and fluent, and he had gray eyes too, and tawny skin, due, some say, to a dash of tar, but no matter—he had the look, and it took him far, to the White House doorsill. It was there that he balked and said *I am not fit*, shook his head, his vapor hair, *I am not fit* he said—and still he walked that look, that head, those pin-striped clothes inside. Once within, he rued him more—*I should never have been here* he mourned—and yet there he was, redolent of bays and laurel and adorned, it almost seemed, in drapes and purple. He had the look!

Alas, even as he had known, the hue imperial went, the horse-power, the forceful bearing, and how then did time pass in the house of numerous rooms? Whither did he wander when the cards lay scattered and the bottles killed, when dearie Nan had left the closet, gotten up from among the rubbers and umbrellas, hiked her skirts, and gone away? What did he think as he toured the halls, peering back at betters peering from the walls? *I am not fit*, did he say, and what did he feel for the frayed cuff, the soiled collar, the honor grayed as if to match his hair? How did he beguile the nights, how while away the days, how did he stand the millionth handshake, break the brambled maze of eyes? How did he rise those nine hundred mornings, what did he see in the mirror's candor, and did he straightway moan *I am not fit* or wait till later, when there were decrees to be signed, bills, treaties, pardons, warrants for the death of others? Did his mind turn to his God damn friends, Albert, Harry, Jess, did he yearn for chips and face-down aces, for sour mash, for a chaw of plug and a brass spittoon, or, as he dawdled over some document (Elk Hills, did it say? naval reserves? Casper? where in hell was Casper?), did he moon about his dreary dearie, did he long to die . . .?

V. I. Lenin, 1870–1924

THAT LITTLE BALDPATE FROM SIMBIRSK
: sermon to a dying planet :

> . . . he was hard to tell from a man. No red satin domino
> set him apart, no deformity, no sulphurous smell,
> nothing but a Jew-blood tinge on his mother's side. That
> kind had overthrown their tables once before. That
> kind you had to kill, and they tried.
> —A More Goodly Country, p. 233

He looked like some of you, one of many and much the same,
an ordinary member of a humdrum race, with less hair, perhaps, than
your heads wear, and a little more span to his face, and save for the
sense he gave of seeing beyond you, of seeing, you might say, what
wasn't in sight, you'd scarcely know him as the Outcast of Heaven,
Prince of the power of the air. What!, you'd've cried, this unimposing lawyer in clothes bought off the rack, this astringent provincial
the black and fallen angel!—another, maybe, but never he.

Still and all and even so, he it was, though in his going to and
fro in the earth and walking up and down, he showed no sign of
an ill-made foot, nor wore he the garb of scaresome story. He demeaned himself well, as if he'd never been in Heaven, never known
a hell that held a candle to our own. To sight and seeming, he was
quite as any other—except, as said, for that far-seeing eye.

There were some all the same that knew him from the start, the
changers of money, the venders of doves. They that dealt in silks
knew him, and in cotton from the Nile, and they knew him that
grew the wheat, the wool, the fragrant weed—they didn't need the
domino or the smell of the burning yellow stone. They could tell
Old Nick at the dawn of day or dark. Had not his brother swung
as a plotter (something about an infernal machine), and had he
himself not drunk from the Jacobin sink? Consider the company he
kept, all the sour and greasy croakers, all the *frondeurs* of his time,
and note, if you please, that he fled them and the scene when a revolt
was put down in Nineteen-five. Is it any wonder they knew him

[274]

at a glance, those that drew the dividends? — how could they miss the Serpent's hissing, how fail to light on the Sire of Lies?

They shook their heads at the sealed train that sped from Schweiz, watched its lights disappear toward Stuttgart, toward the Baltic ferry, Malmö, Stockholm. He was the fiend of all fiends, and he should've been shot when found, on the spot or the run or against a wall, not stuffed with pâtés and tucked in a wagon-lit. Once in that car, he was all but rid of, dead at a say-so, a covered cough, but no one nodded, no one gave the word: instead, he was sent on his way, and there was deuce to pay at Helsingfors and more at Finland Station. Thousands came to meet the train, to unseal the car, to greet Satan the First, the latest Czar of Russia, and he was borne away on their shoulders through the dim April evening — he was home at last, the little baldhead, and all aburn to overturn the tables of the changers and the seats of the sellers of doves. It was a doomful day, and even from a great way off, the sounds of spellcraft could be heard, and seen was the glow from the Lake of Fire.

For three years, they tried to kill him, and to kill as well his multimillion imps. From all six sides of hell, they tried to quell his hellion hosts, and never did they doubt that they fought against the forces of the Pit: they were Christian soldiers, they thought, and their enemy was the damned. They were up against all the stored-up spite of the ages, all the rankle of insult and injury, all the dreams of revenge, and fearful of the harm they'd done, they only did the more. From the White Sea to the Black, they slew whatever moved and even what did not, they shot the living and shot the dead, and when they got to Simbirsk, they plugged the very stones the bald one might've trod. But they were dying too, among the lilacs along the riverbank and in the orchards where the green apples grew, and they were found in grainfields and marshes, drowned in the Don and Dnieper and in shallow pools of rain.

But worse than death was their fear of the Red Disease. Would the import legions become infected, the Czechs and Magyars, the Polanders, the Letts, the Finns, the Japs, the armies of the limeys and the French? Were the Yanks immune, the Serbs, the just-defeated Dutch? Or might all such soon be lost to the nonfilterable virus now rife in the world? And it was so, even as they dreaded at Broad and Wall — there were refusals to obey, strolls in the woods, flight under fire, high and low treason, and, beyond all these, an aversion to shooting those who were crying *Bread and Land!* On 'Change, they

[275]

knew it was over for a sixth of the earth, and they knew it too on the Bourse, in the cathedrals and the warehouses of the rich. A fraction had been lost, and lest it cost them more, they withdrew—whereupon at Smolny, the baldhead said *We shall now proceed to construct the Socialist order!*, and the godless work was done.

To undo it one day became the Christers' ever-after aim. It inspired all speech, it imbued each written word; it was put before famine, pestilence, the convulsions of Nature, the rights of man, and the meaning of Him that had lain in the manger. It justified spies, assassins, secret treaties, it explained novel weapons and tryout wars, it made smaller still of the small—the pastoral conscience and the scientific mind. After all, the objective was a good one, the retrieval from Old Nick of a sixth of the earth, and they meant to do it before he took the rest. They had to stop him, and when at last their hour came, they tried to do as the Lord had done—cast him down from Heaven.

I beheld Satan, said He, *as lightning fall.*

They too, Christians all, made a fall of fire, and in numberless numbers, those beneath it died. Some simply flooded at the mouth, as though their streams of blood had overflowed, and in the middle of a word, a thought, a heartbeat, without finishing a stride, they ended. And there were some that caught fire afoot and burned while standing, and some, shielded by a wall, a roof, another body, turned to bursting blisters, and each, the dead and the not-yet-dead, stank of rot within and void outside, and to eyes that still could see, all greenery was gray, as if trees and shrubs had put forth ash.

How art thou fallen from Heaven, O Lucifer!

There will be a black rain soon, black as the bark of the camphor, and in the dark of noon, there will be the silence of the night, Truly, as the prophet has said, *thou hast destroyed thy land, and slain thy people.*

The Styx is gone, but so, alas, is the Mississippi.

THE BURNING OF JIM IVY

Everybody down there knows everything.
— Memphis *News-Scimitar*

It was quiet under the steps of the stoop, dim down there and cool, and to the boy, hidden by the latticed siding, it was a hiding-place, a den in which to lie in wait. He let sand pour from his hand as he gazed through diamonds of lath, through shrubbery and gossamer, at a Sunday afternoon. On the big road, no car had passed for a long time, and in the still dust, a bird bathed, a bunting, and a gun-dog lay in the sun, on the run in slumber, but no people went by, and the only sound the boy could hear was a crying, as from a crowd at some far-off game. It came in a single tone, and it made him fall asleep.

When he awoke, the sound seemed nearer and more varied, and soon it broke into voices and the voices into words, and now cars spun up the dust, and doors began to slam, and above the boy's head, two pairs of shoes trod seven treads to the porch. Two rockers rocked for a while, and then his father said *Well, that ought to learn the nigger a lesson.*

> Every man in Rocky Ford was on the hunt, but even so it took them two full days to run him to earth. No one had known which way he was headed: he might've made for Tippah county and Tennessee, or, more likely, he might've followed the Talla-hatchie to lose himself among the oaks and beech and shortleaf pines of the sheep country. But he could've gone straight up in the air, the nigger could, and still they'd've found him. Along Hell Creek, it would've been, or out by the shut-down mine at Winburn—somewhere they'd've smelt him sweating and drug him out of his hole in the ground. And they did, finally, and all the way back to Rocky Ford he was hollering *I didn't do it! I didn't do it!*

The boy heard his father hawk and his mother laugh, and he heard their chairs creak, cracking sand, and through a fine downdrift of dust, he looked at the sun outside, at pieces of sky in the trees, at a black girl in the road. The word *crazy* came to mind, and he watched for her crazy signs: the sounds she made that made no sense, a head that shook as if sprung, sudden passes at nothing, sidewise locomotion, like someone on a ledge. *That was one hollering nigger,* his father said. *Hollered from there to here.*

> When they got back to town, the victim, a white female, was still laid up, so they took the nigger to the hospital and showed him to her there. They turned him everywhichway to give her a good study of the man, and in the end she said that while she wasn't sure, Jim Ivy looked like her attacker. That was sure enough for about six hundred people in and around Rocky Ford that Sunday afternoon, and what they did was hold a parade out along the big road, and clean to the edge of town, the nigger hollered *I didn't do it! I didn't do it!*

Crazy, the boy thought as he peered at the black girl at the roadside. She'd been there when the parade went by with Jim Ivy, and she was there still after it came back without him: twice she hadn't seen it pass her, hadn't been aware of the shouting, the flags, the smell of gasoline. She'd simply stood where she was, her head jigging, her hands dabbing at what? what?, and speaking the words that animals spoke. *He was one sure-God hollering nigger,* the boy's father said.

> Out past the last house, there was a glade in a loblolly grove, and that's where the parade ended. In the middle of the clearing, they drove down an iron stake, and they chained the nigger to it, him all the time hollering *Oh God! Have mercy! Oh God! Oh God!* But he was praying to the wrong man, and the fact is, there was no right man in the whole crowd of six hundred, and no right woman, either. He could've hollered till he was white in the face, and they still would've built a fire around him and then tried to quench it with gas. *I didn't do it!* Jim Ivy cried. *Oh God, I didn't do it!*

The boy wondered what the black girl would do if there were flames around her feet, if her dress were climbing her body to join her smoking hair. Would her head stop quivering as if on a wire, would her hands dab at fire instead of nothing, would she speak then in words, and would he understand?

Everybody down there knows everything, someone said to the *Scimitar, but not an officer in Union county will point out any member of the crowd. We're all neighbors.* Jim Ivy wasn't one of the neighbors, though: he was a slumpdown chump of jerky, still asmolder, still in chains.

One of the chairs stopped rocking, and the boy heard his mother say *I'm hungry,* and he heard his father say *I'm hungry too,* and he heard his mother say *What kind of hungry?,* and then the other chair stopped rocking, and the boy's father said *Your kind of hungry,* and pairs of footsteps led to the door. Inside the house and going upstairs, the boy's father said *That nigger sure learnt a lesson.*

Under the porch, the boy stared out at the black girl in the big road. What would she do if he tied her to a stake and set her afire, would her head stop shaking, would she cry *Oh God!,* would her hands be still at last . . .?

Eugene V. Debs, 1855–1926

A SPEECH IN CANTON, OHIO

*Whoever when the United States is at war, shall
wilfully cause insubordination, disloyalty, mutiny,
or refusal of duty in the military or naval forces,
shall be punished by . . .*
—Espionage Act, 1917, as amended

From a bandstand in Nimisilla Park, not far from the parallel
roadbeds of the Interurban and the Wheeling & Lake Erie, he addressed a gathering of some twelve hundred on a Sunday afternoon
in June, 1918. It was a scorcher even for the place and the time of
year, hot enough to make the sky shake over the baking tracks and
ballast, and nary a jacket could be seen on the twelve hundred shirts
being ironed by the sun on the backs of the crowd. But it could've
been a heap sight hotter, and still they'd've turned out to hear what
Gene had to say. Many of them had never seen him before, but
precious few hadn't been told of how he leaned forward when he
spoke, of how he'd poke at them with his finger (*I felt as if he was
hitting me in the nose with it*), of how each would feel the words
were meant for him alone. What they saw up there on the platform
was a tall, bald, string-gutted old specimen of sixty-three, a rail of
a man homely enough for two, what with those cupped ears of his
and that cute-angle beak, but once he began to speak — *Comrades,*
he said — he seemed to change from plain to fair. Something happened to his gant face and his flimsy figure, something got into that
high thin voice, something made it stay on the air like the sound
of crystal — *Comrades,* he said — and for every man below him on
the grass, it became a brand-new expression, one coined for them
on the spot, and yet somehow they all understood it as an end to
divisions. With that, heat or no heat, they pressed closer to where
he stood, mingled their sweat and cigar-smoke: they wanted more
of what he'd brought them from Terre Haute, more of that good stuff
he had in his mouth, and it didn't much matter that their neighbors
stank or gobbed on their shoes. Well, he had more, and he gave it
to them.

[280]

He was there, he said, to speak for labor, to plead the cause of those who toiled, and he felt it an honor to put it forward, to serve those whose very lives were service. But these were hardly the best of times, he said, they were a cold and parlous season in history, imperative, unsparing, a winter of the mind (*Whoever when the United States is at war*), and it behooved a man to use great care in choosing what to say and how to say it. Still, while he couldn't say all he believed, he'd be damned if he'd say what he *didn't* believe, which was this — that the war was a just one, fought under flowing banners for the good of all men. He was no suck-up, he said, no licker of spit, and any day, sooner than kiss a jingo's ass, he'd piss on freedom and go to prison.

He said those things. Those were the things he said.

He was born over on the Indiana shore of the Wabash, a good four hundred miles from that bandstand in Canton, and in a frame house not even a little bit better than the ones next door, he lived there still. It had a railed-in porch, and when the weather was fine (he had a bad back, lumbago or something), he liked to sit there in a rocker and chew the rag with anyone who slowed down or stopped, and if they kept on going, he'd wave as they were passing by. There'd be days, though, when he'd see nobody, say nothing, merely sit: he'd be deep in a book he'd read a dozen times before, a book by a Frenchman about a stolen loaf of bread, and for him on those occasions there'd be no sights or sounds outside the pages: he'd be in it with the wretches and their rags. The book, or a fresh copy of it, stayed with him all his life — that there should be both bread and hunger!, he thought. Maybe that's why so many went out of their way to walk his street and go past his door; maybe the things he felt about bread were in the air, and though he was with Valjean and Javert, unaware of them and their greetings, in some way they seemed to improve. The lonely, the lowly, the desperate, none of them knew how it happened, none saw his magic, his particular medicine, but all seemed better than they'd been before.

He'd made some mention of prison, he said, he'd spoken of preferring it to keeping his mouth shut, but there was nothing new in that, because never was there a time in history when a few hadn't put freedom of speech ahead of freedom itself and mouthed their way to jail, the theory being that there was more liberty inside than out. A loony notion, most people held, and maybe they were right, maybe it was true that the few were simply wrong in the head, longing for the Cross and the vinegared sponge and itching to die for the crowd—maybe it was so, he couldn't deny it. But suppose this, he said from that bandstand in the park, suppose no one had ever made that lunatic choice, chosen to speak when speech was a crime, suppose they'd served themselves instead of time—we'd still be wearing skins, he said, and snotting through our hands.

Those were the things he said.

At fifteen, he was firing locomotives for a dollar a day, small pay for burns and scalds and the danger of dying in a ditch. He was as tall then as he'd ever get, six-two or thereabouts, and spare as a spike-maul, and though he liked the work, his mother didn't

A BOILER EXPLODED NEAR VINCENNES ON FRIDAY LAST, KILLING THE ENGINEER

and she made him quit to become a clerk for a wholesale grocer. It was a dull grind alongside those runs he'd had on the Terre Haute line, it never stirred him, never caught his mind. On the warehouse air, there were spices, teas, and herbs, but what he breathed was steam and smoke: at heart, he stayed a rail. In the evening, when he shut his ledgers, he didn't linger to dwell on cloves and fennel and darjeeling: he made his way to the yards, where other rails were, and there he forgot about firkins and canisters—the talk was of unions, and young Gene listened. They held him in good regard down at the roundhouse; they thought there might be something going on between those cocked ears of his. He read, they noticed, he read all the time, things by Tom Paine about rights and reason, things by some frog about the miserables—he was always gabbing about the miserables. Therefore when the brotherhood organized a firemen's local, they picked a man to lead it who no longer rode the footboard—Gene, six feet two of lean meat. He was twenty years old and on the way to where he ended.

In those days, he said, his grip was always packed. In behalf of the brotherhood, he was always off to somewhere or other, always boarding a train, often as blind baggage, and now and then he was kicked out into the snow, the sleet, the rain, whatever the weather was doing at the time. *I rode on the engines*, he said, *I slept in the cabooses, I ate from the pails of swarthy stokers* — he was twenty-five years old, and he was making the union go.

Some who were there that sunny afternoon say that he kept his coat on all the way through that two-hour speech — he was the spareribbed kind, they said, and he never felt the heat. If so, he must've staved it off with his own, because he was talking against the war in Europe, and he hated it, he said, and hated those who'd brought it on — the Prussians of Prussia and the Prussians of Wall Street. Wherever found, they were one and the same: they spoke different lingos, and they wore different clothes, but the man didn't live who could tell them apart. Who could tell the rich apart? They had one love, one desire, one God, and its name was Plunder.

Those were the things he said.

He'd worked as a scoop for two-three years, four at most, but looking back from that balustered porch, he must've felt that he'd never left the road, that he was still stoking for those cornfield runs, still pitching in chunks of his life along with the chunks of coal. When he wasn't lost in that Frenchman's book, when he was just rocking himself quietly, and no one was passing by, he might've been thinking of fireboxes, of steam domes and ash pans, of sights once seen from rights-of-way, forests, farms, children waving, he might've been remembering the Mollies, the bomb in the Haymarket, the town of Pullman — Pullman, he'd've thought, the workers' paradise, a small and perfect garden in a great imperfect world. He'd not have forgotten its parks and pleasances, its green stone church and its wheel window, the theatre in the Moorish manner, the blocks of flats with a crapper for every two and a tap for every five. How vivid still that feudal Eden, where the pay was cut a nickel from 20¢ an hour! Sitting there and rocking gently, he'd've clearly heard Mr. Pullman say *There is nothing to arbitrate*, clearly seen a strike begin that he knew the union could not win. But he'd led it all the same, because the men had desired it, and for a matter of days, it'd gone well: no train entered or left Chicago, the rails grew rust, and there were naps of dust on the palace cars and the cold engines; in stalled reefers, food went bad, and no mails got through with bills and bundles and *billets-doux*. In the end, though, the soldiers were sent in, and the strike was lost — to wedding invitations and postcards with pictures of the Falls. That wasn't enough for the railroads and the rich, for the Government and that Pullman son-of-a-bitch: they had to put Gene in a cell for six months to show the people who really ran the planet Earth.

On his Eighth Street porch, he sat looking away through those gold-rimmed specs he wore, as if his pale blue eyes could see the past. If so, he saw the reading-room of the Woodstock jail, where a photo was taken of him with a book in his hands. Only he ever knew whether it was the volume of Shakespeare he'd brought along, or the speeches of Ingersoll, or *Wealth Against Commonwealth*, or that favorite of his wherein he read of Fantine, Cosette, and a fateful loaf of bread.

> And he said that all through the ages, wars had been waged for wealth, not for the commonwealth, for spoils, not for the good of man. The masters had always declared such wars, he said, and the serfs had always fought them, lost their lives while the others won the world. To the crowd, to the white-shirt glare spread out before him that Sunday afternoon, he said this— that their real enemies were those who, in the name of liberty, sent them off to be slain. They were our own Junkers, he said, full brothers to the Prussian kind, and their only god was Gain.
>
> He said those things to the people. Those were the things he said.

Four days after delivering the speech, he was indicted by a Federal grand jury, and on being tried, he was found guilty of having intended to subvert the armed forces of the United States. He offered nothing in extenuation, he made no plea in abatement: he'd known that his words were being taken down, he said, and he denied none of them. In fact, he'd go even further: war was odious to him, he said, and he'd spoken against it because in his view it impeached the social order and shamed the Christ the Christians vaunted. He was listened to in silence, and when he'd finished, he was sentenced to ten years in the penitentiary, first at Moundsville in West Virginia (*I never met a kinder man*, Warden Terrell wrote. *He is forever thinking of others, never of himself.*), and then at Atlanta, where he became Convict #9653.

Whoever when the United States is at war, shall wilfully, etc., he shall be clad in prison gray, a blue shirt, and canvas sneakers, and he shall sleep one of six in a cell of springless bunks, and he shall eat mush in the morning, slum at noon, and beans at night. He shall be limited to one letter a week, and that to his wife, but on Independence Day, he shall have the privilege of writing to the person of his choice (*There are six of us in one cell. My five companions are the finest, and I love them all, a German, a Jew, an Irishman, and two Americans. I have no complaint. I am in perfect health. All's well*).

It was to his brother that he wrote on the Fourth of July, but he didn't tell him that he couldn't eat the slubber he was given, the hash, the liver, the mutton stew, he didn't let on that his heart was arrhythmic and wearing out, that he could hardly breathe in that cell for six with those he loved so well, his Germans, his Jews, his Micks, and nary a word did he say of the stink or the heat, the weakness he felt, the pains in his back, the loss of weight. He merely said *The prisoner to whom we sent a little money for tobacco two years ago has been very kind to me;* he merely said he was quite serene.

But when a visitor journeyed from afar to see him, the serenity she found was that of coming death. She raised such a ruckus, there and in Washington, that he was moved to the prison hospital and put into what was called the kick-off room, where dying lags were taken to await the final roll-call, a small enough place with a cot, a table, and a couple of chairs. There was hardly space for the bareboned man and his two-three books, one of which might've been written with him in mind. Somehow or other, he didn't kick off in the kick-off room, and, who knows?, it could've been due to one of those books.

People were always after him to petition for a pardon, but Gene didn't have the right kind of knees for begging or the horns for pulling in, and besides, he had no use for Mr. Wilson, nor had Wilson use for him: *I know that in certain quarters of the country there is a popular demand for the pardon of Debs, but it shall never be accomplished with my consent.* He needn't have fretted: Gene wouldn't've said Uncle even to Uncle Sam. And hell, with Wilson out there, the company was better inside.

For Gene, truly it was better. He loved all those lifers, all those bank robbers and counterfeiters, and he talked to them as if they were still a part of the world, still worth respect, still human, and slowly they came to understand that he meant the things he said, that though they called him Little Jesus, he wasn't made of tin. On his walks through the yard, they simply followed him around, a cloud of hangers-on, and at ball games they vied for a place at his side or

anywhere nigh. They asked him for advice, they brought him letters to answer on letter-day and also the Fourth of July. He gave them
shares of his tobacco, and when theirs ran out, he left off smoking
and threw in his own. He taught English to some, one of them an
old wop who said *Mister Debs justa like God,* and what chocolate
he came by went to the lungers in the tb ward. Little Jesus, his name
was in that house of lowlives. It must've been the lowlife way of
saying thanks to someone they'd heard was dead.

They were proud when his Socialist Party sent a delegation to tell
him that for the fourth time he'd been nominated for the Presidency,
and they were joyous too: they thought that when elected, he'd pardon himself and set them free. He announced that he intended to
conduct a front-porch campaign from his residence in Atlanta
(laughter); at least, his opponents would know where to find him
(laughter). No convict had ever run for the office before — run, so to
speak, while standing still — but Gene wasn't fazed by bars and walls:
he ran all the same, and for a stationary candidate, he got a slew
of votes, some nine hundred thousand, and he'd've gotten two thousand more if those in the pen had had a say.

The election was won by a Mr. Harding, an Ohio man from Bloom-
ing Grove, and he was nothing like the stroke-struck cove whose
place he took. He was cut from different cloth — and cut on the bias.
He was a loose one, Warren G., a poker-playing soak, a chaser of
the girls, and he no more fit the White House than tits would fit
a boar. Even so, dreary, venerean, smoke-stained man, he seemed
to know that something was wrong where Gene was in jail and his
friends were not — his God damn friends! He gamed with them and
drank the same drench, they were his liars and arrangers, they stood
guard while he jigjigged with Nan — and then they gave away
Wyoming while he looked for his pants. His God damn friends!
Something was wrong, he must've thought . . . or maybe there was
no thinking to it, just a weakness for an old man who'd lived long
and done no harm, a soft spot for one of the few in whose coat there
were no holes. Whatever it was, he couldn't rest till Gene was let
go. It was the one good act of his life — but how many, he may have
thought, how many do more?

On the Day of the Nativity, 1921, the warden sent for Gene and
gave him a brown suit of clothes, a winter overcoat, and a five-dollar
bill, and then he took him through the corridors to let him say goodbye to his beloved mail-thieves and murderers. What they said back

he never learned, because all he could hear as he passed their cells was a storm of sound from two thousand men: it was a walk in the wind! Two thousand voices called out to him in a great and constant roar. They must've called out his name, *Gene! Gene!*, and on that day of days, how could they not have hailed Little Jesus! *They need me,* he said as he went through the gates, *I hate to leave them,* and for a long way down the road, he could still hear the tumult, and if he grew less sad when it died away, maybe he knew he hadn't really left after all. He had a certain book in his satchel, of course, and that helped too.

Home again in Terre Haute, he sat on the porch, sometimes with the book and sometimes not, and as before he waved at passersby, he rocked his chair, or if thinking of firemen, Pullman, Nimisilla Park, he sat still for a long time and saw nothing, not even the book he held in his hand. All men were miserables, he may have thought, imperfect but striving, striving and falling short. Some day, though, some day . . . and there he may have smiled.

William Mulholland, 1855–1935

THE WATER-BRINGER OF LOS ANGELES

There are some things we'll never tell.
— Bureau of Power & Light

When he landed at San Pedro from wherever it may have been—
Galway, was it, or the Cove of Cork?—a ten-dollar bill was pinned
to his britches, and that was all he had to sink or swim on, all he
had to do him—and do him is what it did. He started as a ditch-
tender for the pueblo (a rather fitting thing, Ireland being full of
ditches and the ditches full of micks), and before you could say *Erin
till doomsday!*, he was the bureau engineer. At the beginning, his
story is fragmentary—no one wrote it down daily, no one noticed
the rounds he made—but it was said by some that what schooling
he'd lost he found beneath the lamp, that he read himself fly by
kerosene. And so it may have been. He may well have learned from
the printed word, won his degree in Hydraulics at a table in a kitchen,
cap-and-gowned it in some closet commencement—so it may have
been. The trouble was, though he knew what he knew, which was
water, he fell a little short about the earth.

That lifelong love of *agua*—how did it come to be? Was it in the
zanja madre that the love arose, was he a water-thing himself, a
sprite, a haunt, might the mother ditch have mothered him? But
whatever its source, the passion grew, expanded to reverence and
in the end to an adoration that seemed to some profane: he worshipped water; water was his Mary. What could he not have told
of the viscous element, what property was he blind to, what numbers,
what hydrostatic law, what had he not read of pressures, friction,
motion, what equation for a flow from a constant head? Ah, when
it came to water, that self-taught ditcher was the nonesuch of the
age: he built nineteen dams for the Pueblo of the Angels, and the
angels of the pueblo cried for more.

Better by far if he'd then and there shut the books and technical
journals, put away the papers and reports, better if he'd left off testing
theories, least of all his own, better if he'd sat by the seaside awaiting

Poseidon. Instead, alas, he built another dam. The San Francisquita, it was called, the Little St. Francis, though it really wasn't little, not at all. It reared from the bottom of a canyon in a gravity arch that measured 700 feet from wing to wing and nearly a third as tall, a concrete block containing 130,000 cubic yards of pour. Held back by that widespread crescent were 40,000 acre-feet of water piped in from Inyo a couple of counties away. The angels drank to the dam in champagne. It was the public toast of the pueblo, that great stone rampart, the town's talk, and some made a note to walk it one day, to take in the view from its topmost step. Few ever did and maybe none: there was too little time.

What of the engineer in those last lullaby moments? Was he still at his books and bulletins, his tables, charts, and findings, was he still boning up on the traits and tricks of fluids? Or down below the base of awareness, deep in the hardpan of his mind, was there some slight seepage of unease? Had whisperings (whose?) begun to tease his sleep, a humming as of insects, a wind as of their wings? Was he wondering now, and long too late, about another element: how firm was the terra beneath and abutting the dam?

If doubts he entertained, the chief was a quiet host. He said little about the damkeeper's calls (*She looks bad*, the man had warned, but, hell, he'd always been afraid up there at the lake, always in a jelly about a break), but even so, he may have weighed the wing-wall leaks, the cracked steps that were packed with oakum, and, worse still, the fault on which the dam was laid, a crustal fracture that contraposed two kinds of stone, neither of which was holding water.

The western buttress of the dam was a ridge of red conglomerate, a clastic rock composed of fragments of shell and coral, volcanic glasses, and crystals of granite, permeated by bonding stubstances and pulverized by frost, rain, and running water; there were interspersions of gypsum, however, stringers with little more bind than chalk. Due to the fault in the floor of the canyon, the steep hill staying the eastern end of the dam extruded a dissimilar formation. There the rock was schist, a metamorphic compound of quartz and mica with laminations of talc; these tended to make it slip on its plane surfaces, much like a deck of cards.

She looks bad, the damkeeper had said.

The chief engineer, though, how did he fill the final hours, how did he still his fears? Did he dwell on those magnitudes of concrete, did he down doubt with weights and dimensions, did he bank on mass and the force of gravity, did he tell himself that nineteen other dams had stood? Was such his bet—that having never yet failed, he never would? And when he seemed still to hear those insect wings, those murmurings, *she looks bad she looks bad,* did he turn his mind to thoughts less loon, to angling from the parapet, next Sunday, say, in the afternoon . . .?

If so , the dam was gone when the Sunday came. It went one night in a great roaring comber a mile wide and tree-top high, a surging spate that tumbled blocks of concrete as if they were foam. Every structure in its course was smashed to flinders and carried away, every house, barn, bridge, and wall, orchards were plucked from the earth, root and all, and track was torn from ties and relaid upside-down. For a week, dead animals and parts of dead animals were fished from a brown river that ran out into the Pacific as far as Santa Cruz. There were human dead too: four hundred were drowned in that sweetwater freshet, and another hundred were never found. *She looks bad,* the damkeeper had said, and for him she was bad indeed: he was one of the missing.

And the chief engineer? Immigrant with only a tenner to eke, self-taught builder of twenty dams (nineteen standing)—what of the engineer? Oh, they built him a memorial fountain where water plays in his name.

Alvan T. Fuller, 1878–1958

ROSINA SACCO AND LUIGIA VANZETTI

*I can understand the sorrow that overwhelms you,
but I can do nothing.*
—Gov. Fuller, Aug. 22, 1927

The evening was well along when the two women were brought to his chambers in the State House. On being shown into his presence, they kneeled at once to beg him in Italian for the lives of their men, the brother of one of them and the husband of the other. Speaking through an interpreter, they implored him for more than an hour to spare the condemned from death, awaiting them now in the next square of the calendar.

Did he sit or stand for their pleas and prayers, did he share their anguish and agonize too, or did his mind stray from the sallow women to the sheen of his Gainsboroughs, did he preen himself on his clubs, the Brookline Country and the Union Boat, did he gloat over his forty millions, his summer place, his Back Bay stack on Beacon?

Through an hour and more of supplication in two languages, was he ever once moved, did he doubt his ground however briefly, or did the sound he heard make him languorous, as if the water were running for his bath? Would the women still be here for the voltaic moment, he may have wondered, would Luigia be calling on him softly, would Rosina be telling her beads? In the end, he had to end it, and he said *I can do nothing*, and a mile away in Charlestown, a shoemaker and a fish-peddler were as good as dead.

At one minute before midnight, the Governor left the building and betook himself—where? to his summer place in New Hampshire, to one of his clubs (the Essex County, the Algonquin), to a card-game, a whorehouse, a saloon? He did not see the two women on the steps, he did not hear their weeping.

Ella May Wiggins, c.1900–29

THE GASTONIA STRIKE

*The mill owners here have been mighty good
to their folks.*
— a North Carolina preacher

It wasn't much of a strike. It only took a couple of days before
the flush wore off, and the rush of blood became a walk, only two-
three days till the millhands tired of commonist talk and honed for
the sound of spindles, the pound of power looms. A day or two in
the open air, and back they tracked, and they didn't seem to care
that the strike had been lost—what did it matter? For a while, they'd
made a noise out there in the road, and they'd heard some jaw about
a union, but never having seen one in the Smokies, where they came
from, they took it to be a bullshevik word with no ptickler meaning. All they could swear to was that they drew no pay on the picket-
lines. There was no cash-money in carrying signs, or making a fist,
or singing such things as

> The boss man sleeps in a big fine bed
> And dreams of his silver and gold.
> The worker sleeps in an old straw bed
> And shivers from the cold.

It was true enough, God knew, but it didn't quit the rent, so back
they went for their two bits an hour: the men, that is—the women
and children got somewhat less. A day or two or maybe three, and
there wasn't much left of the strike—a tore-up sign, a picket-line
pore as a snake, mostly yankee jews, and there was your strike, lost
in the whirring of the spindles, the stomping of the looms.

Not for Ella May, though. She was still there outside the fence,
still churning away with a stick and a square of cardboard, still shaking a fist at the windows of the mill, still singing about the boss
man and the bossed, as if she'd never heard that the strike was lost.
Ella May—who the hell was Ella May? A nobody, you'd have to say,
a scrub come down from some farm in the hills, her past left behind

with the trash of the seasons, blackened stubble and the dust of leaves, rags, tins, flakes of paper ash. No great shakes was Ella May, a chunked little woman of nine-and-twenty with one fine feature, eyes. Apart from such, she wasn't much to behold; in fact, after nine babies without a breather, she looked a little shrunk and not a little old. There's no telling what her tits must've been with all that sucking—like pockets, maybe, pockets pulled inside out—but her face was plain to see, and there were shrivels in it, as though she'd left her teeth at home. *I'm the mother of nine,* she said, *but four of them died with the whooping cough. All four at once,* she said, and in a few more weeks, she was dead herself. For Ella May, only then was the mill strike over—over, yes, but it was never lost.

She hadn't ever made more than nine dollars a week, she said, and with a family of nine, that came to about a dollar a kid, God damn it!, one God damn dollar to do for a kid!, and when those four came down with the cough, she asked the super to let her off nights and put her on days, but he wouldn't switch her, the son-of-a-bitch—a sorry man, she called him, *the sorriest man alive*—and four children coughed till they coughed themselves away.

Ella May! When others cast their signs aside, she was an army vast with banners, and where she marched she was many. She never gave up—*We all got to stand for the union,* she said, *so's we can do better for our children, and they won't have lives like we got.* Ella May! She was on her way to a meeting when five company gunmen shot her. Fifty people saw it, swore to it with a Bible oath, but a jury found the guilty innocent, let the guilty go.

> *If the mill officials get it in for you, they will get rid of you.*
> —a Gastonia minister

Well, they got rid of Ella May, yet when they go through the gates of the mill, there are some who say they can still hear her singing *Let's stand together, workers, and have a union here.*

AL CAPONE et al

the beetle-headed, flap ear'd knaves

How seldom they die in bed! The fall, the failure, the lingering ailment, all such are for another breed. These go from the world with the world as witness. They lie in gutters, alleys, banquet halls, they sprawl in black and white, they appear on Page 1. Sheeted and lathered, they bleed from barber-chairs, and their striped shirts are further striped at games. In riddled cars, they hold stiff poses, they root for swill in garbage-cans, they drown in sewers, vats, and public toilets. Not for them the tubercle, the trypanosome, the vascular catastrophe — they shun the unseen disaster, they die for Page 1.

THE GOD WITH THE GLASS HEAD

Only members may execute orders
on the Stock Exchange.

—rules

In His temple, none but these may change money at the tables, no one else may trade in doves, for this is not that house where the blind come and the lame. What prayers are offered here are not for sight and not for soundness: they're for canned meat and dotted swiss, for the horseless carriage and the dynamo, for carbon, crude, and the fragrant weed; here the lamb bleeds for monograms, numbers, fractions, lots; here men pray for gain.

How they leap and lunge, how they flay the air as though to throw their hands away! How they prance, how they mill in the moil, how they shrill and dance! And then a bell rings, and they curse and joke, they launch paper planes on the smoke and shivaree. A few launch themselves from a thirty-ninth floor, and they do not float. Halfway through a taxi-roof, they are members no more, and they may not trade in doves.

THE MANAGEMENT OF LABOR

We don't tolerate rough stuff in the
Ford organization
—Harry Herbert Bennett

That was just pie for the Simple Simons. What they didn't tolerate in the organization was *organization:* at River Rouge, all you had to do was say *union,* and you were a sheeny agitator rousing the rabble, and you had no more rights than a roasting ear in a shithouse. The plant was stiff with spies, and what the spies missed, the snitches guessed at. They peached when you pissed and even when you didn't, and they listened, those narks, they noted the kind you chose to mix with, gave you marks on your manner (open? furtive? in between?), on your tone of voice and frame of mind. With that many eyes and ears around, you weren't going to roll any handbills into the toilet paper or whip up trouble on the line: you were going to keep your trap as tight as your ass and put a nut on each bolt as it passed you by. You'd make no speeches to the shift coming on, nor would you hand out fliers to the one going off: you'd do your work, take your pay, and go home to bed till the next day dawned. If you did otherwise,

. . . if you tried to organize

We let the jewboys get as far as the Overpass,
let them climb the steps from Miller Road
and walk halfway across toward the gates,
and then we closed in on them, trapped them
up there with us in front and us behind
and nowhere to jump but over the rails.
If they had that in mind, they soon forgot it:
they had other things to think of, a sore head,
for one, and a kick in the balls, two more,
and they got off cheap if that was all.
Four of them, we had, four Hebes in city suits,
one wearing glasses and another one fat,
and there they stood, walled in between us,

[296]

and damn if they didn't sort of smile,
as if what we meant to do was shake their hand:
well, we did, never fear, and all the rest beside.

The fat one, we wooled him with his own coat,
pulled it up his back and down his face,
made him play at blindman's buff
while we beat him loose from his whey.
It was good work—all who saw it said so—
especially the part where we knocked him over
and spraddled him out like an eagle,
four of us pinning him down, legs and arms,
while a sixth booted his nuts up to his neck.
It was good workmanlike work, after which
we stood him up and threw him down the stairs.

Good work as said, but there was just as good
around Gate 4, and maybe a little better,
like the handbill guy we sapped from the rear
and then stomped on till we broke his back,
or take the nigger we picked up and flung down
like a God damn sack, all the while whaling away
at his belly because as everybody knows,
you can't hurt a coon by hitting his head,
or take the woman we jabbed in the tits
when she wouldn't give up her throwaways—
it was all good work for good pay, ten a day
for busted noses, skulls, ribs, and jaws,
and for making a girl puke
when we punched her in the twat. . . .

We don't tolerate rough stuff, Harry said.
And who in hell was Harry?
They say he could trace his line to Plymouth Rock—old stock,
they claim he was, the gist, the stuff of history—and, who knows?,
they may be right. Maybe his far-back blood did stain the Pequot
forests, the Deerfield plain, and Malvern Hill, maybe it did found
this family of men, this last best enterprise, and extend it to the
western sea. It may be, it well may be, and none the less so for that
his father won his honors painting signs. This Harry, though, who
and what was he?

No one seems to know very much about him, or else mum's the
word with those that do. The certainties are far between and few,
but he did, *on dit*, join the Navy at seventeen, and it's rumored too

he had a four-year hitch, after which he knocked around on the coast of Africa before coming home to Michigan, to Dearborn, to a job with Henry Ford. The Devil knows what the old son-of-a-bitch saw in the ex-sailor, and there are some who say that Henry knew, and the Devil didn't. But all say, and of this they're sure, that Harry'd do anything Henry ordered, and moreover he'd do it on the selfsame day. He hated, therefore, what Henry hated, and the list was long, from Jews to books, and betwixt the two were unions, Wall Street, booze, and change. Change—to Henry that was the blackest beast of all. He didn't know that his own black beast had changed the world. He wanted the nineteenth century to last forever—and maybe that's what he saw in Harry, someone to save him the past, to stave off time. They were close, those two, one the father, almost, and one the almost son, and while Henry rolled the new world in, Harry made it look like the old.

He did that with a private army of riffraff three thousand strong— any ruffian with a blackjack, any bruiser with knucks, any gunman or con on parole, any thug, wrestler, tackle, or pug—all served Henry as the Medici were served, as though his flag too was six red balls on a field of gold. They turned up all over the place, in the mill and out. They were at the bins and in the crappers and on the line next to me and thee, they were in taverns, doorways, streetcars, and even in your dreams; you were eavesdropped at home, and your lunch- box was rummaged while you worked; you were shadowed, warned, bulldozed, and sometimes beaten; you were stretched out, sped up, underpaid, and laid off—all to show Henry that Harry could handle you.

In time, though, Harry came to think he owned the works, lock, stock, and the Boss as well. As it turned out, he hardly owned his ass, and like those bygone unioneers, he was flung down the steps of the Overpass. It was called a retirement, and he spent it somewhere on the desert, and (the Devil knows) he may be living there yet. His pastime was painting—landscapes, portraits, and possibly signs.

ON THE WAY TO JOY ROAD

I was a born mechanic.
—Henry Ford

He was only ten or twelve the day that steam engine went past his father's farm, a machine to haul machinery with, traction for a reaper. A great grim ant, it seemed to be, an emmet of iron, and he must've stared at its thorax-boiler, at its wheels and valves and pistons, the whole insectival morph, and even then he may've known, may've read in its smoke and heard in its noise, all the smoke and noise of the years ahead. *I was a born mechanic*, he said, but if so, he must've been born then, at ten or twelve, when that engine went by in the dust of Greenfield Road.

From there, it was only a mile or so to Joy—he could almost see it from where he stood—but he was in no hurry to reach the crossing, and it took him seventy years. He had engines of his own to build—cars, they'd be called—and in his head that day, he may've seen his little black ants take shape, mandible, feeler, ptopodeum, one a minute he'd make, his machines for moving machines. *I was a born mechanic*, he said.

From the farm, he could gaze out over the prairie to where Joy and Greenfield met a mile or more away. Seventy years he'd wend that mile to end in a grave at the junction, the born mechanic dead. What would he know then, he may've wondered, that he hadn't known at ten, what would he have acquired as time went and he with it—would it come to more than numbers, would people people his mind, or would they be numbers too, hired for five a day and fired for a smile, a piss too many, or a snitch too few?

From the farm that day, he may've thought ahead to Joy and Greenfield, and from there he may've looked back through seventy years at a black formicine engine and wondered what he'd done to the earth. Would he see himself as a mechanic then, would he still be only a fixer of watches, a maker of devices, someone with a kit of tools and a coil of wire—or would he ponder his thirty-two million

Hymenoptera and fancy he'd made another world? Would he have become a Creator, that bringer of swords, that hater of Jews—or would he never have grown from the age of ten, would he be the boy mechanic of old lying in a Joy Road grave?

FREIGHT TRAIN ON THE SOUTHERN

> *That is not the train I was on*
> —Victoria Price

Of course it wasn't—how could a grown woman have ridden on a toy train, a string of little reefers, flats, and tankers, forty-two pieces of painted tin a foot long each and drawn by a footlong engine? There on a trestle in the courtroom, they gleamed in the dimness; they gleamed, and so did the tracks they stood on, and many in attendance must've honed to roll the Tom Thumb cars, to stroke the locomotive, many must've dreamed back the years as they stared at the childish things that were set down before them. Not she, though. *That is not the train I was on,* she insisted, and, true enough, she never was, nor could she be made to touch it.

No, the train she'd ridden was higher, wider, far less handsome, a way freight Memphis-bound from Chattanooga, a mile of cars, each with its number, capacity, and stencilled herald—Monon, Wabash, Central of Georgia—and all with some chalked-on scrawl, ciphers written in hobo-code. That was the train she'd been on, that chain of red-leaded rattlers, tanks on wheels, gondolas filled with coal, with sand, with chips of chert.

That is not the train I was on, she said, and she could hardly look askance at the scaled-down model on its narrow-gauge rail. *It was bigger, lots bigger,* she said, and she was enraged at the suggestion that the replica be taken for the real. It was exact, she was told, made for this one occasion, not meant to be played with, not a toy at all: it was the very train in small that she'd caught in the Chattanooga yards on that cold March morning. But she would have none of it— *That is not the train,* she kept saying, *that is a toy*—and she never changed, nothing ever changed her. Nothing, and sure God not that damn Jew lawyer!

What did he take her for—a fool in the tules? She didn't hook any ride on a kiddie choo-choo, she didn't get raped by no nine niggers on a pissy Christmas present—she got it put to her on a full-size freight by nine black full-size bucks, eight of them pinning her to a bed of flint while the other forced her lily thighs. That didn't happen over there on that table, Mister New York Jew; it happened an hour out of Chattanooga just across the Tennessee line. It happened nine times, she swore, and she hollered all the while, and though she remembered little else, she did remember this—one of them saying *You ain't hollered none till I put this black thing in you.*

It made no nevermind to her that Olen Montgomery was all blind in his left eye and nigh so in his right, or that Willie Roberson, what with a chancre on his membrum and a clap in its tract, could scarcely walk even with a cane, and as for two of the nine being under thirteen, who said boys couldn't ride a cock horse? Nothing swayed her, and nothing made a juror doubtful: she could've been, and was, a whore by trade, and still her word would've been good against all Africa.

And so it proved through a long generation of trial and appeal. Always it was held that no white woman would spread for a black, not even a spraddle-leg, and therefore what this one had sworn to was true as blue and maybe more so. Alabama never managed to kill that crew of nine, but on the other hand, the Jew never did get them off, and there they stayed, on Death Row, till the State wore itself out and let the niggers go. From first to last, it was nineteen years before eeny-meeny-miney got to moe.

In all that time, and all the time since, did anyone ever wonder about that set of toy trains, any lawyer, any witness, any bailiff, any of the nine, did anyone ever fathom the white slut's rage? Why did she seem to glitter, to vitrify, when she was shown those miniature cars, the engine and tender, the neat caboose? What did they contain for her that no one else seemed to see and that she couldn't face? *That is not the train I was on,* she said—but was she not on it till the day she died? Well, who can say now? She never did, and she's been a long time dead. But what about the trains, what about those forty-two little cars, the ten-wheeler pulling them, the caboose at the rear . . .?

A CRUELL AND FEIRCE STORME

The rain are fallin.

1. School in a Kitchen Corner*

The rain are fallin—the words are chalked on a strip of black
linoleum tacked to the wall, and below them are written a row of
numbers, 1 through 10, and, in a double row, the letters of the
alphabet. There are two pupils, both boys and both black, and they
sit facing the inscription, their gaze on a crooked stick that a black
girl, standing nearby, is pointing directly at the 7. Somehow, though,
it seems to include the sentence above it, where the world is being
told what the children already know—*the rain are fallin*

The Natchez Democrat papers the walls,
old pages sealing older, or peeling
to censor sense from ads and headlines
    It is a Real Sale of Such Sweeping
    That People Will Come from 20 to 30
and in crayon someone has scrawled

                    F
                    L
                    A
                    D

and not far from this vertical cryptogram
hangs the candor of a calendar
generous with January,
and the eyes move,
the eyes move from right to left,
follow the crooked stick
see the 7,
read that *the rain are fallin*

---

* photograph, Library of Congress, 1939

In the corner, on a three-drawer dresser, a coal-oil lamp with a
sooted chimney, a box of striking matches, a small tin, a smaller
jar, a dish, a frayed scarf of dotted cloth, but no books, no maps or
globes, no blocks to build with, no treasury for the mind—in the
corner, nothing but the letters, the numbers, the Word on the wall
in chalk: *the rain are fallin*

> The eyes move from right to left,
> reach the margin,
> the hard edge of the earth,
> take in a splintered mantel,
> an enameled pitcher (chipped),
> a shaving-brush,
> three flatirons hanging from the hob,
> the last things on earth,
> and then they go from left to right
> along the wall
> and learn once more of rain,
> *the rain are fallin*

2. A Woman, Upper Portion*

She stands against a block of shade, the black solid made by a tar-
paper shack. A hole in space, it seems to be, and from it only her
head and chest emerge, the rest of her withheld as if unworthy of
the sun. On her soiled sweater, a safety-pin appears against the days
to come of wear and ravel, and from its collar a column rears, thin
and sinewed, the wrinkled scrag of a withered phiz

> Her face is a high look down at a desert,
> a calm of coulees and dry streams
> converging on the sink of her mouth
> and the baked-out lake of an eye,
> a shrunken place from which she gazes
> a little to her right and a long way off
> to where sight ends and mind starts seeing,
> and if she finds there that wall
> and those words in a kitchen corner—
> > *the rain are fallin*—
> be not dead to her repose,
> but dread it as a warning

---

* photograph by Dorothea Lange, 1939

3. A Gate in a Barbed Wire Fence*

The wire is slack, and the fenceposts lean, and the gate opens on nothing, leads from weeds within to weeds outside, from waste to wild. It was a place of grass, a granary once, liquid in the least of airs, land a sigh would seem to squander, or a bird passing by. But nowadays all green is gone, the wheat, the maize, the long-awned rye, and the gate gives on desolation

> It used to be good growing-ground,
> that strip between the two Canadians,
> loess, the soil was called, from *losen,*
> meaning loose, or land that would pour,
> a fine and flaky loam high in lime
> gotten from shell and mammoth bones —
> well, anyway, that's what they tell you,
> the ones that know such mortal matters,
> and they say too that it was aeolian,
> that is, of the wind, a gift of the wind

> If so, the wind was an Indian giver,
> and what it gave it has taken away,
> undoing in a day what it did in an age,
> sweeping up earth in a curled black surge
> two miles tall and a hundred long
> and sending it off across the world,
> a rolling semi-solid storm of land,
> and God knows where its fine flakes fell,
> where rich in lime it fell as rain

Between its hasp and hinges, the gate hangs shut, a partition in an empty scene. Here and there, a tin or a stick appears, a scoured plank, a tendril of wire, but the pickings, this clump or that blade, are too poor to come for, and no bird now does, no black widow, no jack or locust, not even the pneumonic plague, for the people have gone to where, they hope, *the rain are fallin*

4. On the Banks of the Hudson**

Rack-and-ruined piling runs out from shore between a shanty and a hulk, and all, the shack, the wreck, the pier, seems to have been stranded here by a higher tide, cast aside to settle in the silt, never

---

* photograph, Farm Security Administration, 1938
** photograph by International, 1932

to ride the river again, never to come and go like the water, a movable and wandering thing. And the men in the scene, one on a stringer and one in a chair, they too may well have been marooned, left where they sit and stand, there to shrink in the sun, rot in the alluvium, sink, and be forgotten

> All this litter will some day disappear,
> and there'll be a park in its place,
> a pleasance beside the stream,
> and those who come to walk or play
> will not fancy, never dream
> that underfoot a man still stands
> astare at nothing in his shirtsleeves
> and another still sits in a chair,
> nor will they be aware of the riparian mansion
> or the yacht submerged in slime,
> nay, they'll learn no lesson at the riverside,
> they'll stay in the sun,
> never know
> > *the rain are fallin*

5. Sharecropper's Bedroom*

The floor is made of rough-sawn 1x12 planking, weathered and scrubbed, worn clean, like the deck of a ship. There are no chairs, no mats or curtains, no tables, lamps, or pictures, only a bedstead cattycornered and a shotgun on a wall, and if it's falling anywhere

> *the rain are fallin*
> > here

6. The Sleeping Man*

He lies sidelong on a stone step, his head pillowed on a sheet of cardboard. He wears a cap turned askew, so that the bill shades an ear, and if there are sleeves on his shirt, they fall short of those on his jacket, the cuffs of which are frayed. A hand reaching across his body seems to be half of a self-embrace, and he may have dreamt well, who knows? — three buttons of his fly are open that the other hand failed to close

> *the rain are fallin—*
> > so it says on the wall in that kitchen,
> > and so say the 7 and the a b c

------

* photographs by Walker Evans, 1936, 1932

MY DEAR GENERAL PERSHING, SHE WROTE

> *I trust you can see your way clear, dear General Pershing,*
> *to give him the recommendation necessary to advance him*
> *to the grade of Brigadier General.*
> —Mary P. MacArthur, 1918

She was writing of her son Douglas, a colonel in the Rainbow Division, fighting at the time along the Moselle in Lorraine. It hardly required saying, she said, that he knew nothing of the letter and the appeal it contained, the implication being that had he so known, he'd've forbidden both. No, dear General, the impulse was hers alone: it was her hope and ambition, she said, to live long enough to see her son made a General Officer, and therefore, as it were, it was her own life too that she was submitting for preferment. And she subscribed herself, with great esteem, etc.

She need scarcely have been concerned for Douglas. He was no longer a boy, ramping around after his father, who was Captain of Company K in the 13th Infantry. All that was back in the last century, and he was long past the days at Fort Wingate, which was hard by the Navajo reservation, past Selden too, down in the White Sands country of the Chiricahuas: by the time that letter was written, the Indians were hostile no more; they were starving to death or already dead. Douglas was thirty-eight years old when his mother sought that star for him, gold, not unlike those he'd brought home from school. She didn't seem to know he'd outgrown the lizard hunts, the pony rides on the dry *bolsons*, the skirts he wore instead of britches. Such things were now no more, but there she was, pulling a sleeve for her feminized son: she must've thought he squatted to piss.

She took it for granted, she wrote, that her dear General was familiar with her son's achievements at the Point—98.14 per cent. of all the merits it was possible to earn, a record second only to that of Cadet Robert E. Lee, set in 1829. She also assumed that her dear General was aware of the preference that Douglas had always shown for service in the field, for any duty, as she put it, that would allow him to share the rigors endured by the troops. If she was aware that they called him *the Dude* and *the Dandy* and sometimes *the Stick*, she did not reveal the fact to her dear General, nor did she allude to the dresses Douglas wore till the age of eight. He got his star, finally, but not through her letter. There were better reasons, and not the least was his three-star father. *My dear General Pershing,* she said, *I am taking the liberty of writing you a little heart-to-heart letter* . . . but she was wasting his time and her ink. Douglas pissed through his fly now, and he did so standing up.

In those days in France, his skirts were gone, and in their place were flaring pants and glaring boots, a riding crop, a ringless cap, quite rory-tory, don't you know, and the stub of a manly cigar—*the Stick*, they called him, *the Stick*. He was on his own now, and he required no letters to ease his way. By the time the fighting ended, he wore a motley of ribbons for his campaigns and decorations, among them those for two Purple Hearts and seven Silver Stars—ah, *the Dude*, *the Dandy* with the broken hat, he came home a Brigadier.

*   *   *

No letters were ever written in behalf of Walter Waters. His mother, if she could spell, never heard of General Pershing, and his father, in a ditch or at a trade, was a three-star nobody. He was born in Oregon, Walter said, but it might've been Idaho, or even Montana—how did he know except by being told? Anyway, it was probably somewhere up in that corner of the country, though none can say for sure, for few knew that he was present and fewer that he'd gone: he was a thin cloud, and he cast a mere mar as he passed across the earth. There were no Captains in his line, no foxed photos of mule-teams, drill and repose on the post, guns, flags, and barrack rows, there were no medals on velvet, no uniforms, no memories of gypsum dunes and pronghorn chases and Krags being fired on the rifle range—there was nothing

> so many leave no trace; only a handful still have a name in some annal and a known place of birth. Who were they, that they survive the histories on their stones—in what did they differ from the forgotten? Were they better-boned than the rest of their breed, were they finer-made and higher-minded, were they nearer to Heaven? Or did they merely have mothers who wrote to the General?

No one wrote for Walter Waters.

Of his youth, all that's left is the word that went around, the guesswork of idle moments, the absent-minded notions, the things men said when there was little to say. None of it is actual, and yet none of it is false. Taken altogether, it sums up someone's life, and the someone may be he. If so, none of his vita suggests the hero. He was merely a member of the National Guard, merely a medic with the Field Artillery, merely a sergeant after three years of service, and when the war ended, he became even less, a name and number on an archive list.

After his discharge, he or the one who wore his suit tried to find a job, not anything at all, not simply a hole to be filled for so much a day, but a place to start his line of kings. He found no such beginning in selling and repairing cars, in being a baker's helper, a harvest hand, a capper in a cannery. Wherever he lit, he found nothing, and on he went in his long migration from hope deferred to disenchantment, and the years passed, and his way lay ever downward.

It must've come as no surprise that he had company: many another were headed for nowhere too, and numerous among them were they who'd served in a war now thirteen years done with, all but the bonus promised by a grateful country, and that still thirteen years away. They'd be old by then, he told them, they'd be well on the road to hell, where all roads ended. Their pleas went unheeded, he said, their petitions were unread—a grateful country had forgotten them, and, out of sight in the forty-eight states, they'd stay there out of mind. Their proper place was where they could see the Capitol, because only there would they be seen and only there be heard.

From Portland, after three hundred of them had made him their leader, they set out along the Columbia for the east, an over-age army, weaponless and unrationed and with no more shelter than their hats. They were eighteen days on the roads and rods before they saw what they were looking for, the high white dome on Jenkins Hill. By then, others were on the way, from the bayou country and the Finger Lakes, from somewhere on the Wabash, the Gunnison, the Aroostook, from the Staked Plains and the savannas, and from where the lupine grew and the columbine—and soon there were many where few had been before. In time, they became a contingent of twenty-eight thousand, some in sack suits black once and green now, and some in dungarees, a great creased corps of down-and-outers, wind-worn, ganted-up, and in the main ashamed.

No door opened for them in Washington, no house received them, and in their shirtsleeves and cracked shoes, they roamed the vistaed avenues, strangers among familiar views. Bands had played once, crowds had blown them kisses, and paper flakes had fluttered down, but they were bindlestiffs now, and no banners were flown in their honor, no hearts were warm but their own. They wound up in hallways, ballparks, and buildings partly razed, and on the flats that bounded a creek, they reared themselves a city of debris, a mean city near a city that was set on a hill, and there they dwelt in shanties made of piano crates, sheets of tin and cardboard, cars that would not run.

They were there for months, sleeping on straw, on bare springs, on furniture found in vacant lots, and sometimes on the ground. They begged for food in forage squads, and when picking over garbage, they chose the choicer streets. They washed their clothes and bathed in the creek, they crapped in an acre of crappers (at one time or another, they all had the trots), and swamped by speeches, spells of rain, and their own excreta, they somehow lasted into the summer of the year, thinner than when they'd started, worn down further, emptier in the mind, and blinder, seeing far less with their far-off eyes. And with the coming of the dog days, they learned that they had lost. Under the great white dome they could see from the mud-flats (cast iron, cost a million, height 285 feet), the Senate had voted the bonus down. They'd come and spoken, all those thousands, but they'd not been heard.

Only some of them went when told to leave, went everywhichway but toward Nebraska (nobody was there from Nebraska), went forty-seven ways off into their grateful country, went out along the tracks and roads that led from shakedowns here to shanties there, went home to machinery rusting in last year's weeds, to missing steps in a stoop, to washing lynched against the sky, to doorways, benches in the park, apples 2-for-5 for passersby, went from cold shoulder to even colder, from things of naught to less than nothing, went to the devil and never came back. The rest stayed, and soon, on that riparian *Champ de Mars*, Sergeant Nobody met General Gent.

* * *

Against an army of ragamuffins, the General (two stars now), the Yankee Dude the Dandy, led a battalion of infantry, a squadron of cavalry, and a tank platoon, and to avoid the possibility of a repulse (by what—bricks, barrel-staves, shit-grenades?), reserves from Virginia were ordered on the way. The Stick wore his skirted coat, his black and blazing boots (glass vases!), and five rows of ribbons. As he watched the ragtag run, he must've given thought to starting another row—a bit of silk for his Mud-flat campaign, a little bar of brown.

The sergeant? Oh, he ran too, ran off to nowhere in particular, made no mark there, and died, they say, after another twenty-seven years in the shade.

SHIKATA GA NAI

What happened, happened.
—Japanese saying

They wore tags, all of them, a narrow strip of cardboard hanging from a button by a string, and coming along a street somewhere, or plodding across a bridge, they might've been goods in motion, a procession of merchandise offering itself for sale. The elderly, as in a will-less dream, drifted with the flow of the young, and toylike children were buoyant on the stream. Passing before the curious at the wayside, they might've been wares on display, a showing of faces, fashions, but only the children stared back at blue-eyed staring.

The ticketed people were on their way to banishment, but not beyond the pale of their country: their place of exile lay within it, at an inner confine called Topaz, Tule, Manzanar, and they were moving now toward its towns in the desert, toward league-long reaches of mesquite and ocotillo, toward shimmering scrims of heat and winds that were made of dust. They were headed for trains of passé cars, days and nights of empty views, for a compound called Minidoka, Gila, Heart Mountain, deep inside the compound land. Their tar-paper mansions waited under the sun, black ovens, and they'd sleep in wet-down sheets and bleed from the nose in the heat. Infants would wilt and die, and blistered by blown sand, families and friends would bury them among the creosote bushes, and on a stone some day one would be known as Jerry.

It would not be long before the old ones sat gazing off into the distance as if there were nothing near they cared to see. They'd look out across scrub and sage at a dim sierra, a wedgwood band at the base of the sky. They'd sit quite still in the midst of movement, they'd be unaware of the roundabout commotion, hear none of the cries and collisions, none of the running feet, and not a word would be heard of the traffic on the air. They'd be somewhere in the far blue mountains: their past, the best of life, was there.

The young, if they dreamt at all, would dream at night: their days would hold no bygone vistas. There'd be shacks to mend, doors that didn't fit, cracks in the shrunken floors. Who would moon over blue buttes and pompous clouds when there were snakes to roust and centipedes? There'd be winds to deal with and force-fed dust, there'd be the range of the seasons, the mile-high heat and cold, there'd be barrens to claim, sand-burs to burn, thistle, arrowgrass, and there'd be a need to learn and wait.

The price-tagged children in doll-size clothes wouldn't know that watch-towers weren't trees. They'd suppose they simply grew as they'd grown, with ladders instead of branches and lamps instead of leaves. Nor would they know that warnings were on the walls, signs on the wire, tethers on their perfect feet. They'd play, shrill, sit in the sand and seem to think, they'd chatter at the soldiers and never know they were guards who'd kill. They'd never be afraid, never be sad, bereft, abused, and yet one day (*shikata ga nai*) they'd begin to hate: what happened would happen to them.

Atomic Bomb Test, Trinity, N. M., 1945

OF ONE WHO MISSED THE SECOND CREATION

*After a few days he was perfectly
all right.*
—Gen. Leslie R. Groves, U.S. Army

His name is never mentioned, as if it doesn't matter, and no one
gives his age, his race, his rank and regiment, but, strangely, his place
of birth seems to matter much, for all agree and all assert that he
came from Tennessee—Tennessee, they say, in explanation

he was a soldier at the Base Camp
ten miles south of the Shot Tower,
and at five in the morning,
half an hour before the second world,
he came back to the barracks
from a weekend whirl in Alamogordo,
and, all used up and drunk on beer,
he fell across his bunk and dreamt
of vague rooms, bars, hallways, dim spaces
where he dimly saw swirls of skirt
and girls' faces,
dreamt, maybe, of Tennessee
in those last thirty minutes before
sunrise
over the lava beds and hills of gypsum,
a white desert called the Journey of Death,
and in the dream he knew nothing
of being alone,
of the empty cots in the empty shack,
was unknowing of the void in sound,
of running water, laughter, collisions,
morning renewals of last night's spite:
he dreamt in private of Tennessee.
Nor during those thirty malted moments
did he know of the quiet in the open air,
the white-sand stillness outside the walls,

[314]

he was dead to the grand excitement,
the held breath, the extra heartbeat,
he had no share in the doubts, the mystery,
he was unaware.
He did not know of the cold, the overcast,
the now-and-then lightning, the fine rain,
nor did he hear the wind blow,
the switches being closed, the whispers
and someone saying *Too damn scared to piss,*
he was deep asleep, he was unaware
of idling motors, the ticks of passing time,
unaware of the five-minute rocket,
the two-minute siren,
the ten-second gong,
unaware of staring praying fearful men,
unaware of a great light growing,
a sun that made the sun seem dim:
he slept and dreamt of Tennessee.

The shock-waves blew him awake,
but when he opened his eyes,
whatever he saw was seen by his mind:
he was blinded.
He missed the eight-mile cloud,
orange, peach, pink, and purple,
he missed the behavior of animals,
the trembling dogs, the sweating horses,
missed the belief and disbelief of men,
the jigging,
the handshakes,
the slaps on the back,
missed the wonderment,
the misgivings,
the faces that said *What have we wrought!*
They gave him morphine to stop his raving,
and after a few days he was perfectly all right

His name is never mentioned, but all agree that he came from
Tennessee. Doubtless that's where he now is, if still alive. He did
get his sight back, though; so if dead, he didn't die in that same blazing panic. He'd been there for it all, and nothing had happened.

THE UGLY SKY

*As I lay there, looking up at the ugly sky, there
was a faint smell of wild chrysanthemum.
Alongside my cheek stood a torn, flowerless stem.*
— Dr. Takashi Nagai

He was at or near the College Hospital when the bomb was dropped from a height of thirty thousand feet, and all through its fall of fifty-two seconds, he might've been doing any of many possible things. Yet even he could not have said whether he'd been standing or seated, whether speaking or silent, gazing from a window or lighting a cigarette: he remembered a stunning blue-white flash, but nothing else; he never knew how he came to be lying in the ash of grass, looking up at the ugly sky.

He was unaware of the ruinous stroke of sound, of heat that put a vitreous finish on the earth, of fire instant and everywhere in which all that would burn turned suddenly to slag—dogs, cats, and people became scoria, as did insects, birds in flight, and trees, but he never learned why these things died and he lived. All about him, the smell of wild chrysanthemum over pinches of char that'd been an old woman once, or someone's pet, or an unknown passerby, and from such small remains a blue-gas soul went up to join the ugly sky.

Lying there in the carbons of the city, he couldn't recall whether he'd picked the flower that was still on the air—nothing of the past moment, the past hour, came back to fill his mind. He watched smoke pile up from smoke, build itself by the mile, saw it spread and set the morning sun, and soon outsize drops of rain began to fall, oil-black and oil-cold, and without knowing why he should rise, he rose, and through unastonished eyes he took in pulverized brick, iron that fire had brought to a bubble, steel rail wrought like wire, a trolley in which a cinder driver still drove his cinder fares.

His watch had stopped and with it time, and he wandered without purpose, drifted where the wind blew or whim drew him, and he passed bodies skewered on bamboo splinters, smashed by bolts of

molten metal, shredded by flying glass. In the river, a foam of dead
floated among exploded fish, and tied to a boiled mother bobbed the
dinghy of a premature child. Others wandered with him, naked,
hairless, smeared with shit, and they held their arms free of their
bursted sides, and from seared backs the skin hung down in rags.
All stared at nothing, as if there were nothing at all to see, and
through open mouths they screamed without sound, pleaded for what
they could not utter from those that could not hear

      The flies were quick to return,
or were they new ones that came
to feast on pus, piss, and broken blisters,
on the roasted squabs of children
and the colons of the old?,
and when disturbed,
they took wing humming,
winged atoms,
and coming down,
they clambered over corpses
till cooked meat looked alive,

and a man with burned hand
was seen to soak it in water,
from which then blue smoke emerged,
and when the man stooped to drink,
he died,

and many noted an unbearable odor,
that of drying squid,
and they brimmed over with vomit,
a thin yellow liquid,

and they passed things
with their faces melted away,
with nothing left but teeth,
and in one such head
the teeth spoke,
asking for water,
and children laughed
as though they'd lost their minds,

and there was a pumpkin field
bare of pumpkins save for one,
a woman's head with a gold tooth,
and her eyelids were open,
but she had no eyes,

and women bled from the uterus
though it was not their menses time,
and there was blood in urine too,
in stools,
in sputum
and faces were blown to double size,
and at such things
the mad children laughed,
and at a mother giving tit
to a dead infant,

and walking in their own silence,
screaming unheard in an unheard-of hell,
a host of the living would soon be dead,
indeed, for most malaise had begun
with the rays they bore within,
and even then they suffered fevers,
epilation, purpura, necrosis of the gums,
and already their platelets were fewer,
their appetites weaker,
their sperm counts nil,
and it would've shaken them to know
how their bones would glow in the dark —
they were decaying on the go,
dying in a dream of living,
a scream without a sound,

A faint smell of wild chrysanthemum, he thought, and as he roamed among the dead, it may have kept him alive. He dwelt on the broken stem he'd seen — what color had the blossom been, how lush its ruche of leaves? A smell of wild chrysanthemum, he thought, but why did he name the flower when he meant the smell of the leaves? He tried, tranced and almost airborne, to evoke their silvan rankness, that of weeds, but the more he sought it the further it faded. Still, he kept on pursuing it, and that may be why he lasted under the ugly sky.

But not forever.

Dr. Takashi Nagai
b.1909—d.1951
leukemia

David Greenglass, 1922–

BABY BROTHER

Little Doovey
—Ethel Rosenberg's pet name
for her youngest brother

So little is known of him that no face or figure forms from the fragments that come to mind, as if, drawn from some medley of parts, they compose nothing distinct, nothing entire. In his photographs, he seems to have been caught in motion, and where descriptions have sought to hold him still, the words blur and their meanings change. Beyond that, little: hazel eyes, someone has said, and others have guessed at weight, height, and inner nature, but even if such things were certain, they'd merely be spare pieces summing up to nothing more.

Ethel was seven years older than he, and almost from his birth she took care of him, took care of her little brother Davy, or Doovey, as she called him, from the Jewish way of saying David. Six in number when he came, the family was piss-poor: the father was a fixer of sewing machines for sweatships, a small living, hardly a living at all, and the mother, at her household tasks, drudged the livelong day. To Ethel therefore fell the charge of looking after the latest born, and if anyone knew him well, it was she. She knew the color of his hair and the color of his eyes (who better?), she knew his birthmarks, if any, his wens, moles, lentigo, and she knew the size of his personal parts. She knew the build of his body, the proportions, the grace or the lack; she knew, and few with her, whether he had an extruded umbilicus and dimples on his back. It was she who watched his eight pounds grow, toyed with his pink and faultless toes, it was she who fed him, hummed him to sleep, wiped the flows of mustard from his thighs. *Little Doovey*, she may have whispered, *little brother Dave.*

He grew, and she did too, and while he was becoming, she became, and one day as she looked upon him, she may have found that wonder had given way to understanding, and what she saw then may not have been the quite flawless, the still immaculate figurine.

Instead, she may have seen the grown-up in the making, may have known from certain signs that his best had been reached, that all the rest would be frailty and failure. Was there not about him, she may have thought, a lack of response, an impersuadability, was there not, at five, at six, at ten, a thickness of texture, a trend away from fine?

By then, he no longer required her keeping: he was quit of her hands, her admonitions, her lullabies; he was Little Doovey no more and free to find or avoid the sharp corners, the hot surfaces, free to venture forth into Sheriff Street, a man-to-be, and learn the ways of slumdom on his own. From now on, there'd be trash-can standards to set against the pattern of the home. There'd be other books than Ethel's dull ones (what was *Kapital?* who was Engels?), there'd be other aims, other songs to sing, other pleasures, among them the secretory raptures of the dark. If she perceived these East Side lowerings, these pushcart things, she may have spoken out, tried to stay them, sought to bring him back (maybe she reasoned with him, maybe she dragged him along to some lecture, to her singing school at the Met, maybe she gave him another book), but if so, she did no good. He was *grob*, her baby brother, tumid, coarse—perfection's pink was gone.

He wasn't much at studies, he didn't beat the Dutch—sad to say, he was openmouthed, and sadder still, dense. At Polytech, where he enrolled to (how did he put it?) better himself, he worsened, taking eight courses in mechanic arts and failing in them all. Thereafter he whiled away the days at handball, odd-job wiring, working as a clerk—doing nothing, really, dreaming dimly, thickly yearning, flowing down some twilit stream. He was headed, it seemed, from little to less . . . but his saving grace was a block away. On the ground floor of a Rivington Street walkup, there was a small store where cotton goods were sold, and behind it dwelt the family of the proprietor, a hunky Jew named Printz. One of his treasures—perhaps the only treasure of the one-time miner, oiler, slaughter-house worker—was a daughter Ruth, and he lost her to Little Doovey when she was eighteen and he twenty. She was said to be a smart one, with a gold seal on her high school diploma, but true or false, whip-smart or stock-stupid, she could outthink her husband, who could hardly think at all.

She it was who'd harped on betterment, who'd urged Little Doovey to consider his brother-in-law Julius, a graduate engineer, pointed the way to Polytech, mourned when he stumbled there and fell. She must've been a hard rider, that youthful Ruth, so envious, so avid, so ridden herself, that she put him to a ditch he couldn't carry, a fence he couldn't clear. She never knew, as Ethel may have known, that he was no great shakes, no *Macher*, that at best he was a fixer of other men's machines. She couldn't bear it, the thought alone was too heavy, that her own was second-rate, and therefore she came to hate and fear the paragon, the graduate engineer.

Four months after their marriage, Little Doovey was drafted into the army, classified as an automotive machinist, and sent to a motor and tank pool in California. Thereafter, over a two-year period, he was shifted from post to post, coming to rest finally on a mesa in New Mexico, a place about thirty miles from Santa Fe. It was called Los Alamos, a name he'd never heard before. It meant *poplars*, and if he knew that, he may have wondered where the poplars were, for nearly nothing grew there—scrub, yes, and on the steeps of the barrancas Spanish bayonet and ocotillo, but little more of green. He may have wondered as well at the shops and forges, each of them new, at the barracks, the wire fences, the guards and badges, and most of all at the somnial air, the sense he drew of being quartered in a dream. He was a long way from where Sheriff crossed Rivington, far from the hue of the crowd and the street-cry: one of many there, here he was one of the few. Little Doovey, high upon a mesa with the makings of a bomb!

On being discharged at war's end, he returned to—where but that street-crossing a block away from Williamsburg Bridge. He was three years older now, but no better off than before. He'd learned little in those years: he was still the same inept joiner, founder, machine-fitter that he'd been at Polytech. Lost in the profundities of Los Alamos, infinitely small amid all its genius, diminished, in fact, from his actual size, he must've come home knowing that he was going nowhere—and had it not been for his mother, to nowhere he'd've gone. Somehow or other, she contrived to raise the money to buy him a share in a business run by her son-in-law Julius, the graduate engineer.

From the outset, the partnership failed to flourish. Julius had scant regard for Little Doovey, to him merely a *Dummkopf*, while he, to David, was the scholar of the family, the *Gelehrte*, a down-the-noser, a finder of faults, and in all truth there were many to be found, for Little Doovey, alas, was a fool. At a lathe, a press, a power-punch, he was something less than the machine itself: he seemed to stand between its potential and the result, and often enough there were crudities and imperfections, more his own than the obedient engine's. These lapses, measured in lost time and lost custom, were written in red, and as trade shrank, quarreling grew, and then red too were the words that flew the air. So flawed was Little Doovey's work that Julius appointed one of their employees to superintend it, whereupon the dispute swelled and became a feud. The wives, Ruth and Ethel, were now drawn in, and true it must've been that much was said that was better censored, that became a part of mordant memory.

In those days, Little Doovey was often absent from the shop: he'd go home for lunch and stay, run household errands or roam around loose, or merely sit on a dock and stare, but always, whatever he might be doing, he'd stew in the juice of rage, and the pole of his wrath was Julius, the graduate engineer. He couldn't endure the contempt, the rebukes, the unremitting blame, he couldn't bear the shame of doing as he was told. Who was Julius, that he could issue the orders while others did the work? What gave him the right—that degree he held, that B.Elec.E.? How much did a piece of parchment prove? After all, how far had Julius gone with what he'd gotten from his books, where were his diode tubes, his telegraph, his incandescent lamps? His heights were there in that machine-shop, Little Doovey thought, and no higher than his own. And why, a man might think, were they not a little lower? He'd spent three years on that mesa in New Mexico: the air was rare there, and rare too the air that fed his mind; he'd been among the great, which made him greater—indeed, he thought, he was a creator too, and alongside him, what was Julius?

In time, he may have come to believe that he'd helped to build the bomb, that when others despaired, he'd come up with some essential, some spanning of a void, some realization of an abstraction—in time, surely he so believed. The truth, of course, is that he contributed nothing, less than a molecular fraction, less even than the shadow of a fraction's dust—on the contrary, what others brought, he took away. He listened (in his paltry presence, who would not have talked?), and having listened, he remembered—phrases, formulae, equations, diagrams—and bore them off in his head. Little Doovey, thief of fire! When they came to his home to arrest him, he was warming some milk for his child.

They demanded the names of his co-conspirators. They wanted

the names he knew, and once he blew the gaff, he'd be cleansed, they said, or nearly so. It was as if he had the syph—he was impure, he was told, and he could cure himself with the 606 of names. The names, they said, two or three, and he'd be nearly free to go—name them, they said, name those he linked with spites, humiliations, sudden laughter unexplained, cite some of the envied, they said, the sought-after, the eloquent, the comely, surrender the ones he'd never led, peach, they said, on comrades, neighbors, kinsmen, wives. . . . To save save himself from death, Little Doovey gave them Julius, and then he gave them Ethel too.

A long time later, they were sentenced to die in the electric chair, and while waiting in the Detention Room of the courthouse, Ethel (for what reason? for what possible reason?) sang *Un bel di vidremo* to Julius at the other end of the hall, sang it so well, so far beyond the anguish of its own lyrics, that the guards outside her cell applauded. On another day, as she was being led to the Chair in a gray cotton smock and felt slippers, she did not sing, but all the same she may have thought she heard applause.

At eight minutes after eight that morning, what was Little Doovey doing, what was passing through Baby Brother's mind? Was he thinking of his sister, just then dying, or of Julius, the electrical engineer, for six minutes past electrically dead?

Oh, it was one fine day. . . .

OH GOD, WHEN I GO DOWN

let me go down like an oak
felled by a woodsman's ax.
— motto on his office wall

He went otherwise: his liver failed him, and he died of the poisons his body produced. Toward the end, there was leucin in his urine, and tyrocin too, and it turned yolk-yellow, almost orange. His head shook at times, and his hands were never still, and, weak and somewhat vacant, he took to falling down. The four-pound mass in his abdominal cavity was smaller than before, harder in texture, and bile, instead of flowing into his duodenum, was absorbed by his blood, and he was soon dead of his own humors, a saffron suicide. The jaundiced stiff was borne in a flag-draped casket to the Capitol, where seventy senators came to view it and some of them to mourn.

A big, slovenly, jam-packed man, a whole kit and caboodle of pipes and organs, he all the same made no few wonder whether he was quite as fraught as he seemed. For all his fullness, were there not voids within him, were there not dark intervals that he'd striven and failed to fill? There was about him a suggestion of unstable rest, of a child rapt for the moment, but apt at the next to self-excite, explode. A child — was that it? is that why little could hold him long and less could take him away? is that what those who wondered saw, the child expanded, larger, louder, more unstaid, but still as he'd been before, timid, clumsy, friendless, shy? Was he a child, short-armed and thick-fingered, without the skills of other children (a bear cub, his brothers called him, though unlike such he never played: he was a solitaire)?

Why was he so? What was in the blood he was given, the Wisconsin air, the one-room school he went to, the catechism? Why did he squirm among strangers, sweat, shake, look at the floor? What happened to him back there at the beginning, what made him run when callers came, what was said to him, was he doubted, slighted, denied, or was nothing said at all, had silence fallen, and did he fear

[324]

it, flee it, hide? And where did he go in his flight, to which stall, which hayloft, and what did he hate when he got there, what did he try to kill? A drear time, he must've had of it, with himself his only company, with only himself to outdo. How young was he when he knew he was unequal to others, lacked their grace, their looks, their ease, at what age did his betters enrage him—they were all his betters—and make him take revenge?

If that was what he sought, a quittance of his condition, he never got it. He rose in station—for a time, he did outdo himself—but his arms were still too short to suit him, his head still trembled, and he drew no friends to the last. With those forepaw hands of his, he mauled his enemies—they were the people's enemies! he said—but the people were in dread of him too, and they shunned him, ran as he'd run once, and he was lonely of *their* choosing now, he was still in that stall on his father's farm, still trying to kill something and not knowing what till his liver gave out. He knew then. In the yellow haze of those final days, he knew.

ON REFUSING TO ANSWER

What do you think you are—a martyr!
I think you're a God damn fool!
> —a friend, 1951

You had dangerous thoughts, they said: in the round of your head swirled the smoke of subversion. It dwelt, they found, in the aqueduct of Sylvius and the fissures of Rolando, it spanned the twain of hemispheres, it tainted too the cells of Purkinje, and when they put you on the stand, they'd find proof of what they knew in the membranes and meninges of your mind. There in those gyri, those gray and white meanders, the vapors of revolution rolled. Behind your teeth and eyes, they claimed, deep in the fosses of your brain, plans were being framed for an alien order, one that put the top dogs at the bottom and the bottom at the top. You were a danger, therefore, to them that bought and sold in the temples and them that trafficked in doves.

When made to appear before them, you knew that you stood among the priests and the Pharisees, that soon you'd be tendered silver for the mention of a name. And though so it was, they didn't demand a Jesus from the garden beyond Kidron—they'd settle for less than a Savior, they said, a cheaper brand of merchandise, a smaller size would do. Give us, they adjured you, the equivalent of the thieves; surrender, they suggested, some unimportant lives, the faceless, the unheard-of; arraign the put-upon, the sodden rejectamenta, the dreamer, the dejected; cast blame upon those that none will ever miss. We'll doom the sons-of-bitches—all you do is spell out whom.

It struck you as strange, their offer of absolution: we'll wash you, they said, of the deep-dyed sin, the doing-in of your brother; we'll relieve you of guilt, we'll speak to your God, tell Him how you anguished, say it was we who constrained you, we who turned the screw. Come, they said, how hard can it be to peach on a nobody, a nix or two, a pair of treys? What stays you, the stares of those whose nights are long? What gives you pause, what debt do you owe to drawers of water, to the ruck that sits below the salt, what writs run that you dare not scorn?

You gave them nothing, and they paid in kind. There were no badges of honor for you, no cordons, ribbons, wreaths of laurel. From then on, you were without a country, a wanderer within it, an internal outcast. You'd worked yourself loose, like some minor component of a giant machine, a shim, a grommet, a superfluous spring, and ground by its shaking, you made a small sound for a while and then fell silent, as if you'd worn away. *What do you think you are—a martyr?*, you heard your friend say.

How could he have thought you'd so suppose when you'd never felt the thorn, never endured the nail? He knew, as you did, that you'd merely chanced on your hill of skulls and pondered on the purpose of the pyre. How, a martyr, when you were your own victim?—you'd chosen the stake, you'd lit the fire. *I think you're a God damn fool!*, he said, and in the ways of the world, you were, but did he deeply believe his words, or did he simply say them, having found them in his mouth? Why his anger?, you sometimes wondered, what harm had you done him in giving none but yourself away? What made him mock you? What did he note in a Simple Simon, what could he not bear to see and hear? Or was he seeing and hearing himself, was he on the stand instead of you, was he giving you away?

Charles A. Lindbergh, 1902–74

HE RODE UPON A CHERUB

*and did fly: yea, he did fly upon
the wings of the wind.*
—Psalms 18.10

And for doing so, which none had done before, he was lauded in
the sung and spoken word, lyricized, borne home under whipping
pennants, and there, in crumpled clothes and hatless, driven between
two walls of roaring. A June day, it was, and yet, for the paper storm
the people made him, the squalls, the flurred scraps all flouncing
downward, it might well have been a winter's time and snow that
blurred the air. Truly, though he'd flown upon the wind, it almost
seemed as if the wings had been his own, as if the quills, the carpals
had been appended to him, two great pinions for a flight from
Heaven. But why almost, many must've mused: they *were* his
plumes, they grew from *him!* And for long thereafter, he was thought
to be a Given Thing and splendid, a sun that shone on moons. What
reverence due him went unpaid, what knee bent not, what praise
was muted in his radiant presence? He was a deity, and before his
sacred and adorable light, too bright to gaze on, men turned down
their eyes. . . .

And then the star began to lower, and few could give the why and
wherefore, none could fix the day or year. What had he done or not,
when did he start to fade? What word had he uttered or withheld,
what comparison had he made? What medal too many, what fatal
hat had he finally worn . . .?

WHO KILLED COCK ROBIN

I, said the sparrow,
With my bow and arrow,
I killed Cock Robin.
— nursery rhyme

He didn't want a long funeral, he said. He didn't much care whether dirges were played or prayers read, and he'd just as soon no fuss was made with flowers, flags, and speeches of praise. A hymn would do him, he said, or a psalm he was known to prize, and then a place in the earth to await the call to rise. A small turnout would please him, he said, a well-loved few in the open air, and no funeral at all would suit him best.

The one he got is going yet. They set his coffin on a flat-bed farm wagon, and, drawn by a pair of mules through the streets of Atlanta, it has gone far further than its four-mile route to the grave. Some hold that it reached there long since, that they saw it put in the ground, covered with fill and squares of turf, and left to wither six feet down. But for many, aye, for most, that pair of mules is still on the way, still plodding urban pavements and the clay of rural roads, and no one knows when their sounds will cease, the ringling of harness, the gnash of wooden wheels — some say they may last forever, some say the funeral will be long.

From the window of a toilet, a shot was fired diagonally across a backyard dump for stained and worn-out things, for torn screens, broken chairs, rags, cartons, sprung springs. It was aimed at a balcony seventy yards away, and traversing the distance at a velocity of thirty miles a minute, the bullet found its mark, a black man's head, in one-thirteenth of a second. Being soft-pointed, the ounce or two of lead expanded on impact, blowing out the jawbone and disintegrating the spinal column, wherefore the man could not have heard the explosion — the report was not yet there — could not have seen the face in the windowframe, the trash in the yard, the leafless trees, could not have known he was dying and would in a little while be dead.

Photograph of a toilet

It wears the slubber of years, the grease, the slime, the melded
smears of sullied hands. A smoke, as from some vast erasure,
soils the dado and the plaster, and the tub and sink and stool,
if ever white, are dinged with dirty rinsings. The window is
open. From it, above a litter of pipe, paper, and suppurating mat-
tresses, a balcony can be seen seventy yards away.

After the shooting, the shooter left the toilet and crossed the hall
to his room. Putting the rifle in a box and taking up a small handbag containing soap, toothpaste, hair oil, and shoe polish, as well
as a pair of pliers and a tack hammer, he went downstairs to the
street. There, in a nearby doorway, he abandoned both the box and
the handbag and drove off into the darkening maze of Memphis—

                                                he,

    meaning Eric Galt,
    or Ramon Sneyd,
    or Harvey Lowmeyer,
    or John Willard,
    or James Earl Ray,

                                                he,

    meaning a buyer of standard brands
    of shaving cream
    of shampoo and headache tablets,
    of vitamins and beer,

                                                he,

    meaning someone born in Alton, Illinois,
    the first of nine children
    gotten by a traipsey father
    (boxer, farmer, mechanic, section-hand,
    jack-of-all),
    and a pretty girl (they say),
    shy and quiet but making do,
    who later took to drink and died,

                                                he,

    meaning a rude and taciturn kid,
    small for his age, slipshod, and dishonest,
    stealing from a teacher in his eighth grade,
    stealing all his life, in fact,
    or as much of it as it took
    to get to that rooming-house toilet,
    but always, in each of his many crimes,

seeming to have planned nothing
further than the crime itself,
as if he couldn't see beyond the deed
and thought he'd be free to go.

Who killed Cock Robin?

He did,
but first he joined the army
when the draft blew on his neck,
a peacetime volunteer,
and awkward for the blunder squad,
and there he stayed for his hitch,
ungifted, thumbfingered,
couldn't tell up from slaunchways
and wouldn't know down if he fell,
bell, it was all he was able
to find his hair,
and when it came to screwing,
he got the syph and a clap
as if they went in a pair,
et enfin, mes amis,
they discharged him out
as too damn dumb even for a dumbjohn.

I killed Cock Robin.

I,
meaning James Earl Ray,
or Ryan,
or Raines,
or Galt,
but not right away.
I had other things to do,
such as swiping a typewriter
in L. A.,
El Pueblo de Nuestra Senora,
getting caught like a chump,
and drawing ninety days.
I had to ride the rods at twenty,
lift a roll of coins from a till,
and get nailed with pounds of silver
that I couldn't explain away.
I had other things to do,
I had to stick up a hack in Chi, Illinois,
for a gain of eleven dollars

and a two-year loss at Joliet,
and I had to lose three more
for forging money orders,
and by the time I got out,
the score since my army days
was six years in jail to three on the street.
But even so, I wasn't done
with the things I had to do.
I still had to rob that market in St. Louis
for $190
and get pinched in half an hour,
I still had to be called habitual
and sentenced to twenty years,
serving about seven before I got away
in a hamper of fresh-baked bread,
I still had to do all those things
before

                              I killed Cock Robin,
and one year later,
I did.
As Harvey Lowmeyer

                         (or was it Ramon Sneyd,
                          or John Willard?,
                          I forget now).

I bought that Remington in Birmingham
and took it to Memphis,
took it to a room numbered 5B
catawampous across the hall
from a toilet.
I put only one shell in the magazine—
don't ask why because I don't know.
But one shot was all I needed
once I got that black man's head
in the crosshairs,
one shot,
and he was dead.

                              I killed Cock Robin.

The man he killed,
the one he called Martin Lucifer King
and Martin Luther Coon,
the black face in back of the circled cross,

he too knew the law's embrace.
Arrested, charged with, tried, convicted,
jailed,
released,
arrested again early and arrested late,
arrested for kneeling in a public place,
arrested for praying (to whom? for what?),
arrested for his race—
Christ, he was always getting pulled in
for some no-account nothing,
like sitting where only a white ass sat,
like marching without a paper permit,
a pass from Mr. Master!,
like loitering, as they put it,
when all he'd done was carry a sign,
or speak from a car,
a bandstand,
a flight of steps.
They didn't care for the way niggers listened
to his high-tone words
that somehow the low-down understood,
they wanted him to run
when they said Git!,
they wanted him to shit himself
when they showed him a gun,
they wanted him to quit pointing
at the road that led to white uptown.

I killed Cock Robin,

I,
meaning James Earl Ray,
but with equal truth,
he might've said they,
meaning every man Jack,
the devil and all of us
who weren't black.
We,
we bought that 30.06,
we drove it from Alabama to Tennessee,
we lugged it to Room 5B,
we stood in that tub in the toilet,
we took aim,
we fired,
we.

We—and it made no difference where we were or what we were doing at the time, casting from the Hatteras beach, logging on the Klamath, or merely jazzing in the grass—we all did it. We killed Cock Robin.

But we gave him a long funeral.

Viet Nam, 1968

MY LAI 4

We were shooting at everything.
Everybody was just firing.
—a private, Charlie Company

It was point-blank murder.
—a sergeant, Charlie Company

It never happened.
—a private, Charlie Company

The birds put the men down in the wrong My Lai. On the maps of Quang Ngai province, there were six My Lais, and they all looked alike from the air—a clearing ringed by thatch-roof huts, an atoll in a patchwork sea of paddies. Flying in at fifteen hundred feet, the pilots didn't know that My Lai 4 was guerilla-free, that it was filled with mama-sans and children and men long past the fighting age. They didn't know that they weren't over Pinkville, as they supposed, and that no one below them was armed; they didn't know that the little figures they saw were merely living one more day as they'd done before, the elders at work and the young at play.

When the birds broke open, Charlie came out firing at the world, at whatever moved or failed to move, at the mama-sans, the boys and girls, the black-pajamaed old, firing at the whole damn undoing world, at doorways, dogs, cattle, shadows on the ground, *it was just firing*, a general shoot as at varmints impounded in a pen—but no pest ever screamed as the people did, none ever rocked its dead and died in the middle of a wail, never was there a jackrabbit roundup where eyes implored to less avail. *I seen bodies everywhere. Everyone was being killed.*

It was no long time before all Charlie grew aware that nothing was firing back. There were no shots from the hootches and the trees, and no grenades were thrown from the dikes and bunkers. There were only the pleas of upraised hands, strange cries, sudden dispersions. No soldier was blown to rags by a mine, no flags fell, no one fled the field: they were immortal that day; they killed at will and everywhere and took pictures as they went

They drug out this fifty-year-old dink
and pitched him down a well,
and then somebody
pulled the pin of a hand-grenade
and dropped it in after him,

and there was a bunch of women
and little children,
crying,
kneeling and praying,
and we went by them one by one,
like we was taking turns at pissing,
and shot them in the head,

and there was another bunch
of about eighty,
and when we got the order
to kill them,
one guy got off five clips of M16,
the women all the while
holding their children behind them
and hollering *No VC! No VC!,*

and there was an old man
hiding in a hut
with his wife and daughters,
and when someone got them out,
someone else said,
Don't let none of them live
and blew their heads off,

and there was a young slope
leading a water buffalo,
and they told him to run for it,
and when he wouldn't run,
they shot him
and the buffalo,

and there was about a dozen soldiers,
all of 'em shooting at a cow
like it was a road marker,
and they kep on firing till it fell,

and there was a woman
that they found hiding behind a bush,
and they pulled her out

and shot her,
and you could see pieces of bone
flying through the air,
after which somebody took a picture,

and a soldier killed a cow
with a bayonet
and another chased a duck
with a knife,
and people,
men, women, babies,
were herded into bunkers,
and grenades
were lobbed in,

and there was a soldier they found
all hunched up
with his face in his hands,
and he was crying
and saying
he shot people
because he was ordered to,
and they tried to calm him down,

and there was a girl about twenty
laying on a dike
with a hole in her gut,
and a medic was treating her,
not much you can do for a belly-wound,
when an officer came over,
put his weapon on automatic,
and emptied a clip into her,

and there was a woman in a paddy,
and the same officer brung her down
from about a hundred meters,
wasn't a bad shot,
and then he went up close
and shot her several times
from couldn't've been six foot away,
anyhow so close
you could see her clothing jump
with the blast,

and listen!,
all the time the shooting went on,

the guys was laughing,
running from place to place
and laughing,
calling out their score and laughing,
cursing,
drooling,
coming in their pants,
killing and coming
and then looking for more.

                    It never happened!
              It never happened!

But it did happen,
and kept on happening

            everyone was just shooting
                  at anything
              and everything,
                  it was like nobody could stop.

   They were touching off the hootches
with their cigarette lighters
and shooting the people
when they came out burning,
and there was a soldier
that sprayed automatic
like he was wetting the place down,
and, come to think, he was,
with slant-eye blood,
and when a clip was gone,
he rammed in another,
and it was a funny thing to him,
must've been,
because he was laughing all the time,

and there was a soldier
that couldn't stand to watch
any more killing,
couldn't stop it and couldn't watch,
so he walked away
and sat down under a tree
and shot himself in the foot,

but there was others that *could* watch,
and one of 'em seen a soldier

kneeling down with a grenade launcher
and firing into a huddle of gooks,
KA-PLOCK!,
and shreds of people flew,
and he done it again and again,
KA-BLAM! KA-BLAM!,
and the whole wide world went red,

and there was another watcher,
and what he seen was this,
a friend, a best friend,
reaching into a passel of women
and plucking out a kid,
a little girl,
couldn't been but five or six,
and he taken her into a hootch,
and after a while,
he come out buttoning up,
and what he done then is,
he chucks a grenade back in,
KA-PLOWIE!,
his best friend,

and there was an old woman that survived
(how? how!),
and she said
when the Americans came down from the sky,
they were soon in her hut,
firing,
and they killed her husband,
her son,
her two daughters,
and seven grandchildren,
and she said
I am too old, I just want to die,

and at the edge of the village,
there was a stack of bodies,
and a kid,
tiny,
a shirt-tail kid,
he come along crying,
and he was ascared,
and he picked up a hand to hold,

just stood there holding a dead hand
and crying,
and a soldier,
range thirty meters,
killed him with one snap shot—

                                It never happened!
                        It never happened!

but it did happen.

They killed five hundred that day,
suffering only one casualty,
a soldier who was shot in the foot.

J. Edgar Hoover, 1895–1972

THE WICKED WALK ON EVERY SIDE*

> . . . dirty, filthy, diseased women. . . .
> —J. Edgar Hoover

Why did he hate them so? What befell him in the womb, what did he see from the crib, what went on in the room next door? What did they deprive him of, what did they emit that corrupted the air, what was he unable to bear, what bent, what turn of mind, what centrum could he never find? What did he derive from his Switzer mother, what did she smear on her tits or feed him by spoon, what flea did she put in his ear?

Dirty, filthy, diseased women, he said.

But which did he mean and how did he know? Was one of them tried and found to be so, or did the Book stay him, confine his sin to the palm of his hand? Did the crabs come on commingled hair, did the blueballs catch him or the spirochete, or did he kneel at keyholes and listen through the walls? What had they done, those carriers of desire, and what had he not, what fears had fled him for seventy-seven years?

> At the age of four,
> he poses for his picture
> in a sailor-suit of blue serge,
> a serene little Jack
> with six black buttons on his shoes.
> Gazing from the seas of one century
> to those of the next,
> he seems quite certain of his shipmanship,
> his skills in navigation:
> at four, in his small fine clothes,
> what wind can fail him,
> what shore forbid . . .?
> But, alas, he's only in costume,

---

* Psalms 12:8

and he'll never square the yards,
never steam away—
the fixative will decay,
and he'll disappear.

Dirty, filthy, diseased women!
He got even with them—he hounded their wicked cocksure men.

Paul Robeson, 1898–1976

THE MOOR OF PRINCETON

Among white men, I am always lonely.
— Paul Robeson, 1934

There were some who thought he'd known bygone times and sacred places, brought traces along in his bone and blood; he lived, they held, as one who'd lived before, and he was not at home in their nights and days. How could he not have been lonely among the whites?, they said, how, coming from this myth or that legend, how could he not have been a one-and-only in the sycamored streets of Princeton?

Born there in the parsonage of his father's church on Wither-spoon — African Lane, they called it then — he'd wander as soon as he learned to walk, stray the graveyard across the way, range the fields where the battle was fought, ford the slush or dust of the Trenton pike, and stand there staring at Princeton. He'd stare past the Dean's house and its cast-iron porch, its keyed lintels, its windows of twenty-four lights, stare at grass he'd never tread, paths that led to rarer heights. How could he not have been lonely there under the catalpas, under the chestnut trees of Princeton?

From where he stood, at the foot of African Lane, he might've seen his life to come as a repetition of the one he'd spent before, and he might've wondered, having borne it once, at the need to bear it again. Nothing would change: there, hard by the rutted road through Princeton, he'd know that no pain would be remitted, no spear withheld, nor would the sponge this time be sweet; there, engraved in snow and grown in ivy, he might've read what was on the way, another round of the same.

He'd see his blinded mother burn and die when a coal ignited her dress (flowered, striped, polka-dotted, which?), and his father would lose his pulpit (why?) and fall to hauling ashes for the rich — he'd see these things of his second life, for they'd happened once before. He'd see other towns he'd one day live in, Westfield, Somerville, and he'd see streets with other names than Witherspoon, Jackson, Quarry, Green, but always he'd find an African Lane, and therefore, wherever he went, he'd still be in Princeton, he'd never shake off Princeton.

They'd let him school at Rutgers, though he was bright enough for better, and he'd excel at college games, but he'd never dwell within the walls, never make a white friend, never dine in the dining halls, never attend a dance: he'd bed and board in Jigtown and jig there with his own. Four years would he spend on the Raritan, and halfway to the end, when his father died, he'd wait on tables to meet his fees, he'd tend furnace and rake up fallen leaves. All that lay ahead, in his second life, but he'd see it in advance, from his first.

A child in the dust of Princeton, the Princeton rain, he'd see the years of the Great War, he'd see blacks fight in the whites' war — there it all loomed, on the gates of Blair, the blocks of Stuart Hall. And in the summer of 1919 — the Red Summer — blacks would die for swimming in Lake Michigan, and in Tulsa for stepping on a white woman's foot. One by one, he'd see them all from Nassau, see them shot, beaten, hanged in Knoxville, Waco, Omaha, see them from where he began, on the road that ran through Princeton.

In the Harlem days, as he passed shops and stoops and doorways, as he wove through crowds, came to corners, hove to at crossings, people would speak his name — That's Paul, they'd say — and all would know which Paul was meant and be glad for a while they were black. Maybe you were in one of those crowds, maybe you stood near him at some curb, peered at the same goods in a window-display. You too lived in Harlem, and you and he might've made way for each other once, brushed sleeves, your worlds so lightly grazing that neither was aware of the touch. But if someone had said That's Paul, you wouldn't've turned to look — no Paul you knew was black. And so it took you long to learn that he knew you, that half a life back he'd seen you through the trees at Princeton.

He'd seen beyond and all around you, seen the white mass you were a part of, the cause of his despair. He'd seen himself go among you with his voice, his look, his presence, and his anguish, seen and heard himself sing for you, watched himself play the Moor in a black and purple doublet, seen you become almost heedless of his race. He'd be drawn to Spain, he'd entertain between defeats, and one day, to what remained of the Lincoln Brigade, he'd bring himself to say The people are a powerful source of power.

But he'd get no power from you and yours—you were the kind that took it away—and on another day he'd die, and you'd wonder at times whether he'd seen himself dead when he gazed ahead from Princeton. *Among white men,* he said, *I am always lonely.*

Father Charles E. Coughlin, 1891–1979

A MESSENGER OF GOD

to the American people
— Msgr. John Ryan

He came to them once a week for years and years on Sunday after-noons, and to some, *hearing a voice, but seeing no man,* it was a Second Coming and he a second Christ, and what they heard was the Word made air, the Word ethereal. It was called the Golden Hour, that special time of day, and with no small reason, for to those who listened, the things of the world seemed to change: the lackluster grew luminous, the leaden began to flash.

They'd collect in the streets for that hour, they'd be drawn out-doors to stand in a crowd, they'd drive the roads to be one of many at a storefront, an open window, a corner of a square — they'd join for that hour, all those parts and parcels, and *hearing a voice,* they'd cease to be smithereens. And for them, there was a meaning in the voice beyond the audible meaning, a power greater than the power shown, and it was as if they somehow fathomed these unknown things.

To thirty millions came that freighted sound from few knew where — a Savior was among them, unseen but there, in that tran-som, on that porch, under that tree in the park — and they were sure, they were sure that with the morrow, the hard times would end, wheels would turn, smoke would show on the sky. The wind would die, they thought, and the dust die with it.

One day, all that was foretold in the Golden Hour would come to pass indeed, the earth would flourish and the sparks would fly, but by then there'd be sparser assemblies, there'd be places amid them where the sward could be seen, faces less rapt than they'd been before, and as men spat and children played, shrill grew the voice to those still heeding, and there'd be rash appeals from the tower on Twelve Mile Road (Blame the Jew!, the standard form on a standard fre-quency), and the people, seeing the man now, would spit a little fur-ther while their children ran.

Richard M. Nixon, 1913–

FATHER TO THE MAN

We had our arguments within the family and there
were times when I suppose we were tempted to
run away. None of us ever did.
                                        —Richard M. Nixon

No, none of them ever did: they stayed for more, they never
strayed. But what, he may have wondered, what if he'd done what
he thought of, scribbled a screed, pinned it to the screen, and gone
out into the suspiring night, drawn deep of jasmine, orange, oleander,
and run . . . to where? how far toward where? But *none of us ever*
did, he said, none, and least of all he, had ever forsaken himself and
fled, none had ever taken the road that led . . . to what? to where?

It was just as well he never tried: he'd hardly have gotten to the
door. For him, and he knew it, there was nothing outside but danger
that began where the five stone steps descended from the lawn, went
down into the swirl of an unknown world. It drew him, that roundabout suction, but never through his skin of windows, walls, and
shiplap siding. He was safe there within . . . but all the same he
was tempted, he said, he could feel the force of the outer persua-
sion, and when his feet failed to run, to walk, to stir, even, he may
have tried to respond in his mind—to *imagine* going, just to *im-*
agine!—but when fancy faded, he was still inside.

He must've been aware early that he was sequestered by himself,
container and contents in one, his own restrainer, and he studied
not to care for the things he saw through his look-out eyes: he'd live
on the safe side, he must've resolved, the inner side, the white-frame
four-square skinful of *him*. Thrice on Sunday, therefore, he attended church (some say more), and he gravely fished, bent pin and pole,
in the water-district reservoir, he stole fruit and swam in ditches,
he split his scalp in a fall from a wagon (eleven stitches!), he chored,
he odd-jobbed, he read useful books, wrote themes on topics of public
interest, made his schools' debating teams (Resolved: That insects
are more beneficial than harmful), won this game, lost that race,

boned up, burned the midnight oil (or gas), earned the name of Iron-ass . . . but he never ran, he must've rued, never ran away.

There were Nixes in the thirteenth century and Nikesons in the next, but what they did before they died no Nixon ever knew; clay once, they were dust now, and so too such as may have fought on the Brandywine, fallen between the graves on Cemetery Ridge. There were no immortals among the family dead, no suns that would never set: there were only fading records in nutgall, only stories told at reunions spun thinner all the time—it was a low-lumen line.

The lessons taken on the violin, the work done in orchards, fields, packing-plants, the goods sold in stores, the windshields wiped, the *helping out* at home, the activities, the activities unending! He entered contests, edited papers, stood for student office, he danced, he tried out for no matter what, he cheered for 'varsity, he thrashed, throbbed, whirled around, some part of him always seemingly involved in sound or caught in motion, oscillating, reciprocating, grinding—he was one of his own beneficial insects, chafing, rasping, as if to set himself afire.

It did no good. He could see all his life from its near beginnning, there from the foot of the Chino Hills, he could see year after year of the rest, a strung-out procession of identicals, and though he must've longed to make it change, he knew he never would. When the parade ended, he'd be just where he started, still in his house of skin and quite as ill at ease. He must've felt that he had no real right to be anywhere, out there in the cold or holed up in his pelt, and from afar, across that Yorba Linda lawn, he must've seen a day dawn when he was only a Nikeson of the past, an entry made in fading ink.

What was there about him, or what was there not, that cost him quality, lost him poise? what did he comprise that diminished him, what did he omit? why did he perform for mirrors and memorize? why was he always urgent, even while silent, even standing still? why did he seem to plead, and for what and from whom, what did he need? what did he have too much of, too little of, nothing of at all—taste? tact? the *bon ton*? dash? why were his clothes correct but wrong, why were his postures *im*posture, his gestures apt but for other meanings, his phrases coined from tin? why did he try so hard, why did he feel less than the least . . .?

None of us ever did, he said, but oh God, if he could only have run away!

[348]

THE WAR THAT WAS FOUGHT IN YOUR HOME

They seemed to be fighting it just for you, at your convenience, your command. Silent and unseen, they were an electrical disturbance of the ether until, with a movement of your hand, they changed from waves to rays, came to life nine thousand miles away to kill or be killed at your feet. You could dine while you watched them, you could smoke and drink, or if you willed, you could stroke your poker, you could think of gain, revenge, of loves past and loves to come, you could see queer species burn as you savored metrics, *when lilacs last, lilacs out of the dead land,* and you could turn your head if pain offended, if the dead were rude and stared.

A slight manipulation, a touch, a twist, a pressure, and soon, in a black vacuum, a small world grew behind glass. It was a strange place, and seen however often, strange it always stayed. The trees, the roads were forever unfamiliar, the houses too if houses there were made of leaves, and those six-inch things were an unknown people, even the ones with three-inch guns. And the flags seemed strange, like flags on the moon, and strange too the turbid streams, as if the water had already been used, and it was strange to see rain there when it was clear here, rain on rice grass, rain on fallen rain. You heard firing, you saw flame flower and the flowers fume, and there were cries and quiet, and flight and stillness, and a strange sight they made, the old with their trash and children.

There you sat with you own trash, books, clothes, azaleas, and a coiled cat, and you could, with a wave of your hand, make others wage a war for your eye alone, make strangers come far through space to die near your cash, your throbbing canary, your suitful of you.

Printed in March 1984 in Santa Barbara & Ann Arbor
for the Black Sparrow Press by Graham Mackintosh and
Edwards Brothers Inc. Design by Barbara Martin.
This edition is published in paper wrappers; there are
300 hardcover trade copies; 200 hardcover copies
numbered and signed by the author; & 26 copies hand-
bound in boards by Earle Gray lettered and signed by
the author.

JOHN SANFORD is the name of the principal character in *The Water Wheel*, a first novel by Julian Shapiro published in 1933. Adopting it as a pseudonym, the writer has used it ever since. Born in the Harlem section of New York on 31 May 1904, he attended the public schools of that city, Lafayette College, and finally Fordham University, where he earned a degree in Law. He was admitted to the Bar in 1929, and at about the same time, influenced by his friend Nathanael West, he too began to write. Published at the outset in vanguard magazines of the period—*The New Review, Tambour, Pagany, Contact*—he soon abandoned the legal profession and produced through the years a series of eight novels. Concerned always with the course of American history, he interspersed his fiction with critical commentaries on the national life from the Left-Liberal point-of-view. As a result of such dissent, he was summoned before the House Committee on UnAmerican Activities, and for refusing to cooperate with it, he was blacklisted. In spite of difficulty in obtaining publication, he continued to write in his chosen vein, ultimately stripping his work down to its historical content only. During the several years last past, he has written four books of creative interpretations of the Land of the Free: *A More Goodly Country, View From This Wilderness, To Feed Their Hopes,* and the present volume, *The Winters of That Country*. All four titles derive from a single passage in William Bradford's *History of Plymouth Plantation*. John Sanford has been married to the writer Marguerite Roberts since 1938; they are long-time residents of Santa Barbara, California.